ENVIRONMENTAL ETHICS AND FILM

Environmental ethics presents and defends a systematic and comprehensive account of the moral relation between human beings and their natural environment and assumes that human behaviour toward the natural world can be and is governed by moral norms. In contemporary society, film has provided a powerful instrument for the moulding of such ethical attitudes.

Through a close examination of the medium, *Environmental Ethics and Film* explores how historical ethical values can be re-imagined and re-constituted for more contemporary audiences. Building on an extensive back-catalogue of eco-film analysis, the author focuses on a diverse selection of contemporary films which target audiences' ethical sensibilities in very different ways. Each chapter focuses on at least three close readings of films and documentaries, examining a wide range of environmental issues as they are illustrated across contemporary Hollywood films.

This book is an invaluable resource for students and scholars of environmental communication, film studies, media and cultural studies, environmental philosophy and ethics.

Pat Brereton is Head of the School of Communications at Dublin City University, Ireland.

Routledge Studies in Environmental Communication and Media

'There is a saying that "without vision, there the people perish". In *Environmental Ethics and Film* Pat Brereton beautifully illustrates and makes the case for the capacity of films to help us tell new stories and provide visions of the "human condition" in an age of complex and global ecological challenges and opportunities. Brereton sees film as neither a substitute for political activism nor mere "escapism". Rather, it creates the conditions for transformation, new understandings and the fusing of normative, affective and above all imaginative interpretations of the present or alternative visions of our planetary future. In film's capacity to appeal to our imaginations about human relations, we have different and more accessible resources for new narratives and ethical responses than those given by scientific readings of those relations. This book is an authoritative and accessibly written account of how film can do much more than simply paint dystopian, nostalgic or utopian accounts of our planetary condition. It can help in remaking a better, more ecologically sustainable world.'
— *John Barry, Professor of Green Political Economy, Queens University Belfast, UK*

ENVIRONMENTAL ETHICS AND FILM

Pat Brereton

LONDON AND NEW YORK

from Routledge

First published 2016
by Routledge
2 Park Square, Milton Park, Abingdon, Oxon OX14 4RN

and by Routledge
711 Third Avenue, New York, NY 10017

Routledge is an imprint of the Taylor & Francis Group, an informa business

© 2016 Pat Brereton

British Library Cataloguing-in-Publication Data
A catalogue record for this book is available from the British Library

Library of Congress Cataloging-in-Publication Data
Brereton, Pat.
  Environmental ethics and film / Pat Brereton.
      pages cm
  1. Environmental protection and motion pictures.
  2. Environmentalism in motion pictures. 3. Motion pictures –
  Moral and ethical aspects. 4. Environmental ethics. I. Title.
  PN1995.9.E78B84 2015b
      791.43´6553--dc23   2015009707

ISBN: 978-0-415-74727-1 (hbk)
ISBN: 978-0-415-74728-8 (pbk)
ISBN: 978-1-315-79715-1 (ebk)

Typeset in Bembo
by HWA Text and Data Management, London

Printed and bound in the United States of America by Edwards Brothers Malloy
on sustainably sourced paper.

CONTENTS

ACKNOWLEDGEMENTS

This book received financial support from the Faculty of Humanities and Social Sciences Book Publication Scheme at Dublin City University.

Permission has been sought and gratefully received for re-framing sections from previous publications around ecology and film including:

'Cinema, Ecology and the Environment', Chapter 22 in Anders Hansen and Robert Cox (eds), *The Routledge Handbook of Environment and Communications,* Routledge, 2015.

Hollywood Utopia: Ecology in Contemporary American Cinema, Intellect Press, 2005.

'An ecological approach to the cinema of Peter Weir', *Quarterly Review of Film and Video* 28(2): 120–134.

Smart Cinema: DVD Add-ons and New Audience Pleasures, Palgrave, 2012.

'Irish eco-Cinema and Audiences' (with Pat Hong), *Interactions: Studies in Culture and Communication* 4(2): 171–199, 2014.

'Screening Green Business: An Ecological Reading of the Greatest Business Movies' (with Pierre McDonagh), *Journal of Macromarketing,* 30(2): 133–146, 2009.

'Eco-cinema, Sustainability and Africa: A Reading of *Out of Africa, The Constant Gardener* and *District 9*', *Journal of African Cinemas* 5(2): 219–235, 2013.

'Appreciating the Views: Filming Nature: *Into the Wild, Grizzly Man* and *Into the West*' in Stephen Rust, Salma Monani and Sean Cubitt (eds), *Ecocinema Theory and Practice*, Routledge, 2013.

'Farming in Irish Film: An Ecological Reading' in Sid Dobrin and Sean Morey (eds), *Ecosee: Image, Rhetoric, Nature*, SUNY Press, 2009.

I would also like to acknowledge numerous scholars and students who have read various drafts of these chapters and record my thanks for various very helpful suggestions and insights. These include: Pietari Kääpä, Alexa Weik von Mossner, Michael Doorley, Bert Gordijn, Donal O'Mathuna, Alan Kearns, Pierre McDonagh, Dave Robbins, Pat Hong, Padraig Murphy, Trish Morgan, Neil O'Boyle, Brenda McNally, Eileen Culloty, Fiachara O'Broichain, John O'Sullivan, together with DCU undergraduate and postgraduate students, especially the masters in ethics students on which some of these ideas were road-tested.

1

ENVIRONMENTAL ETHICS

Literature review

Overview

Why are some people in Western society actively concerned with protecting nature and natural things, while others are not, and what motivates people in the first place to become involved in environmental protection? These are very complex and loaded questions that preoccupy environmental communication scholars and are difficult to answer. But by focusing on contemporary fictional film with their often engaging environmental themes and storylines, we can at least begin to explore some of the debates embedded within environmental protection and its related ethics. I will explore how mass audience films and their use of a creative imaginary, display a range of cautionary allegorical tales that help to promote greater awareness and debate concerning the central importance of environmental ethics for the very survival of our planet.

Introduction

Adam O'Brien in a review of a recent reader on eco-cinema (Rust *et al.* 2013) asserts how my research tends to place 'a remarkable degree of faith in cinema's capacity for wonder and hope (of the kind we might associate with André Bazin or Stanley Cavell)', and speaks to Hollywood's 'somewhat tentative move towards a more provocative evocation of nonhuman agency' (O'Brien 2013: 221). While at first sight, fictional cinema seems to be a poor substitute for effective and direct engagement with a range of environmental challenges facing the modern world, nevertheless, its global reach in itself means Hollywood has an important role to play in promoting awareness around environmental ethics and helping to construct new modes of popular engagement through the visualisation of environments, drawing on a long romantic history around the therapeutic representation and evocation of nature.

A tremendous amount of moral thinking and the development of ethical feeling and perception is undertaken when reading literature or watching films. In fact it is not an exaggeration to say that for most people the mass media are the primary way in which they acquire ethical attitudes, especially within contemporary culture.[1]

This study seeks to explore how contemporary commercial Hollywood cinema, together with a very small number of more art-house eco-imaginaries, as I describe them, pose varying responses to environmental crises and often more concretely and creatively feature the global concerns of environmental ethics, while encouraging *us* to take things into our own hands.

Building on an extensive environmental investigation, beginning with *Hollywood Utopia: Ecology in Contemporary American Cinema* (Brereton 2005), this study will focus specifically on a number of key environmental and ethical debates embedded within contemporary popular films. The films appeal to audiences in very different ways, as we face the long-term consequences of climate change, as the number one environmental and ethical dilemma. At the outset, while acknowledging the dangers of over-exaggeration concerning the innate power and influence of cinema, environmental communication scholars still need to risk such dangers, by highlighting and examining every way possible that film might help to emphasise the primary importance of our fragile environment and call attention to the often conflicting ethical issues surrounding us. Cinema as a broad-based and influential medium can greatly assist in the process of framing what audiences might think and imagine, while at the same time actively engaging with, and provoking responses for publics and communities across the world.

Frequently successful Hollywood films with their universal narratives, at least unconsciously, strive to do this by bringing all peoples and nations on the planet together with a common purpose, while tapping into a latent hunger for connectivity within a broadly conceived ethical system of values. The Hollywood dream factory can produce what I will categorise as 'creative imaginaries' and 'ecological fantasies' – framed across a range of ethical registers – which feed into the global consciousness of world audiences, often negating issues of race, class and even ethnic divisions. While such 'feel-good' ecological fictional narratives can be easily criticised as vacuous, or even dismissed as just promoting and endorsing grand symbolic gestures and simply upholding the status quo, they still remain significant, if only for keeping the environment at the centre of human consciousness (Rust *et al.* 2013; Ivakhiv 2013; Weik von Mossner 2014).

At the outset this study recognises that it is difficult to get across the deep environmental and radical ethical message, as it is politically unacceptable in most quarters to simply insist that the global economy ought to shrink to become environmentally sustainable, while using less carbon-based energy sources in the longer term. Most in the West, in particular, appear addicted to 'affluenza' (wealth and affluence), as a more destructive form of conspicuous consumerism, while embracing the long-term expectation of continuous economic growth. Alternatively, at the other extreme, a stoical, resilient or frugal ethic that seeks to promote less overall consumption and general conservation demands a radical re-shifting of established economic, political and cultural norms. Less industrial development and less wasteful growth is considered critically important as an underpinning (post)economic model to build a future for environmental sustainable and ethical living. Lifestyles, by all accounts, will have to change to accommodate this and *we* need to prepare for such a radical transformation carefully. This study suggests that somewhat paradoxically fiction film can serve as a useful sounding board for such scenarios and sometimes a range of audio/ visual stimulus provides an effective creative imaginary to set up and explore many of these radical environmental and ethical hypotheses, while suggesting if not always fully fleshing out possible solutions to our planetary environmental problems.

Each subsequent chapter will focus on a small number of contemporary films and survey others to illustrate the diversity of environmental ethical issues that are addressed, both overtly or implicitly, and at the same time explore how environmental ethics and values have preoccupied and informed mainstream cinema over the last few decades. The following sections will begin by defining the scope and definition of environmental ethics for this study. Then I will explore some of the core concepts used to investigate the growing corpus of eco-films. Most notably this will include analysis of anthropocentrism and biocentrism, together with related environmental ethical precepts that underpin subsequent chapters, including 'the tragedy of the commons', 'land and wilderness ethics', 'lifeboat ethics' and 'otherness', together with the most pervasive notion in the literature, coalescing around the term 'deep ecology'.

Definitions and scope of environmental ethics

As a relatively modern phenomenon, environmental ethics remains an all-encompassing concept which is *inclusive* rather than exclusive and causes problems in trying to create and maintain strict guidelines following any definitional terms of reference. Studying environmental ethics through film is a way of getting behind the headline news and often using mythic and allegorical storylines to explore what's at stake across a wide range of environmental problems, across a broad selection of films discussed in this volume. Indeed, environmental ethics is partly concerned with why something that happens in the world should be seen as a 'problem' at all (Palmer in Keller 2010: 41). At a macro level, this introductory literature review will highlight a number of fundamental critical ethical debates which have particular purchase for film analysis, including: the valorising of indigenous peoples and the notion of 'otherness', as theorised by Emmanuel Levinas; alongside Garrett Hardin's influential notion of the 'tragedy of the commons', which explicitly draws on the premise that people are *de facto* competitive and that capitalism is the 'natural' form of economic life, with the commons reflecting a state of nature. Hardin's well-used concept, together with his engagement with 'lifeboat ethics', are both grounded in a form of egocentric ethics, which can in turn be rooted in an atomistic, rather than a mechanistic, metaphysics of human agency.

A so-called 'tragedy of the commons' is particularly useful for coalescing environmental film analysis and occurs when individuals, sharing a resource held in common, act in their own self-interest and the collective result progressively degrades the collective resource. This phenomenon is illustrated most pointedly by the classic Hollywood western with representations of cowboys placing more and more cattle (or sheep in some cases) on land held in common, and having to fight over scarce allocation of communal water sources in particular. Such a scenario calls attention to the ethical allocation of scarce resources and will be re-evaluated most pointedly through an examination of a wide range of contemporary film across several chapters.

There are at least five basic assumptions implicit in such a broadly environmental ethical perspective: 1) everything is connected to everything else; 2) the whole is greater than the sum of the parts; 3) meaning is context dependent; 4) process has primacy over parts; 5) humans and non-human nature are one.[2] The progressive manifestation of environmental ethical assumptions remains an idealised dream of a pure environment movement that does not have to worry about the material consequences of such a philosophy. Nonetheless such ethical precepts actively inform and underpin specific textual analysis of many of the films discussed in this volume.

This work will examine how such perennial environmental and ethical assumptions are conveyed both directly and implicitly through the cinematic medium, while exploring how these specifically might relate in the long term to the more ephemeral nature of cinema and film study. This environmental ethical engagement remains by all accounts under-developed in the broad-based film academy, while becoming a growing preoccupation for a branch of eco-film theorising, which this volume extensively draws upon.

The notion of 'lifeboat ethics' for example can most usefully be used to examine contemporary films like *Wall-E*, *All is Lost* and *Captain Phillips*, explored in Chapter 2. Environmentalists apply the metaphor of the earth as a fragile 'spaceship' to reflect the ethical dangers of pollution and degradation of the ecosystem, alongside exploring all forms of waste and management of scarce natural resources, which is also alluded to in a study of the 2013 Oscar winner *Gravity*. The limited capacity of any hypothetical lifeboat is, of course, called into question with regard to the so-called carrying capacity of the land, or even the sea for that matter. Relating to the 'tragedy of the commons', an environmentally ethical farmer, for instance, will allow no more cattle onto a pasture than it can withstand. All the while knowing full well the consequences of overloading the habitat and the prospect of erosion, which might set in together with weeds taking over, thereby losing the long-term inherent wealth and nutrients of the land.

To reiterate, if land is designated as part of the commons and is open to all usage, this may not be matched by a corresponding responsibility by individuals to protect the commons. Every user will have different needs and the pervasive danger is that there might be no overall control or regulation on its usage. Furthermore, in a 'crowded world of less than perfect human beings, mutual ruin is inevitable if there are no controls. This is the tragedy of the commons' (Hardin 1974: 3).[3]

Mainstream philosophies and Hardin's (somewhat unstated) underlying assumptions include for instance that people are naturally competitive; that capitalism is the 'natural' form of economic life and that the commons also remains the most efficient and progressive notion of a marketplace, as it infers strict regulation and control. Most explicitly, this underlying assumption can be applied to the mindset and cut-throat world view of Western finance, as evident in films such as the *Wall Street* franchise and most recently *The Wolf of Wall Street*. Meanwhile, the very influential ethical theorist Emmanuel Levinas certainly informs the literature in film studies, recalling especially the representational concept of otherness.

Levinas (1906–1995) is widely considered the most significant ethical thinker in twentieth-century continental philosophy. Levinas regarded the demise of humanism, coupled with the horrific trauma of the Holocaust that marked the twentieth century, as fundamentally challenging to all forms of ethics. At the same time, he has always been profoundly wary of the so-called rhetorics of nature and of connectedness to place (see Hatley *et al.* 2012: 2). For Levinas, ethics is precisely the disruption of egoism, of a life that centres on the self and is thus focused around decentring the subject. Levinas also lays the foundation for the disruption of any ethical stance that places too much emphasis on the instrumental dimensions of the self's relations with other human or other-than-human beings (Hatley *et al.* 2012: 5). Hence a deep love of nature, following this line of thinking, can at times be construed as another form of egoism.

The appeal of a Levinasian philosophy that valorises this particular notion of otherness, especially for film studies, lies in its ability to go beyond the surface of an image. Cooper (2006: 24), for instance, provocatively finds in the face-to-face encounter between the subject and other, the prospect of being witness to an infinite time that persists outside of the real-time present. Thus, Sam Girgus' (2010) important Levinasian film study finds in instances of the close-up, in particular within Hollywood films like *The Grapes of Wrath* and *The Searchers,* a certain aspect of the image that is both transcendental and infinite. Meanwhile, Butler (2004) suggests an inherent paradox in the ability to record the surface features of the face – which could be extended to encapsulate nature and landscape for instance – without succeeding in presenting its unrepresentable aspects. It is this paradox that is suggested which must be retained in representations through the cinematographic medium (Butler 2004: 144). This notion can equally extend to various forms of ecological manifestations and help to explore a range of ethical paradoxes, alongside the more obvious enigmatic quality of the face. The catastrophic sublime of nature *in extremis* following climate change – as evident for instance in *The Day After Tomorrow,* or alternatively the eco-cautionary number one blockbuster success *Avatar* that is extensively examined in this volume – speaks to such aesthetic debates (see Taylor 2013).

Calling on the specific role of ethics as a method of exploration around how disparate groups of people can and should behave towards each other, there has been a palpable shift in emphasis around how these relationships are manifested and cultivated within a moral framework. This shift is philosophical, concentrated on the (largely abstract) figure of the 'other' within a dominant, hegemonic social environment. Early attempts at establishing an 'ethics of the other' however (which can include protection of the environment conceived of as other) – at least in continental philosophy – have stemmed from an idea of otherness as an oppositional term; a 'them' who are not 'us', who may, at best, be tolerated for their difference, even as we are aware that their otherness is suspect and probably dangerous. More recently, philosophy has developed a far more incisive enquiry into the characteristics of alterity itself.[4] These concepts are particularly relevant for the whole area of environmental ethics, as especially embodied through the characterisation of indigenous peoples, who have frequently been appropriated to actively help valorise the specificity of a more harmonious ethic of nature, as explored in Chapter 3.

While most pointedly, Holmes Rolston claims that 'the challenge of environmental ethics is a principled attempt to redefine the boundaries of ethical obligation'. At its most basic level, Rolston perceives environmental ethics as vital, simply because the survival of life on earth depends on it. Consequently, the main concerns on the world agenda for the new millennium include: 'war and peace, escalating populations, escalating consumption and most significantly large-scale degrading environments.' These concerns are all interrelated and underpinned by various conceptions and even pragmatic approaches to environmental ethics and films examined later (Rolston in Keller 2010: 41).

Framing cinematic environmental risk: fatalism and the precautionary principle

Environmental scholars have become preoccupied with all aspects of framing risk and its management. A dominant strand in scholarly analysis of the representation of the environment through news for example, be it fictional or factual documentary, is concentrated within a focus around 'framing'. Lakoff (2010) argues that 'environmental frames are the (typically unconscious) conceptual structures that people have in their brain circuitry to understand environmental issues' (Lakoff 2010: 74). Such scholars contend that changing people's environmental frames, 'to engender (necessary) awareness and action in the face of global warming and climate change is compromised by pre-existing dominant environmental frames, perpetuated by vested ideological interests, and evidenced by their prevalence in the news' (Lakoff 2010: 70–71). Similar arguments are also made with regard to fiction film, with its dominant ideological status designed to perpetuate the status quo, rather than apparently promoting and legitimising a revolutionary deep ecological and more pro-active environmentally ethical mindset.

Salvador and Norton's critique of *The Day After Tomorrow* for instance – one of the few disaster movies to explicitly utilise global warming as a plot device – argues that the human capacity to avert the apocalypse is strategically removed in the film. They suggest that 'whereas in ancient and biblical tales, humans were subject to the power and principles of the gods or God: in the secularised version of the flood myth expressed in *The Day After Tomorrow*, humans are subject to the power and principles of nature' (Salvado and Norton 2011: 51). Weik von Mossner (2012) also provides a very balanced review of a range of scientific and audience studies of the film's effectiveness in promoting environmental changes in perceptions, while noting according to Beck and others, such audio-visual spectacles have a 'direct visceral effect on the viewer'. In many ways this contemporary evocation of nature in extremis can be contrasted with the more recent and less effective Old Testamont filmic epic *Noah*, which is also examined later.

According to other critics, fictional film potentially 'enfeebles environmental advocacy' as it offers a representation of environmental risk where 'there is little left to do but wait for and survive the purification brought by nature's retribution' (Campbell 2013: 60). Referring explicitly to films like *Twister*, *Volcano* and *Dante's Peak*, Kakoudaki (2002) and others argue somewhat fatalistically that nature across these explicitly coded films is presented as an 'agent of destruction' and 'outside of human agency or responsibility' (ibid: 120). She further states that 'human *responsibility* thus is removed from the main encounter of the films'. As a result, the new apocalyptic films 'are not about ethics or choice in averting disaster' (ibid: 121, original emphasis). This aspect of apocalypse and fatalistic 'end of the world' disaster narratives is extensively covered in Chapter 8, which focuses on a more evocative environmental reading of *Melancholia* and *The Tree of Life*.

Campbell (2013: 15) believes that there remains a clear differentiation between the 'call to action of an environmental advocacy documentary such as *An Inconvenient Truth*, and the passive experience of disaster movies like *The Day After Tomorrow*' and how this raises a question over 'how factual entertainment programs attitudinally represent risk and disaster'. Re-reading a range of disaster and cautionary tales across a number of chapters in this volume, the study will attempt to explore some of these varying, even contradictory, ethical positions.

Unfortunately, it has to be left to a subsequent volume to reveal how a wide range of polemical documentaries and other new media modalities effectively speak to such factual debates within environmental ethical praxis. Buell most notably concludes that many advocacy documentaries, much less fictional narratives, depict a vision of 'natural' disaster as spectacle: 'but this vision is not meant to shock us into our senses and make us seek alternatives'. Instead, he suggested, it is 'directed at transforming apocalypse into exciting entertainment for the multitudes' (2010: 31 cited in Campbell 2013). Their representations of disasters are not warnings intended as environmental advocacy, or a call to action, but rather offer a vicarious pleasure, a version of 'seeing nature as sublime, but the sublime in the sense of the pleasure of terror in the face of the power of nature' (Wheatley 2011: 244). Others including Adrian Ivakhiv would concur that such a reading re-enforces an impotent attitude that suggests a subsequent weak engagement with environmental ethics. While this approach informs readings of films in this volume, it is certainly not the only interpretation, which has validity for audiences. This study will seek to explore and highlight more benevolent and positive environmental readings of various successful commercial films.

Core elements of environmental precautionary principles, which also feed into an environmental ethical reading of a number of narratives in this volume, include the following:

- pre-action: willing to take action in advance of scientific proof;
- cost-effectiveness of action: taking into account issues of proportionality;
- safe-guarding ecological space: promoting resilience as short-hand for self-reverence;
- legitimising the status of intrinsic value: without degenerating into dangers of essentialising 'nature' as never changing;
- shifting the onus of proof and the burden of proof that nothing bad will happen and shift this responsibility to the developer, who wants to exploit some natural resources;
- meso scale planning; looking forward to a 25–100 year time frame into the future;[5]
- paying for ecological debt: in the short and longer term remains a most pressing precautionary principle, leading to most prescient global concerns.

Chapter 8 in particular will feature some of these attributes.

Concurrently, while the costs of climate change and continued economic development and growth are already becoming major global issues, the solution posited by utilitarian and more contemporary ecological ethicists and policy makers revolves around mutual coercion, and at one extreme consenting to a form of sustainable regulation of resources and even calling on a radical strategy of de-growth. At the same time this study and approach recognises the dangers of 'greenwashing' and the legitimation of more shallow forms of corporate responsibility, evident in mainstream entrepreneurial culture, which in turn can be used to affirm a 'business as usual' strategy, while paying lip service to notions of 'universal sustainability' and deep environmental ethics. All of these loaded, discursive and contested terms are very much part of the lexicon of modern economic, cultural and political thinking and are also becoming infused within eco-critical film analysis. Alongside these core theoretical and ethical philosophies lie a number of other concepts which also underpin this study, most notably anthropocentrism.

Anthropocentrism

As an overarching core concept, anthropocentrism places humans at the centre of the universe. It has become customary in the Western tradition to consider only *our* species when examining the environmental ethics of a situation. Consequently adopting this logic, everything else in existence should be evaluated in terms of its utility for our species, thus committing a form of speciesism.[6] Such emphasis on human agency and the primacy of an anthropocentric approach remains central to the vast majority of storylines in Hollywood cinema, while sometimes this position is tentatively problematised especially within science fictional narratives like *The Planet of the Apes* franchise discussed later in this volume.

Probably anthropocentrism remains the most essential and foundational concept for this study, underpinning all engagement with environmental ethics and representations of humans in nature. This worldview places humans, figuratively if not literally, at the centre of the cosmos and this attitude and mindset certainly corresponds with much Hollywood cinema discussed in this volume. Various critics characterise its importance regarding:

- seeing the natural order as arranged in a grand hierarchy (a 'Great Chain of Being').
- recognising a firm ontological divide between humans and nonhuman nature (metaphysical dualism).
- the idea of nature as a machine which follows the mechanical laws of physics.
- recognising humans alone are intrinsically valuable and that non-human nature is valuable only insofar as it has use-value for humans (good instrumentally for our ends).
- finally, it is suggested humans beings constitute, solely and exclusively, the moral community.

(Keller 2010: 59)

The most extreme critiques of such a pervasive mindset argue that 'anthropocentrism means a diminished capacity for empathy, comparable to jingoism, racism or sexism'. Anthropocentrism, at its crudest, is reduced to 'human chauvinism' (a phrase used by Plumwood) and according to Midgley is 'no more rationally defensible than other forms of chauvinism centred around nation, race, or sex' (Keller 2010: 92). Many of these high-level debates will resonate and be weaved across filmic readings, especially through what are characterised as chapter-level defining themes like eco-feminism explored in Chapter 4, alongside an ontological engagement with what it means to be in tune with one's environment at a deep level, which feeds into several of the subsequent chapters.

Radical ecologists usefully reveal the social and ecological wrongs committed in the name of so-called anthropological modern worldviews. Most explicitly it is suggested that the ecological crisis stems from the fact that modernity's proponents have simply assumed that human emancipation and wellbeing can be achieved primarily by 'mastering' the natural world (Zimmerman 1994: 7). Such human desire for total mastery, alongside a form of innate hubris, feeds into numerous cautionary tales explored in this volume, focusing on the implicit need to de-centre humans as the primary focus of ethical value across the environment. Unfortunately, Hollywood with all its ideological emphasis on individual storylines and heroic resolutions, at first sight at least appears to perpetuate a mastery over nature master-narrative, thereby embracing a very reductive anthropocentric worldview. But several reading across a number of chapters will strive to contest this pervasive presumption.

Many ecological critics of anthropocentrism have argued that the dominant tendency in Western culture (for instance Christianity) has been to construe difference in terms of hierarchy and that 'nature' is purely set up in the service of human wishes. Meanwhile a less colonising approach to nature does not necessarily involve denying human reason or human difference, but rather ceasing to treat reason as the basis of superiority and domination. While an ecological ethic must, according to Plumwood, always be an 'ethic of eco-justice that recognises the interconnection of social domination and the domination of nature' (Plumwood 1993: 20). Other scholars like Bookchin affirms that human beings have a vital role to play as 'ecological stewards' in the evolutionary process and need to be consciously engaged in the negotiated relationship between society and nature, which is echoed in the other major philosophical theory of *inherentism*.

These eco-philosophical debates help re-define what it means to be 'human'. As Campbell asserts: 'at the core of our sense of self is our feeling of loss and the desire for unity that is born of loss' (in Glotfelty and Fromm 1996: 134). Such universal, mythic expressions of loss and the desire for ecological unity can be found in numerous popular films explored in this volume and dovetails across earlier readings in *Hollywood Utopia*.

Deep ecology

Environmental ethics presents and supports a systematic and comprehensive account of the moral relation between human beings and their natural ethical environment, which assumes that human behaviour toward the natural world can and is governed by moral norms. Deep ecologists who have defined the field

like Arne Naess, consider it as having fundamental ethical implications which
include:

- Biospherical Egalitarianism: the equal right of all creatures to live and
  blossom.
- Principal of Diversity and Symbiosis: the richness of forms as ends in
  themselves both within human cultures and the natural world.

(cited in Allison 1991: 25)

Deep ecology evidently goes beyond the transformation of technology and
politics to a transformation of humanity. Its holistic view breaks down any
boundaries between man and nature (Eccleshall 1994: 237) and has come to
be understood by some cultural critics as more radical than the Copernican
revolution. What can be described as 'evolutionary ecology' displaces humankind
from a position of centrality in the universe and on the planet.

Naess (1973) has particularly called for a radical reconsideration of the
'sustainable development' approaches from within a deep ecological perspective
that was beginning to gain currency in environmental government and business
circles in the 1970s; an agenda which has continued right up to current new
generational thinking. Naess claimed that there was a need to rearticulate our
relations with nature in order to dispel and destabilise the mechanistic worldview
manifested within scientific methodology, which has been dominant over the
past 300 years. Central to this thesis and underpinning the philosophy of deep
ecology in particular is the belief that the environmental crisis is the outcome of
a form of anthropocentric humanism that was central to the defining ideologies
of modernity.

Such a deep ecological philosophy further embraces the view that we ought to
extend moral consideration to the entire biotic community, either by extending
to all living elements of the community the right to live and flourish, or by
regarding the biotic community itself as the primary object of moral regard
(Cheney 1989: 117). Furthermore, deep ecologists reject the quick-fix possibility
that the pervasive market can 'correct' misuse and the misallocation of natural
resources and the institutionalised separation of the human experience from
that of the non-human world. This fundamentally challenges the privileges
afforded to dominant ideologies especially around 'progress' and 'development'
that have marked the age of modernism (Andrew 2000: 6), which have also
remained the dominant orthodoxy in the West.

Unlike deep ecologists however, 'social ecologists' (such as Callicott or
Bookchin) do not seek to radically destabilise anthropocentrism. Instead of
holding the belief that this is central to the perpetuation of environmental
misuse, it is claimed that the environmental crisis should be seen primarily 'in
the light of hierarchy and domination' (Andrew 2000: 8).

Social ecology as an ethical position avoids the serious trap of modernity by
contesting the pervasive assumption that humanity is the master of nature and

that humans have the right to dominate other humans. As such, it is an ethical position that challenges the ethics of individualism supported by capitalist systems. Social ecology encourages us to reconsider the role of hierarchies, social structures and political organisation, so that these can be re-calibrated as essentially egalitarian, libertarian and oriented around the meaningful participation and recognition of all members of the community and not just the privileged (Andrew 2000: 9). By all accounts this is a more pragmatic and realisable long-term strategy for environmental ethics as evidenced in some of the films discussed later.

Meanwhile, deep environmentalists like Paul W. Taylor have laid down a convincing biocentric manifesto titled *Respect for Nature*. Central to Taylor's thesis is a life-centred system of environmental ethics, as opposed to a human-centred one. Taylor affirms how we have moral obligations that are owed to wild plants and animals themselves as members of the earth's biotic community. 'We are morally bound (other things being equal) to protect or promote their good for their own sake. Our duties to respect the integrity of the natural ecosystems, to preserve endangered species, and to avoid environmental pollution stem from the fact that these are ways in which we can help make it possible for wild species populations to achieve and maintain a healthy existence in a natural state' (cited in Keller 2010: 176).

Similarly, the *Gaia Principle* – much beloved by the 'creative imaginary' of radical science fiction – shows how everything is connected and exposes how the environment is unconditionally believed to have inherent value and has little to do with the uniqueness or superiority of the human species. Knowledge of this form of deep ecological value therefore remains independent of all human experience and acknowledged to be intuitively 'true' (Simmons 1993: 184). This 'certain tendency' towards deep ecology underpins much of the base line attitudinal approach to all form of pro-active environmental ethics.

Biocentrism: a framing discourse which underpins deep ecology

Taylor's provocative form of 'biocentrism' can easily be decoded as an explicitly deontological manifestation of environmental ethics. He argues that each individual living thing in nature – whether animal, plant or micro-organism – has a good or well-being of its own, which can in turn be enhanced or damaged. Furthermore, Taylor asserts that all individuals who are teleological centres of life have equal intrinsic value (or what he terms 'inherent worth'), which entitles them to moral respect.

Adapting this biocentric outlook on nature, it is envisaged that:

- Humans are thought of as members of the earth's community of life, holding that membership on the same terms as also applied to nonhuman members.

- The earth's natural ecosystem are considered as a totality and recognised as a complex web of interconnected elements.
- Each individual organism is conceived of as a teleological centre of life, pursuing its own good in its own way.
- The claim that humans by their very nature are superior to other species is a groundless claim.

(Keller 2010: 178)

Such radical ethical philosophies at first sight appear too contentious for mainstream Hollywood to contemplate much less address. Nonetheless in an anthropomorphic predetermined mainstream media, some fissures appear to occur which in turn serves to draw attention to these radical alternative ethical modalities. All the while, it must also be recognised that the so-called science of ethics cannot be considered 'to be a statement of fact, but to be fluid, contextual, dynamic, and often times contradictory'. At the same time it would also be misleading 'to suggest that ethical frameworks cannot guide personal and public action in very clear and influential ways'. In many ways, ethics can broadly be considered 'to be that which informs and guides action, from the founding assumptions that we utilise [and] inform our work to the aspirations and goals of that work. It is this consideration of ethics that will inform our theoretical choices, ontological assumptions, politics, aspirations and actions' (Andrew 2000: 4).

As can be seen from these almost polar opposite positions, namely biocentrism and anthropocentrism, how one interacts with the environment is largely determined by one's pre-disposition towards it (Brereton and Hong 2013), and it seems also that most people continue to embrace a strong anthropocentric position that *de facto* supports environmental exploitation and an attitude that nature is merely a boundless resource for satisfying human wants and needs. In Muir's words, 'no dogma taught by the present civilisation seems to form so insuperable an obstacle in the way of a right understanding of the relations which culture sustains to wilderness, as that which regards the world, as made especially for the uses of man' (in Keller 2010: 253).

Environmental issues also affect a drastic shift in the distinction between the political and non-political in ways that seem alien, even taking on board Derrida's criticisms of the well-established liberal-rights-based justice tradition. While Beck takes up the sheer tragic–comic oddness of the metamorphosis undergone by the political in a crowded but finite world dominated by means of production that demand continuous economic expansion: 'class conflicts or revolutions change power relations and exchange elites, but they hold fast to the goals of techno-economic progress and clash over mutually recognised civil rights' (quoted in Clark 2010: 47). By all accounts a more acceptable and agreeable form of environmental ethical engagement has been encapsulated by Aldo Leopold's very broad-ranging philosophy of the 'land ethic'.

Land ethic

Leopold's 'land ethic' rests upon a simple single unifying premise: 'that the individual is a member of a community of interdependent parts'. His vision served to enlarge the boundaries of community to include soils, water, plants, animals and so forth (Leopold 1947: 204). Especially since his 'rediscovery' in the 1960s, Leopold's 'land ethic' thesis has become a central tenet of environmental thinking and the symbiotic relationship he proposes between man and nature has remained the dominant orthodoxy of much ecological thinking.

This position recognises nature primarily as a resource, which contributes to human value and can be seen through the exposition of animism in the Spielberg oeuvre for example, as providing a fruitful site of light eco-utopianism. Building on the growing scholarship in eco-cinema, this volume provides more detailed and specific ethical analysis through textual analysis across more contemporary and mainstream cinema.

Wilderness

Film is a particularly good medium to draw attention to the value of wilderness and the importance of its preservation, all the while recognising its critiques, which in itself appears uncontestable and a core tenet of environmentalism. In particular, one must call attention to the high-class lifestyles of many enthusiasts for nature rambles, wooded mediations or mountaineering, etc., which often demand a standard of living and the temporal luxury and aesthetic cultural capital that is far beyond the dreams of most of the world's population. Most pointedly, one might wonder is nature worship only practically appealing to those who can afford it? Alternatively, do eco-films simply provide a 'cheap' and vicarious engagement with such otherwise expensive touristic experiences?

Evocations around the ethical implications ascribed to wilderness – which nonetheless remain highly contested within environmental philosophy – play into these and other contradictions and call attention to innate paradoxes around wealth and privilege, valorising a 'back to nature' mode of existence that will be explored through filmic readings across subsequent chapters. One wonders, of course, can such an apparently highbrow and elitist sort of wilderness ethics ever be finally democratised? Most pointedly, how can the physically reviving power of the wild – recalling E.O. Wilson's notion of biophilia and the innate love of nature – become available to those living in the slums of Calcutta or São Paolo?

While not being able to fully answer many of these questions, nonetheless their importance remains pertinent in providing rounded critical readings of films that speak to such dilemmas. See, for instance, analysis of the controversial real life tale of a well-to-do college graduate in *Into the Wild* (Brereton in Rust *et al.* 2013). Such questions and concerns so far lack convincing answers, with commercial and by all accounts self-construed and after-the-fact eco-filmic examples in particular suffused within utopic visions of heroism. These narratives recalling so called 'first wave' environmental analysis, often in turn appear to transcend if not ignore the problems of gender, class, ethnicity and issues of wealth (see Selheim 2011: 129–146). Eco-films through their powerful appeal to the raw beauty of nature, often tend to universalise or dismiss such critical injunctions and barometers of power and injustice. But such tensions need to be faced head on for the deep appreciation and challenges of environmental ethics to mature and develop across film studies and within the social sciences generally.

Many critics, including Ivakhiv, also worry that a strictly aesthetic or moralistic approach to eco-cinema fall short of offering critics a sufficient toolkit for identifying and analysing the contradictions – ethical or otherwise – which are inherent in all films. While an underlying dilemma for David Ingram is whether one film style, genre or taste culture is more effective than another in promoting some corrective form of ecological understanding, much less nailing down a clearly defined ethical position. These are all difficult but important questions to consider at all times when analysing film from an environmental and ethical perspective.

Nonetheless, while still a very live issue for eco-film scholars, much progress has been made in cataloguing a growing corpus of eco-cinema and developing effective multi-layered textual analysis protocols for appreciating eco-cinema's range and potentiality, which are cited throughout this volume. In particular, edited volumes like Willoquet-Maricondi (2010), Rust *et al.* (2013), Taylor (2013), Weik von Mossner (2014), alongside new scholarly journals like *Environmental Communication*, are creating a growing body of scholarship that is exploring a range of concerns and embedding effective strategies and theoretical models to assist in this evolving area of study.

By all accounts, ethical or other environmental arguments will only have force if we physically feel them. In other words, if an argument fails to generate feelings, or does not tap into an affective range of public engagement, then it will probably not persuade. This is why the creative imaginary of fiction remains so important in mobilising and framing public opinion, while calling on the extensive power of emotions towards affecting audience responses. Such affective arguments, it is suggested in the literature, work to help motivate audiences by inducing feelings including satisfaction, pleasure, excitement, interest, anger or distress. If they generate no feelings at all, they are unlikely to be persuasive.

At its most basic level, traditional environmental ethics circle around two fundamental moral questions: what kinds of things are intrinsically valuable, good or bad; and what makes an action right or wrong? Consequentialist ethical theories ostensibly consider intrinsic 'value'/'disvalue' or 'goodness'/'badness' to go beyond more fundamental moral notions than so called rightness/wrongness and maintain that whether an action is right/wrong is determined by whether its consequences are good or bad. Such ethical scales of value underpin and mobilise much narrative engagement within film and other arts.

Native otherness and ecological agency

At one level, drawing on social anthropological concepts developed by Mary Douglas (1966), outsiders can be defined as those groups who do not fit dominant models of society and are therefore seen as polluting (Sibley 1995: 120). The American Indian 'other', in spite of remaining firmly in the background within the dominant Hollywood genres, has nonetheless become a primary focus for progressive ecological values (Murray and Heumann 2014). Instead of apparently polluting the dominant culture, these representational agents came to be seen, particularly by white liberal Americans, as saviours who present and embody a more natural and ethical relationship with their environment.[7] This broad trajectory around authentic indigenous agency will be re-addressed through an examination of contemporary films including *Apocalypto* and *Avatar*.

Gerry Mander suggests in *[In] the Absence of the Sacred* that Westerners fear, hate and revere native Indians because they are what must be repressed in order 'for us to function as we do' (Mander 1992: 214). The Native American Indian has come to embody and symbolise a progressive form of ecological agency. This is crudely reflected in Mander's list of binary opposites which characterises dominant 'white' or 'technological' people as he calls them, while embodying all that is socially deficient and ecologically suspect. The myth of the 'noble savage' Indian who lived 'at one with nature', became appropriated by the ecology movement as an antidote to the growing contemporary environmental threat of Western industrial pollution.

The crude division between the so-called primitive otherness of the Native and the white Westerner can be appreciated on reading *The Savage Mind* (1966) by Claude Lévi-Strauss, who attacks the common notion that modern civilisation is necessarily more cultivated than 'primitive' societies. Modern life is not a sophisticated version of a simple life; it is an altogether different life, based on an entirely separate understanding of the world. Indeed, according to Lévi-Strauss, so-called 'savage' peoples with their highly elaborate knowledge of terrain, flora, kinship and ritual, may in fact live a more complex life than so-called advanced civilisations. Such indigenous people consequently can, according to the literature, represent and embody a more progressive ecological understanding and awareness of an earth-centric appreciation of environmentalism.

While American Indians are frequently represented as the hunted prey, they might more accurately be appreciated as the 'natural' owners of such a landscape. They were the first to inhabit the landscape and more importantly helped to build up a complementary rapport with the eco-system. At least mythically and in spite of some contradictory evidence, they created a perfect balance and harmony between humans and their environment. Consequently the Hollywood native representational man/woman has remained symbolically more ecologically harmonious within the landscape, compared for instance with the white colonial Western hero. Some early ecologists sought to suggest that the new settlers simply destroyed this balance, with their symbols of progress; like the train cutting through an unspoilt landscape,[8] or the even more destructive Western notion of property ownership, which allowed land to be fenced off and protected rather than leaving it in its more natural and wild state. Going back even further in American history to before the arrival of the European colonists, *Apocalypto* serves as a useful exposition of early (revisionist) environmental ethical agendas, as set up through a conflict between two different tribal cultures from the same region in the Americas.

Animal ethics and human agency

While utilitarians tend to focus on the balance of pleasure and pain, exemplified by eighteenth-century thinker Jeremy Bentham (1789), more contemporary philosophers and animal activists like Peter Singer (1993) suggest that the interests of *all* sentient beings (i.e. beings who are capable of experiencing pleasure or pain – including nonhuman ones) are affected by an action and should be taken equally into consideration in assessing such action.

Singer embodies this most radical position, as opposed to the more 'normative' anthropomorphic hierarchising of nature with humans fixed at the top of the pyramid; all of these points of view are explored across various readings of animals in film discussed in Chapter 5. Singer most controversially suggests that the anthropocentric emphasis on members of the species *Homo sapiens* is somewhat arbitrary and that in essence this is a kind of 'speciesism', which remains as unjustifiable as any form of sexism or racism. Meanwhile in contrast, deontological ethical theories maintain that whether an action is right or wrong for the most part is independent of whether its consequences are good or bad. But, of course, trying to weigh up short- as against long-term consequences around 'what if' scenarios between animals and humans remains a very contradictory and often confusing set of value judgements. Proponents on either side tend to use 'worst case' hypothetical scenarios, like what if an animal contained a deadly virus; is it therefore more legitimate to terminate them rather than if it was a human. Very different responses for example can be traced when taking into account the immediate slaughter of whole herds of domestic cattle and the burning of carcasses – as witnessed in the last Irish/UK foot and mouth epidemic (yet one should note this is a disease that does not directly affect humans *per se*). In more recent incidences of contamination by horsemeat in the beef food chain across Europe, alongside more deadly filmic viruses portrayed, including bats infecting meat for human consumption in the blockbuster film *Contagion*, a health-risk scenario is created which has particular resonance most recently with the deadly outbreak of the Ebola virus in Africa in 2014. Chapter 5 is devoted to representations of animals on film, which will help reveal many of their broad ranging environmental and ethical implications.

Aldo Leopold, land ethic, wilderness and spirituality

Building on the short definition of land ethic and wilderness discussed earlier, for nearly half a century green thought in literature and more recently in film has wrestled with many contentous questions including: is nature exogenous to the essential relations of human history; for the most part playing roles as tap (raw materials) and/or sink (pollution). Alternatively, it is suggested that nature is constructed as a web of life encompassing all of human activity, comprising taps and sinks, but also much beyond this. Or is nature something primarily that humans act upon, or act through, as suggested by literary scholars like Jason Moore. The growing green literature that has emerged since the 1970s across political ecology, environmental history and sociology, ecological economics, systems ecology, literature and film study, etc., have evolved by opening out and contesting these broad-ranging questions. Most contemporary scholars like Moore tend to agree that humanity is indeed part of nature, while rejecting the Cartesian dualism that puts society (without nature) in one box and nature (without humans) in another.

In any case, one must question a dominant image of raw nature as passive mud and dirt – a place where one just leaves a footprint – as the best metaphor to capture the vitality of the web-of-life. Many contemporary theorists suggest that foundational theories of environmentalism, including Leopold's land ethic and Hardin's tragedy of the commons, among others, suffer from being couched as broad generalisations that reaffirm the construction of binary abstractions around nature and culture. Certainly crude ethical models of land, nature and environment remain problematic. Nevertheless, they at least provide a useful starting point in attempting to signal a more productive and complex evocation of environmental ethics on film.

Furthermore, Hollywood film criticism most especially has to be particularly cogniscent of playing into prescribed ideological roles around 'greenwashing' of ecological discourses, which largely support a 'business as usual' model and perpetuate reductive romantic attitudes and beliefs around nature, including some assumptions prevalent in so-called deep ecological thought discussed above. The pervasive Arcadian, romantic and even sublime representations of nature in particular are often coded as shorthand for a large tranche of proactive environmental cinema, while at the same time remaining grounded in the service of a mainstream environmental agenda. Such assumptions need to be problematised and continuously questioned and critiqued throughout this study of contemporary eco-film analysis.

Jason Moore and other postcolonial and literary critics (who incidentally have had a longer lead into the sub-discipline compared to film scholars) have particularly challenged eco-film scholars, many of whom – including myself – remain preoccupied with categorising and fine-tuning the tools of analysis for eco-cinema. At the outset, it ought to be acknowledged that while the environmental film arena is not short of relevant theory to help explore and develop a robust environmental ethical framework, the sub-discipline of eco-film studies has to decide what to emphasise and prioritise across a broad range of theories. These call to mind useful developments in the literature that range from eco-globalism (Buell), eco-cosmopolitanism (Heise), eco-phobia (Estok), eco-mimesis (Morton), bio-regionalism (Lynch), environmental justice (Reed), and planetarity engagement (Spivak), to cite just a few.[9]

All of these tools and prisms and other related theoretical frameworks can contribute to eco-critical discourses in the future and are essential in avoiding slipping into various predetermined ideological and romantic aesthetic traps when carrying out representational analysis of nature and the environment. However this introductory study cannot hope to provide a comprehensive review of all such broad-ranging trajectories, rather it focuses on a small number of areas that directly and transparently frame the filmic examples discussed in the subsequent chapters.

Some other core themes and frames which underpin this study include, at one extreme, dramatising environmental risk as a primary cautionary tale embedded in much eco-cinema, and at the other end of the spectrum an affirmation of the power of spirituality and feeling of transcendental connectivity in instilling a deep environmental ethic on film. While there appears to be a decided move away from institutional religion – specifically Catholicism in the West – with a corresponding rise in Islamic fundamentalism in the Middle East, there remains an ever-present desire for more proactive and transcendent forms of nature and spiritual expression. This is particularly evident in the continuous hunger for some form of 'feel-good' spirituality across various art formats. While of course such contested generalisations leave much debate, the growing film-religions literature certainly suggests a preoccupation with various forms of spiritual and religious experience as embodied in film. Bron Taylor in *Dark Green Religion: Nature Spirituality and the Planetary Future* (2009) most notably has drawn direct connections with a form of green spirituality. This form of spirituality has particular significance for readings of *Avatar* and *Life of Pi*.

A dominant aspect of religion and the growth of the elusive notion of spirituality, egalitarianism and deep environmentalism, is an appeal to the heart, human empathy and higher values that inspire individuals and societies to transcend narrow self-interest. Science, technology, politics and economics are less able to provide these perspectives and yet such ethereal values can influence humanity. This last function may in fact be a major key for sustaining progress around 'mitigating climate change' (Posas 207: 1). As Beck and Buell have persuasively argued, the success of environmental initiatives hinges not only on new developments in science and technology, but 'on a state of mind that is bound to be influenced as much by the power of images, narratives, metaphors, and by appeals to feeling, as well as by appeals to data, statistics, expertise, and formal reasoning' (Posas 2007: 10).

Film-goers, I would ideally like to imagine, must become critical spectators of Hollywood films, as film in turn proposes answers to the ancient ethical question: how should life be best lived? Meanwhile S. Brent Plate – one of the foremost scholars in religion and film – talks of the religious visuality of film, helping audiences to 'see differently'. This notion of seeing differently can also be applied to an ecological and ethical re-imagining of the visual and aural techniques of film, alongside other aspects of identification and embodiment in film spectatorship. In film scholarship for example, Kaja Silverman develops an ethical subjectivity extensively predefined across the field of vision 'as an active gift of love' (Faber *et al.* 2009: 51). A religious/spiritual lens can certainly be applied and prefigures an environmental ethical position, as alluded to in a short reading of *Life of Pi*.

Nevertheless, for the moment at least, contemporary Western societies seem predominantly influenced and dominated by non-spiritual and by broadly secular anthropocentric principles. Consequently many fear that ethical and environmental problems cannot be systemically addressed, much less resolved, until there is a radical change in this overall ethical predisposition and until publics embrace a move towards more developed spiritual and related eco-centric ethics, which could in turn call on the more progressive environmental values of Buddhist, Muslim and Hindu religions, alongside more progressive Christian ideals. Otherwise, the world is in danger of not effectively concretising, much less planning for the long-term sustainability of the planet. Such global long-term planning and management by all accounts, whether one uses a spiritual lens or not, has to engage with a more eco-centric, or earth-centred approach, which puts nature first, for the long-term survival of the planet. A call to some form of nature spiritual sensibility helps to develop this radical transformational mindset.

This volume remains preoccupied with debates concerning the veracity of filmic cautionary tales in helping to tip the balance in this regard, while at the same time continuing to emphasise the need to promote such a radical transformation. Only time, of course, will tell, but all forms of art, including what I'm calling the 'creative imaginary' of film, which at one extreme recalls the spiritual evocation of the Hollywood audio-visual industry, can have a pivotal role to play in this major transformation of ideas and audience perceptions.

Yet all the while one must recognise the ever-present danger of appearing preachy and being far from 'objective' in analysing such slippery concepts, which remains frowned upon by most academic perspectives. Simply appearing to be overly polemical and narrowly focused in framing such issues is not enough. Eco-centric ethics essentially remains a shorthand template and actively serves as a radical approach to environmental ethics, which encapsulate and remind us of the hidden social processes within our comfortable Western lifestyles, as opposed to the ever-present primal injustice and stark poverty realities within the Third World, for instance. Such a stance recalls the overall price paid in damage to the natural environment, if such holistic yet radical core ethical precepts are not adapted and systematically embraced by *all* on planet earth. Certainly, if such ethical precepts are not firmly yoked to global injustice issues, environmental ethics as a working axiom remains incompatible and finally unworkable with regards to its core values.

An ethical turn to frugality as an antidote to dominant consumption models

This notion draws on the work of James Nash and the subversive virtue of frugality, which seeks to reject the popular assumption that humans are insatiable creatures, ceaselessly acquisitive for economic gains and egotistically committed to pleasure maximisation, as laid out in environmental allegories specifically around business ethics. An ethical turn to deep environmental forms of frugality involves a rejection of the prevailing ideology of indiscriminate, material economic growth that incidentally was at least historically recognised as a Christian economic norm. Embracing this austere form of sustainability appears a long way for instance from the neoliberal mantra of conspicuous consumption, together with balancing all forms of capitalistic valuation and the fiction of ever-increasing economic growth. While probably it is somewhat counter-intuitive to expect mainstream (Hollywood) cinema to promote such a puritanical form of ethics, nonetheless one can recognise the roots of a 'return to' the values of frugality across a range of contemporary narratives, such as *Wall-E* which explicitly highlights the consequences of excessive waste and allegorically valorises the need for adapting more stoical environmental values.

Furthermore, one could frame how such rampant valorisation of over-consumption has consumed a late capitalist world economy, with its focus on the individual and the resulting atomisation of society. In contrast, the concept of frugality promotes a more sustainable consumption model and might even return us to a deeper sense of community and promote a renewed form of egalitarian society. Back-to-nature quests for survival displayed in films like *All is Lost* speak to such a cautionary frugal agenda as explored in Chapter 2. This erstwhile old-fashioned notion also calls to mind current debates and counter-trends cited in the business literature, calling on forms of positive psychology and an ever-present desire for holistic well-being within society.

In representational terms there always remains a significant danger of prettifying or aestheticising poverty using apocalyptic imagery as a strategy to salve Western charity mindsets, while at the same time collapsing environmentalism and justice models onto very different Third World situations. Such dangers are particularly prevalent for indigenous filmmakers trying to create a more 'authentic' and 'meaningful' aesthetic for their own people, such as in the South African film *Tsotsi* for instance, as well as addressing a global audience.

Commentators often speak of finite resources and environmental damage and emphasise corruption as the primary cause for the continuation of poverty in Africa and elsewhere. But of course the West is closely implicated in perpetuating such corrupt practices. This issue is frequently addressed on film, while pushed back in the end on African or other Third World shoulders as explored in Chapter 6.[10] Eco-feminist analysis, which we now turn to, is also a major area of scholarship in this field and helps clarify and anchor a range of theoretical ethical debates, while ensuring the resultant synthesis of ideas become both pragmatic and realisable.

Eco-feminist studies and environmental ethics

The term 'eco-feminism' was first used in 1974 by the French writer Françoise d'Eaubonne, who called upon women to lead an ecological revolution to save the planet (Merchant 1995: 5). The evolving parameters of eco-feminist discourse embrace various positions in relation to nature, rejecting both the view of humans as apart from and outside nature and of nature as a limitless provider for man's needs.[11] Consequently, feminist discourse incorporates an inherent critique of masculinity and its 'values' (see, for example, Chodorow 1979), as well as a critique of rationality and the 'overvaluation of reason'. It was also promoted as a critique of 'human domination of nature, human chauvinism, speciesism, or anthropocentrism' (see for example Naess 1973), together with a critique of the treatment of nature in purely instrumental terms (Plumwood 1993: 24). Ethical norms are continuously tested and very effectively problematised within an eco-feminist discourse.

Sue Thornham clarifies a primary dilemma of this phenomenon, which coalesces around the dangers of essentialism, when suggesting how feminist theorists suffer from having to 'speak as a woman' (Thornham 1997: 2), a difficulty which remains central to (normative) ethical debates and finding an objective voice and an appropriate language for oppositional discourse.

Not surprisingly, ecology as the study of the balance and interrelationship of all life on earth maps onto the essentialising impulse of the 'feminine principle' and the striving towards human 'balance and interrelationship' which is the stated claim of many feminists. Consequently it follows that if these core principles are accepted, feminism and ecology are inextricably connected. From earliest times, nature and especially the earth was represented as a kind and nurturing mother or alternatively, according to Capra, 'as a wild and uncontrollable female' (Capra 1983: 25). Much later, under the dominance of Western patriarchy, the apparently benign if always ambiguous image of nature changed into one of 'passivity' (Capra 1983: 25).[12] Such regressive passive models are most recently contested in what can almost intuitively be considered as eco-feminist blockbusters such as *Avatar*.

Environmental equality as a solid bedrock of ethical values continues to be regarded by feminists like Carolyn Merchant as a primary eco-feminist issue. 'The body, home, and community are sites of women's local experience and local contestation.' For example, 'women experience chemical pollution through their bodies' (as sites of reproduction) (Merchant 1995: 161). Rachel Carson's *Silent Spring* (1962) – one of the founding texts of an ecological/ethical approach to nature and science and co-opted by some as an eco-feminist text

– effectively expressed this paradigm for America in particular, exposing the 'death-producing effects' of chemicals and helping to make the question of life on earth a public, ethical and political issue (Naess in Gruen and Jamieson 1994: 116).

Merchant usefully suggests and promotes a form of *'partnership ethics'*, which can be seen as a more robust form of liberal eco-feminism, avoiding the gendering of nature as a nurturing mother or a goddess, while also avoiding the ecocentric hierarchic assumptions that humans are part of an ecological web of life and thereby 'morally equal' to a bacterium or a mosquito.

The most persuasive and practical avenue for critical research and anchorage in this highly contested area of ethical debate emanates from an eco-feminist discourse, which incorporates an inherent critique of power, masculinity and such anthropocentric 'values' discussed above; alongside providing a general critique of rationality and what some scholars suggest is the 'overvaluation of reason'. Such influential scholarship across most fields of humanities and social science research, in particular, has been recognised as also promoting a critique of 'human domination of nature, human chauvinism, speciesism, or anthropocentrism', together with a critique of the treatment of nature in purely instrumental terms (Plumwood 1993: 24).

As also discussed in *Hollywood Utopia* (2005), Merchant remains one of the most influential writers in this field and her simple four-point model encapsulates the power of environmental ethics to speak directly and persuasively to mass audiences:

- Equity between humans and non-human communities.
- Moral considerations for humans and non-human nature.
- Respect for cultural diversity and biodiversity.
- Inclusion of women, minorities, and non-human nature in the code of ethical accountability.

(Merchant 1995: 217)

While obsuficating the inherent difficulties and contradictions across such essentialising edicts, which in turn can be critiqued in similar ways to Leopold's 'land ethic', feminists rightly contend that both movements (ecological and the women's movement) have nonetheless been libratory and democratic in their outlook, and reformist, even revolutionary, in their politics and ethical framing. Both pose a threat to the dangers of reinforcing traditional forms of (patriarchial) oppression (Merchant 1995: 139) and provide a cogent framework for future investigation. Particularly if the environmental movement does not actively embrace gender or other Third World power politics debates, the *raison d'être* of environmental ethics cannot be extended successfully into the future. This justice-based movement is often categorised as 'second wave' environmentalism, with the first wave somewhat unfairly seen as overly preoccupied with rural romanticism and the valorisation of a very narrow range of environmental agendas. But Val Plumwood most usefully points out, our ability to transcend the ethical and aesthetic categories and discourses that have contributed to alienation from our environment is dependent upon an enlargement of our imaginative capacities (see Gifford and Becket 2007: 9).

As further suggested in *Hollywood Utopia*, '[E]cology has become a new, all-inclusive, yet often contradictory meta-narrative' (Brereton 2005: 11), which is clearly present within Hollywood film since the 1950s. The research from this earlier study 'focused particularly on feel-good films whose therapeutic character often leads to their being dismissed as ideologically regressive. By concentrating on narrative closure and especially the way space is used to foreground and dramatise the sublime pleasure of nature' (Brereton 2005: 11), Hollywood cinema can subsequently be seen to have within it a 'certain tendency' that in turn helps to dramatise core ecological values and ideas. While probably less certain of such judgement calls with the benefit of hindsight, nonetheless the general tenor of mainstream cinema continues to reflect such values.

While the ostensibly codified 'ideological' analytical strategy that focuses on power inequalities across class, gender and race boundaries continues to preoccupy investigations of Hollywood cinema, there is surprisingly still very little critical engagement with the more universal phenomenon of ecology. Thankfully however this vacuum is being reversed by a small number of eco-film scholars and edited volumes including Ivakhiv (2008), Rust *et al.* (2013), Weik von Mossner (2014) and others mentioned above, who have established a coherent body of environmental wisdom and constructive strategies for reading film from an environmental perspective. Nonetheless, I would still stand by the assertion that if so-called ecological/ethical readings are to remain critical, and avoid degenerating into endorsing naïve and essentialising polemics, they must explicitly feature a variety of interpretations and perspectives, while speaking to this under-developed environmental and ethical project.

Concluding remarks

There is a growing need for broad-based empirical audience research to test many of the assertions suggested in much eco-cinema scholarship as cited above. Such assertions include also hypotheses raised in previous papers, suggesting for instance that evocations of nature have helped to dramatise and encourage 'raw nature' to speak directly to audiences, together with their protagonists, who often finally find sanctuary in nature from particular environmental problems. This contested therapeutic expression (see the well-justified criticism by Ivakhiv (2013)) is often I suggest still valorised over and above the strict narrative requirements of the text through, for instance, framing, narrative point-of-view and shot length. Rather than merely serving as a romantic backdrop or a crude narrative *deus-ex-machina*, I *still* like to believe these evocations of eco-nature across mainstream cinema become self-consciously emphasised and consequently help at times to promote a productive ecological meta-narrative connecting humans' with their environment. One wonders also can the power of cinema, speaking through an explicit thematic preoccupation with environmental ethics, be effective in exposing such complex issues and in turn help to dramatise environmental ethics in all its manifestations? The selected readings in the following chapters will set out to explore this potential, which is inherent in the medium.

As signalled also over a decade ago, foregrounding a proactive visual aesthetic capturing the protagonists in the films discussed in this study (*Hollywood Utopia*) including *Grand Canyon* and *Jurassic Park*, alongside more contemporary examples explored in this and other volumes, one wonders whether all these eco-film analysis strategies help to embody and even critique a range of environmental and ethical scenarios. One hopes so. But note, as Ivakhiv points out, 'ecocritics tend to gravitate towards explicitly environmental films', especially those 'that portray nature and its defenders positively', nonetheless rarely has cinema in general 'been viewed through an ecocritical lens' (Ivakhiv 2008: 1). In simply broadening the corpus of eco-cinema, this study addresses a range of mainstream commercial films which might not normally be examined under the environmental and ethical agenda.

The chapters that follow feature a broad range of these environmental and ethical precepts and in turn throw light on a selection of contemporary films to demonstrate how they can contribute to the growing corpus of texts that can be read through an environmental and ethical lens. These include extensive readings of *The Hunger Games, Gravity, Avatar, Captain Phillips, The Road, The Wolf of Wall Street, The Constant Gardener, Apocalypto* and others that have been the most popular and influential films of recent years and are rarely if ever read from a specifically environmental-ethical perspective.

Notes

1 For instance, one recent study, alluding to the major dilemma of climate change, suggests that if 'we're convinced some powerful force – be it God or science – has things under control we can comfortably remain passive. But fear of chaos leads us to take things into our own hands, increasing our motivation and action'. Meijers and Retjens (2014), cited in Jacobs (2014).

2 In holism there is no nature/culture dualism: humans and nature are part of the same organic cosmological system, while theoretical ecologism often focus their research on natural areas removed from human impact, human (or political) etc.

3 Garrett Hardin goes on to paint a bleak picture regarding various other global dilemmas, especially concerning Third World poverty, and even greater inequality being initiated by not dealing with issues concerning population growth, through for instance a 'World Food Bank' notion of a new commons.

4 Through Mill and Bentham (2000), the philosophical doctrine of utilitarianism with its call for tolerance towards the other, and the overarching concept of ethical relativism drew distinctions between those 'who are not us', and 'us'; yet as Midgley (1996) concludes, such an understanding of ethical relativism assumes a society in which cultures are entirely and eternally separate, and will never mix.

5 Most critics speak for example to the short-term consideration of democratic political parties who do not think beyond the next election, which of course does not take into account longer-term implications around nuclear power, much less older carbon extractive energy sources and the limitations of the carbon sink with regards to CO_2 emissions and climate change.

6 Singer coined the term 'speciesism' to explain the irrational prejudice that Bentham originally identified as the basis of our radically different treatment of animals and humans. Because of its mimetic and realistic features, film most explicitly shows animal–human inter-relationships and their environmental and ethical implications.

7 While maintaining only four per cent of world population – USA emits 25 per cent of the world's carbon dioxide (Centre for Progressive Reform 2008). Yet across the world people living in poverty are now more likely to live in unplanned, temporary settlements which are erected on unsuitable land – prone to the risks of flooding, storm surges and landslides.

8 For example, it is common knowledge that the white settlers massacred the roaming buffalo, not for food, as the Indians did, but simply to colonise the land and force it into submission and fulfil (civilised) Eastern economic expectations towards the production of profitable cash crops. Official American policy, as referred to by the historian William Cronon, was designed specifically to starve the Indians by taking away their food source. Nature became an adversary, which had to be curbed even violated to accord with white man's greedy desires (Cronon1992).

9 For instance, calling to mind Leopold's 'Old Testament' style manifesto of environmental ethics: 'A thing is right when it tends to preserve the integrity, stability, and beauty of the biotic community. It is wrong when it tends otherwise' – which was embraced in *Hollywood Utopia* as the supreme deontological principle. Over the intervening years, however, some important critiques of what could certainly be considered as a *de facto* normative proposition for deep environmental land ethics have emerged. At one extreme, Tom Regan (1983: 362) may have gone a bit too far in condemning this holist land ethic's disregard for the rights of the individual as 'environmental fascism'. Under pressure from the charge of eco-fascism and even misanthropy, J. Baird Callicott (1980) has constructively advocated a revived version of land-ethical holism, which has become modified to a position which now maintains that the biotic community *all* have intrinsic value.

10 For example, *The Last King of Scotland* (2006) traces the rise of an African dictator Idi Amin, who was educated in the West, while back in his homeland, African leaders are able to sell their country's resources to buy arms and provide soldiers to maintain their rule and to amass personal fortunes.

11 'Feminists argue that most contemporary political theory, whether liberal, Marxist, or Frankfurt School, works from a model of *man* which is universal, uniform, ahistorical, and transcendent, excluding a model of *woman* which is contextual, relativistic and particularistic. Eco-feminists add that the traditional model of man is alienated from natural contexts too' (Gruen and Jamieson1994: 161).

12 This image of nature is probably the most common preoccupation in much Hollywood cinema. Critics especially cite Walt Disney's fixation with a two-dimensional representation of nature. *Bambi* (1942), for example, illustrates the classic Disney(land) view, as all the animals troop down to see the 'miracle' of a new baby deer. Such a *mise-en-scène* evokes and serves to reinforce the idyllic co-existence of all animals. Only 'man' can upset this utopia.

Bibliography

Allison, L. (1991) *Ecology and Utility: The Philosophical Dilemmas of Planetary Management.* Leicester: Leicester University Press.

Andrew, Jane (2000) 'The Environmental Crisis and the Accounting Craft'. Research Online Faculty of Commerce papers archive University of Wollongong.

Bentham, Jeremy (1789) *An Introduction to the Principles of Morals and Legislation.* Oxford: Clarendon Press.

Brereton, Pat (2005) *Hollywood Utopia: Ecology in Contemporary American Cinema.* Bristol: Intellect Press.

Brereton, Pat and Hong, Pat (2013) 'Irish Eco-cinema and Audiences'. *Interactions: Studies in Culture and Communications* 4(2): 191–99. Special issue on eco-cinema, editor Pietari Kääpä.

Butler, Judith (2004) *Precarious Life: The Powers of Mourning and Violence.* New York: Verso.

Callicott J.B. (1980) 'Animal Liberation: A Triangular Affair'. *Environmental Ethics* 2(4): 311–338.

Campbell, Vincent (2013) 'Framing Environmental Risks and Natural Disasters in Factual Entertainment Television'. *Environmental Communication* 8(1): 58–74.

Capra, F. (1983) *The Turning Point: Science Society and the Rising Culture.* London: Bantam.

Carson, Rachel (1962) *Silent Spring.* London: Penguin.

Centre for Progressive Reform (2008) CPR Climate Change Bibliography http://www.progressivereform.org/ccbiblioecon.cfm.

Cheney, J. (1989) 'Postmodern Environmental Ethics: Ethics as Bioregional Narrative'. *Environmental Ethics* 11(2): 117–134.

Chodorow, Nancy (1979) *The Reproducing of Mothering: Psychoanalysis and the Society of Gender.* Berkley, CA: University of California Press.

Cooper, Sarah (2006) 'The Occluded Relation: Levinas and Cinema'. *Film and Philosophy* 11(2) http://www.film-philosophy.com/index.php/f-p/article/view/83/68.

Cronon, William (1992) 'A Place for Stories: Nature, History and Narrative'. *Journal of American History*, 78(4): 1347–1376.

Douglas, Mary (1966) *Purity and Danger: An Analysis of the Concept of Pollution and Taboo.* New York: Routledge.

Eccleshall, Robert and Geoghegan, Vincent (eds) (1994) *Political Ideologies.* London: Unwin Hyman.

Faber, Alyda and Blizek, William (eds) (2009) *The Continuum Companion to Religion and Film: Religious Ethics and Film.* London: Continuum.

Gifford, Terry and Becket, Fiona (eds) (2007) *Culture Creativity and Environment: New Environmentalist Criticism*, Nature, Culture and Literature. Amsterdam: Rodophi.

Girgus, Sam B. (2010) *Levinas and the Cinema of Redemption: Time, Ethics, and the Feminine.* New York: Columbia University Press.

Glotfelty, C. and Fromm, H. (eds) (1996) *The Ecocriticism Reader: Landmarks in Literary Ecology.* Athens, GA: University of Georgia Press.

Gruen, L. and Jamieson, J. (eds) (1994) *Reflecting on Nature: Readings in Environmental Philosophy.* Oxford: Oxford University Press.

Hardin, Garret (1974) 'Lifeboat Ethics: The Case against Helping the Poor'. *Psychology Today* http://rintintin.colorado.edu/~vancecd/phil1100/Hardin.pdf.

Hatley, James, Edelglass, William and Diehm, Christian (eds) (2012) *Facing Nature: Levinas and Environmental Thought.* Pittsburgh, PA: Duquesne University Press.

Ivakniv, Adrian (2008) 'Green Film Criticism and its Futures'. *Interdisciplinary Studies in Literature and Environment (ISLE)* 2008, 1–28 http://www.uvm.edu/~aivakhiv/GreenFilmCrit.pdf

Ivakhiv, Adrian (2013) *Ecologies of the Moving Image: Cinema, Affect, Nature.* Waterloo, Canada: Wilfred Laurier University Press.

Jacobs, Tom (2014) 'Faith in Scientific Progress Decreases Eco-Friendly Behavior'. *Pacific Standard* http://www.psmag.com/books-and-culture/faith-scientific-progress-decreases-eco-friendly-behavior-87692.

Kakoudaki, D. (2002) 'Spectacles of History: Race Relations, Melodrama and the Science Fiction/Disaster Film'. *Camera Obscura* 17(2): 108–153.

Keller, David (ed).(2010) *Environmental Ethics*. Oxford: Wiley Blackwell.

Lakoff, G. (2010) 'Why it Matters how We Frame the Environment'. *Environmental Communication: A Journal of Nature and Culture* 4(1): 70–81.

Leopold, A. (1947) *A Sand Country Almanac*. Oxford: Oxford University Press.

Lévi-Strauss, Claude (1966) *The Savage Mind*. Chicago, IL: University of Chicago Press.

Mander, Gerry (1992) *In the Absence of the Sacred: The Failure of Technology and the Survival of the Indian Nation*. San Francisco, CA: Sierra Club Books.

Merchant, Carolyn (1995) *Earthcare: Women and the Environment.* London: Routledge.

Midgley, Mary (1996) *Utopias, Dolphins and Computers: Problems of Philosophical Plumbing*. London: Routledge.

Mill, John Stewart and Bentham, Jeremy (2000) *Utilitarianism and other Essays.* Ed. Alan Ryan. London: Penguin.

Murray, Robin and Heumann, Joseph (2014) *Gunfight at the Eco-Corral: Western Cinema and the Environment*. Norman, OK: University of Oklahoma Press.

Naess, Arne (1973 'The Shadow and the Deep, Long-range Ecological Movement. A Summary'. *Inquiry* 16(1): 95–100.

O'Brien, Adam (2013) 'Book Review of *Beyond Green: Ecocinema Theory and Practice*'. *Senses of Cinema* June. http://sensesofcinema.com/2013/book-reviews/beyond-green-ecocinema-theory-and-practice-edited-by-stephen-rust-salma-monani-and-sean-cubitt/

Plumwood, Val (1993) *Feminism and the Mastery of Nature*. London: Routledge.

Posas, Paula (2007) 'Roles of Religion and Ethics in Addressing Climate Change' in *Ethics in Science and Environmental Politics* 2007: 31–49.

Regan, T. (1983) *The Case for Animal Rights*. London: Routledge and Kegan Paul.

Rust, Stephen, Monani, Salma and Cubitt, Sean (eds) (2013) *Ecocinema, Theory and Practice*. AFI Film Readers. London: Routledge.

Salvador, M. and Norton, T. (2011) 'The Flood Myth in the Age of Global Climate Change'. *Environmental Communication: A Journal of Nature and Culture* 5(1): 45–61.

Selheim, Megan Elizabeth (2011) 'Towards a Political Economy of Activist Documentary', masters thesis of fine arts in science and natural history filmmaking. Montana State University.

Sibley, D. (1995) *Geographies of Exclusion: Society and Difference in the West*. London: Routledge.

Simmons, I.G.(1993) *Environmental History: A Concise Introduction*. Oxford: Basil Blackwell.

Singer, Brian (1993) 'Taking Life: Humans' in *Practical Ethics,* second edn. Cambridge: Cambridge University Press.

Taylor, Bron (ed) (2013) *Avatar and Nature Spirituality*. Waterloo, Canada: Wilfrid Laurier University Press.

Taylor, Paul W. (1986) *Respect for Nature: A Theory of Environmental Ethics*. Princton, NJ: Princeton Univeristy Press.

Thornham, S. (1997) *Passionate Detachment: An Introduction to Feminist Film Theory.* London: Arnold.

Weik von Mossner, Alexa (2012) 'Facing *The Day After Tomorrow*: Filmed Disaster, Emotional Engagement, and Climate Risk Perception' in Christof Mauch and Sylvia Mayer (eds) *American Environments: Climate-Cultures-Catastrophie*. Heidelberg: Universitätverlag Winter https://www.researchgate.net/publication/270161666_Facing_The_Day_After_Tomorrow_Filmed_Disaster_Emotional_Engagement_and_Climate_Risk_Perception

Wheatley, H. (2011) 'Beautiful Images in Spectacular Clarity: Spectacular Television, Landscape Programming and the Question of (Tele)visual Pleasure'. *Screen* 52(2): 233–248.

Willoquet-Maricondi, Paula (ed) (2010) *Framing the World: Explorations in Ecocriticism and Film*. Charlottesville, VA and London: University of Virginia Press.

2

ENVIRONMENTAL ETHICS AND ECO-CINEMA

Core textual readings

Overview: eco-cinema

With so much complex theorising around environmental ethics, it remains difficult to anchor, much less differentiate, so many ideas and concepts. Consequently the core preoccupation of this and subsequent chapters is focused around concrete textual analysis of a wide range of contemporary popular films, in an attempt to illustrate and flesh out such ethical debates. Each subsequent chapter will feature a number of narratives that ostensibly speak to various themes and areas of investigation as set out in Chapter 1. This chapter begins this process by setting up how eco-cinema can be read as emphasising divergent environmental registers, across a broad section of mainstream popular cinema. Within this burgeoning sub-discipline of eco-cinema and also drawing on environmental media communications discourses in general, more robust and in-depth textual methodologies can be developed towards understanding and hopefully assessing the broad range of pleasures provided by audio-visual media.

At one level, environmental scholars would like to think eco-cinema 'overtly strives to inspire personal and political action on the part of viewers, stimulating our thinking so as to bring about concrete changes in the choices we make daily and in the long run, as individuals and as societies, locally and globally' (Willoquet-Maricondi 2010: 45). Focusing primarily on art cinema, this radical approach argues that for instance a filmmaker's unique use of long takes and slow pacing can most positively promote contemplation across ecological lines, echoing for instance Bella Tar's embodiment of 'slow cinema'.

Similar to Willoquet-Maricondi, Scott MacDonald argues that certain experimental films can promote an eco-centric sensibility and considers the 'fundamental job of eco-cinema as a retraining of perception, as a way of offering an alternative to conventional media-spectatorship' (Rust *et al.* 2013: 45). Such eco-critics emphasise the benefits of more reflexive, art-house or 'slow cinema', which can in turn encourage the retraining of perception as a necessary condition for greater ecological awareness. These and other eco-scholars suggest that only certain types of independent lyrical and activist documentaries may be thought of as eco-cinema, simply because they are the most capable of inspiring progressive eco-political discourses and action among viewers. Alternatively, it is the contention of this study that it is much more useful to broadly accept that *all* types of film, from the excesses of a commercial Hollywood blockbuster, alongside the most rarefied and explicitly ecological art-house narrative, can consciously or sometimes even unconsciously, highlight specific ecological issues and ethical debates and thereby help situate these concerns within the general public consciousness.

In this chapter I will concentrate on mainstream Hollywood fare and outline some of the broad environmental trajectories engaged with by a selection of films, drawing on familiar case studies such as *An Inconvenient Truth* and popular fiction films like *The Day after Tomorrow*, *Avatar* and *Wall-E*, as well as developing eco-readings of two very recent survival-at-sea features that would not immediately call to mind an environmental or ethical agenda, namely *All is Lost* and *Captain Phillips*.

Introduction: eco-cinema and textual analysis strategies

Environmental analysis tends to emphasise eco-cinema as first and foremost a cognitive, rather than an affective or emotional experience. Cognitive estrangement is set up as the first step by which the desired state of environmental awareness might be attained. By all accounts this is a very narrow, even an elitist, framing, according to Rust *et al.*, who suggest that eco-film criticism's over-arching purpose

> should *not* be to impose a political program – much less pre-defined aesthetic practices – but to help create public spaces for debate and ethical argument over the claims of the environment for a place in political life.
> (Rust *et al.* 2013: 3, original emphasis)

This study essentially adopts and reiterates this broad-based position using examples across a range of contemporary Hollywood films.

Popular fiction film, alongside more conventional preoccupations with nature/ecology in televisual documentaries and animation, remains an excellent forum to promote and at the same time help puncture any simplistic formulations around the complexities of dealing with environmental issues and debates. However, scholarship has to move beyond simply creating a robust definitional and textual-based corpus of eco-cinema and further develop a body of clearly differentiated empirical evidence to help underpin many of the ecological and ethical assertions made in the literature. This empirical research – which is totally beyond the scope of this volume – can in turn help assess and measure future attitudinal changes, especially as eco-cinema hopefully becomes more provocative in its environmental and ethical agenda for its growing audiences.

Leo Braudy's 1998 essay 'The Genre of Nature' is considered by many, including David Whitley, as seminal in anchoring the study of eco-cinema as part of popular culture, which can in turn act as a 'sounding board' or 'lightning rod' for deep-rooted audience concerns. Key thematic and narrative elements in this broad brush approach include:

> a prevalence for protagonists who might be termed 'primitives' – children, animals or Neanderthals; a nostalgia for a lost past in which it was possible to live more simply and authentically, or for residual elements in the present that emblematise 'that past'; and a hunger for what are described as 'ceremonies of innocence'.[1]
>
> (Weik von Mossner 2014: 145)

The unique value of Braudy's definition of what might constitute nature and eco-cinema, according to Whitley, includes 'avoiding the trap of viewing popular cinema reductively, in the way that some strands of environmentally oriented criticism have done' and 'judging films according to rather inflexible criteria of the degree to which they represent the reality of the natural world', while not always taking into account 'the problems of academic rigour involved in identifying cultural anxieties with enough specificity'. In essence this open approach attempt 'to treat audiences and popular films seriously in their own terms' (Whitley in Weik von Mossner 2014: 145–6).

Sean Cubitt goes so far as to suggest

> [T]hough many films are predictably bound to the common ideologies of the day, including ideologies of nature, many are far richer in contradictions and more ethically, emotionally and intellectually satisfying than much of what passes for eco-politic.
>
> (Cubitt 2005: 1)

Cubitt further proposes that while film critics remain preoccupied with the realist image, environmental science deals in effects that are often too vast, too slow, or too dispersed to be observed photographically. Consequently, in a seminal feature such as *An Inconvenient Truth* to be discussed later, there is a cinematic move towards rendering the world as visual data and thereby helping to promote a critical and concrete environmental ethical agenda around climate change.

Meanwhile, Adrian Ivakhiv more radically re-conceives eco-cinema and its ethical predisposition, as a machine that moves us along vectors that are affective, narrative and semiotic in nature and discloses worlds in which humanity, animality and territory are brought into relationship with each other.

(in Rust *et al.*: 6)

Furthermore, Cubitt, among others, confidently affirms that our affective relationships to various environments, as well as human and non-human entities today, are developed to a substantial degree and mediated by our engagement with virtual technologies, such as film (Weik von Mossner 2014: 6).

In describing cinema's complex interactions, Ivakhiv embraces three ecologies of the earth-world; namely the material, the social and the perceptual, while emphasisng a Peircean model of semiotic analysis. His provocative and dense book-length study titled *Ecologies of the Moving Image: Cinema, Affect, Nature* (2013) effectively grapples with a high level of metaphysical and broadly philosophical ideas that call attention to the representations of environmentalism within a growing corpus of cinematic reflections and theoretical analysis.

At the same time, psychologists and more mainstream film scholars frequently affirm a common-sense notion that we cannot expect dramatic changes in worldviews, much less calling attention to ethical predispositions as a result of simply watching a movie. Naturally also, viewers tend to be attracted by the kind of films that fit their belief systems; and possibly as a worst-case scenario, eco-films may end up only preaching to the converted. Yet in any case, mass audiences continue to watch movies precisely because of cinema's ability to reframe a wide range of perceptions and as highlighted in this volume, helping to explain how the medium sets up a broad range of 'what if' cautionary tale scenarios. The late, great film critic Roger Ebert of the *Chicago Sun-Times* often talked of the power of cinema to invoke empathy and allow audiences to step into another world and see reality from a totally different perspective.

For eco-film scholars, cinema enables audiences to begin to recognise ways of seeing the world, other than through the narrow perspective of the anthropocentric gaze that primarily situates individual human desires at the centre of the moral universe and which, as laid out in the introductory chapter, remains problematic for the prospect of engaging with a deep ecological and ethical sensibility. Of course this proposition that film can have a radical effect on audiences is a big ask and demands much more research, including extensive longitudinal studies to test such a broad hypothesis with regards to the power of cinema to explicitly help feature, much less promote, such an ecological agenda.

In the meanwhile, citing a number of extensively written-about eco-classics, one can at least map and frame the radical potential of the film medium, drawing on the limited, small-scale audience research carried out so far, using these texts as primary stimulus. While empirical audience studies can serve to question and debunk some theoretical eco-textual analysis frameworks, I very much embrace the proposition that textual analysis is always necessary to speak to different sides of the same issue and help to evoke and explore the creative imaginary involved in dramatising such complex debates.[2]

The most recent reader on eco-cinema titled *Moving Environments: Affect, Emotion, Ecology and Film* (2014), edited by Alexa Weik von Mossner, situates the most salient recent concerns in the literature around the inherent power, alongside the potential drawbacks of eco-cinema. For instance, the editor describes the primary importance of 'affect' – 'our automatic, visceral response to a given film or sequence – and emotion – our cognitive awareness of such a response' which in the words of Carl Plantinga are 'fundamental to what makes film artistically successful, rhetorically powerful, and culturally influential' (Weik von Mossner 2014: 1).

Some of the questions posed in this volume also speak to Plantinga's assertion and include: how do films represent human emotions and affect in relation to different ethical environments? How do these chosen films influence our emotions while seeing them and after seeing them, and how do they generate ethical meanings? (Weik von Mossner 2014: 1). Meanwhile Ivakhiv reminds us of 'the thick immediacy of cinematic spectacle, the shimmering texture of image and sound as it strikes us and resounds in us viscerally and affectively'. This complex visceral experience of the moving image, he writes, is what 'moves us most immediately and directly' when we are watching film (Ivakhiv 2013: ix). While many of the films explored in this volume use a limited range of spectacle to communicate an environmental agenda, they all actively use more conventional yet effective forms of narrative identification to connect with and speak to mass audiences.

Berys Gaut clarifies this concept of audience 'identification' as central to the cognitivist interpretation of film. The 'question to ask whenever someone talks of identifying with a character', he writes,

> is in what respects does she identify with the character; the act of identification is aspectual. To identify perceptually with a character is to imagine seeing what he sees; to identify affectively with him is to imagine feeling what he feels; to identify motivationally is to imagine wanting what he wants; to identify epistemically with him is to imagine believing what he believes; to identify practically with him is to imagine doing what he does; and so on.
>
> (Ingram in Weik von Mossner 2014: 30)

These aspects of audience identification remain essential as primary modes of viewers connecting across a range of environmental and ethical parameters. Let's begin to explore how some of these environmental ethical and identification debates are set up and communicated, starting with probably the most recognisable title *An Inconvenient Truth*.

An Inconvenient Truth: an environmental tipping point

The most cited example of eco-cinema over its short history, at least from a documentary perspective, remains *An Inconvenient Truth*. The narrative succeeds not only because of its predictions and persuasive cognitive logics, but also because of the deep eco-memories and emotional affect that it evokes. Gore's film – albeit directed by Davis Guggenheim – powerfully argues for a widely held nostalgia for a better, environmentally cleaner world. Gore's very direct message gains rhetorical force, according to another eco-cinema study (Murray and Heumann 2009: 195), by highlighting what can be defined as environmental nostalgia, coupled with its powerful emotional appeal to audiences.

This eco-documentary argues cogently for sustainable environmental policies and an ethic of respect for nature, by invoking both personal and universal ecological memories, as earlier evident in classic science fiction films like *Silent Running*, *Omega Man*, and (even more closely entwined with Gore's narrative) *Soylent Green*. *An Inconvenient Truth* opens with two scenes illustrating two historical memories of the world 30 years beforehand. One of those memories grows out of a meandering river that flowed near Al Gore's family farm,

> a river we see flowing clean and clear through a pristine green landscape. The year is 1973 and Al and wife Tipper float along in a canoe over gentle ripples of the Caney Fork River. Living nature is highlighted here by the river, the foliage that lines it and the fact that Tipper is close to giving birth to the Gores' first child.
>
> (Murray and Heumann 2007: 1)

According to Murray and Heumann, such an affective and nostalgic eco-text helps to create a 'tipping point' in audience engagement and affords the legitimation of environmentalism as a primary ethical imperative.

Riding on the crest of this notion of a global tipping point, while developing a persuasive visual style which draws upon the scientific truth of climate change, actively inspired media producers and filmmakers to permeate their media landscape with images of global warming in diverse fictional films including *11th Hour*, *The Day the Earth Stood Still*, *Quantum of Solace*, *Wall-E*, as well as most notably *Avatar* with its extremely invasive form of mineral extraction. These contemporary narratives, according to a broad range of eco-scholarly research, (including Rust *et al.* 2013; Whitley 2012; Kääpä 2013; Weik von Mossner 2014) draw on the singular inspiration and potency of this small-scale cautionary tale. Consequently *An Inconvenient Truth* probably remains the canonical text for almost all subsequent environmental filmic narratives, both fictional and non-fictional.

Furthermore, at an aesthetic level, data visualisation through an innovative usage of graphs, PowerPoint and other visualising tools serve to reaffirm the documentary's originality. According to Cubitt, *An Inconvenient Truth* most effectively embraces cartography, numbers, graphics and simulations, which are also integral to the explicitly scientific discourse of climate change.[3] Since global events like climate change do not occur in humanly perceptible scales or time frames, they consequently demand forms of representation that can capture massive, but at the same time relatively slow, ecological change.[4]

Godfrey Reggio most notably pioneered the use of time-lapse photography in his eco-parables *Koyaanisqatsi* and *Powaqqatsi*; techniques which in turn feed into evolving tools of representation that help to visualise such large time shifts and effectively capture themes central to a deep ecological agenda. Incidentally *An Inconvenient Truth* specifically foreshadows the 2012 eco-documentary *Chasing Ice,* revealing the inside story of climate change science through the stunning time-lapse photography of James Balog. The visualisation of climate change in such documentaries help to overcome the temporo-spatial problems highlighted as one of the most challenging aspects of environmental communication. Balog's solution employs the use of photographic stills taken from the same vantage point and separated by years; thus presenting the unfolding ecological crisis before our very eyes in breath-taking simplicity through the use of time-lapse photography, like Kilimanjaro's vanishing snows (Cubitt in Rust *et al.*: 280).

At the outset however, we must recognise that climate change is not the only global ethical environmental risk exploited by Hollywood in recent years: one calls to mind for example nuclear war in *Terminator 2: Judgement Day*, deforestation in *FernGully: The Last Rainforest*, bioterrorism in *28 Days Later*, species extinction in *Earth*, population growth in *Slumdog Millionaire*, ecology and religion in *The Tree of Life* and *Life of Pi*, among many other environmental examples discussed in this and other environmental film studies publications.

A cautionary environmental ethical tale: *The Day after Tomorrow*

It makes sense, for instance, that the first fictional film to directly portray global warming was a post-apocalyptic science fiction film set in the future. *Soylent Green* stars Charlton Heston and Edward G. Robinson who play detectives on the case of a murdered food-industry executive. Through the late twentieth century, as the science of anthropogenic climate change became more conclusive, the energy industry and conservative think-tanks led a concerted effort across the mainstream media to frame the issue simply as a theoretical debate, rather than a pressing practical ethical concern.

In a chapter titled 'Hollywood and Climate Change' (Rust *et al.* 2013), Stephen Rust appears to make an unsubstantiated claim that climate change films have primarily influenced a shift in American popular environmental discourse by translating the science of 'global warming' into the vernacular of cinema. Released in 2004, *The Day After Tomorrow* dramatises the extreme consequences of global warming in a science fiction fantasy and earned more than $500 million at the global box office. It offers a window into what Rust perceptively terms, the 'cultural logic of ecology', epitomising the pronounced shift in American popular discourse around the relationship between human beings and the earth that is taking shape in the early twenty-first century.

By the time global warming re-emerged in cinema during the late 1980s and early 1990s, 'a majority of scientists' had become 'convinced that global warming was occurring' (Leiserowitz 2003: 8–9). In the disaster-framed fictional world of *The Day after Tomorrow*, neither scientific consensus nor increased weather anomalies inspired the government or the public to begin mitigating global warming in time to avert disaster. The film's narrative suggests, only when 'Americans finally *see* climate change and *feel* its direct impact within the United States', will 'they accept responsibility for causing global warming and begin to take action in response to it' (Rust *et al.* 2013: 198).[5]

By all accounts, contemporary film research has become more preoccupied with the power of emotional empathy and affect, which is particularly important in promoting a range of environmental ethical approaches to the world, as against more cerebral cognitive engagement as discussed earlier. This of course is not to suggest that emotion and cognition can be so easily differentiated. See for instance the work of scholars like Greg Smith, Nöel Carroll, Murray Smith, Carl Plantinga and many others.[6]

Without voice-over commentary or 'talking heads', as evident in documentaries like *An Inconvenient Truth*, a film works as much through audio-visual affect, as against the sort of cognitive affects identified by Willoquet-Maricondi and MacDonald, and all of which remains central to the eco-film (Rust *et al.* 2013: 46). The significance of these models/interpretative frameworks becomes more apparent when understood in the context of the evolution of film studies, which has concentrated on teasing out form as opposed to content, while attempting to differentiate and analyse various aesthetic strengths. For some scholars, eco-cinema fills a necessary vacuum by simply seeking to speak to and highlight specific thematic manifestations of environmental–ethical concern. Essentially therefore the focus of such analysis involves striving to extract the particular variables and trigger points, which might in turn promote a proactive engagement with the environment.

With its broad strokes, eco-fictional diegesis – what's on the screen – including its use of special effects to simulate extreme weather conditions that help create an environmental creative imaginary, *The Day After Tomorrow* most certainly has the potential to cue and prompt viewers into an active, multilayered, conceptual and sensory consideration of the relationships between humans and their global environment. For instance there have been useful audience studies in Germany and America (see Leiserowitz 2004[7]) focused on public reactions to the film, which highlight the relative power of the storyline to speak to mass audiences across cognitive, emotional and ethical registers. But much more substantial longitudinal studies are needed however to test many of the assertions made in various theoretical studies, while at the same time developing more extensive textually-based eco-film investigation to set up and drive the range of hypotheses addressed (see Brereton and Hong 2013). Let's now move on to a very successful animation feature, which promotes what could be described as a frugal aesthetic and effectively signals the on-going dilemma over the prevailing ethical concerns around environmental waste.

Wall-E: waste and frugality – new modes of environmental animation

Directed by Andrew Stanton, this cautionary animated satire on consumer culture and environmental waste for the modern world – pushing the implicit assertions of *An Inconvenient Truth* to its ultimate conclusion – has rightly received much praise for its engaging storyline, ostensibly set in 2700, long after the earth is smothered by waste and declared unliveable for humans. *Wall-E* bravely features a non-talking waste allocation (analogue-like) load-lifter – the last 'inhabitant' and robot on planet earth – who initially makes friends with a stray cockroach, before finding his true love EVE (Extra Terrestrial Vegetation Evaluator), a pristine (high tech digital) robot sent to earth to investigate if humans could possibly return to their erstwhile 'Garden of Eden'.

Much later in the narrative we find out, 'Buy-n-Large' a business corporation has been largely responsible for the waste explosion on the planet. Its CEO, a bland hypocrite called Shelby Forthright has, as Philip French asserts in his *Guardian* review from 20 July 2008, whisked away the human inhabitants for a cruise on the luxury starship *Axiom*, which has lasted for several centuries. Meanwhile, robots like Wall-E are left marooned back on earth to clean up the mess. For over 40 minutes this 'rusty metal box with ET's eyes' does nothing much but potter around his city space engulfed in filth, waste and flotsam from a dead planet. By all accounts, this is a long way from the frenetic action adventure of *The Day after Tomorrow*, while at the same time echoing the intense (silent) business of stoical survival and even the values of frugality in a hostile environment, displayed in *All is Lost* to be discussed later.

David Whitley provides a most useful eco-reading of the film and its 'mode of emotional identification that includes rampant anthropomorphising' (Whitley 2012: 3) and goes on to argue against the plaudits of most critical analysis, how the chief protagonist nonetheless remains in love with the consumer culture that he so effectively critiques.

Meanwhile, like in *Terminator 2* with its more advanced computer organism T1000, EVE also appears at first to be more suspect and less ethical in her actions, by zapping everything in her way. But soon both learn to appreciate each other for what they are. Eventually during their strange courtship, Wall-E shows off a precious living organic green plant, which was apparently locked away in a safe. As in *Logan's Run, Blade Runner, Waterworld* and many other eco-science fiction narratives, organic vegetation is greatly prized in such a synthetic world. This miracle of natural photosynthesis in turn proves that the planet is again habitable, thereby securing the empirical proof EVE was sent out to discover.

Either way, on a narrative level, the displaced residents of twenty-eighth century earth do not find refuge from the ills of civilisation in the countryside, as is the norm currently in Western romantic storylines; probably because there is no longer a pristine wilderness and countryside to escape to. Instead they have become refugees in outer space in a spaceship that combines the splendours of shopping malls, alongside the convenience of conventional cruise ships. By all accounts a modern rendition and ironic take on Hardin's spaceship ethics. One would almost instinctively agree with Murray and Heumann's conclusion that *Wall-E*'s artificial environments are anathema to the conventional restorative qualities of romantic pastorals,[8] a trope which continues to have echoes in eco-blockbusters like *Avatar* explored later.

In any case within classic children's animation films like *Finding Nemo* and *A Bug's Life*, alongside *Wall-E*, nature and the environment take centre stage. While liberal audiences certainly find *Wall-E* provocative – drawn one supposes from the environmental message posed, displaying its blatant ethical critique of over-consumption, conservative Christians apparently find the narrative alternatively fills a wholesome niche – by essentially valorising deeply felt conservationist values. Such conservatives, according to a review by Charlotte Allen (12 July 2008) in the *Los Angeles Times* particularly detest litterbugs, who alongside all forms of parasites expect others to clean up after them.

As recalled in a Pixar chapter in 'Smart Cinema' (Brereton 2012), the film is reminiscent of Roman times and the crude political strategy of using 'bread and circuses' to keep the masses satiated. This futuristic artificial society was similarly visualised in classic science fiction films like *Logan's Run*, where the populace is controlled by pleasure and spectacle, with its inhabitants not required to make personal decisions, much less forage for food. *Wall-E* follows a similar path, with its more contemporary obese-looking animated humans, drip-fed on synthetic food and thereby becoming more supine and docile in their massive spaceship, having all their corporeal needs serviced by a mechanical under-class. In such an artificial futuristic age, the allegory suggests, humans have lost the capacity to appreciate the importance of scarcity, frugality and striving for basic needs, alongside more normative evolutionary human desires around freedom to control one's destiny.

There was much debate over *Wall-E*'s intended ecological and ethical message and whether it went too far, or not far enough, towards suggesting any solutions for our excessive waste problems. In any case the film effectively plays out a food consumption allegory around how unchecked appetites (alongside more controversial population explosion concerns) pose a major danger to the planet and its inhabitants. Within such allegorical storylines, science fiction in particular offers a cautionary glimpse into a dystopic future in which our insatiable hunger and general rapaciousness threaten to destroy the planet, eating away at our basic humanity, as cogently represented in earlier classics like *Logan's Run* and *Soylent*

Green. These and other ethical cautionary tales and allegories around food and consumption are extensively explored throughout this volume.[9]

Highlighting the connection between film narrative and ethics, MacIntyre (1981) argues that an ethical awareness of the self is connected to the ways in which the individual articulates stories about themselves. Through the philosophical doctrine of utilitarianism with its call for tolerance towards the other, and the overarching concept of ethical relativism draws distinctions between those 'who are not us', and 'us'. Film and literature most especially tries to explore such divisive positions and points-of-view and to a lesser extent call attention to the need to de-centre Western agency as the only model for ethical engagement. To further explore how more contemporary characters reflexively use stories about themselves to frame and cope with very difficult environmental situations, this chapter will conclude by examining two recent sea-faring films, namely *All is Lost* and *Captain Phillips*.

From pleasure cruising to commercial shipping: lifeboat ethics in *All is Lost* and *Captain Phillips*

The late Garrett Hardin (human ecologist) suggested 'to be generous with one's own possessions is one thing, to be generous with posterity's is quite another: a concern for justice for our poor contemporaries has the effect of destroying the environment and cheating future generations' (Jamieson 2012: 193).[10] Hardin ostensibly believed that people in crowded lifeboats were constantly trying to move to the better lifeboats or gain more of their resources. Playing off the earth's 'carrying capacity', which is most specifically alluded to in the narrative back story of *Captain Phillips,* together with the pervasive urge of rich Western individuals, like the Redford character in *All is Lost* to escape from the traumas of social living and literally going into 'wild seascapes', where one presumes nature is in balance, remains an abiding preoccupation.

All is Lost opens with Robert Redford, 1700 nautical miles from the Sumatra Straits on a voice-over narrating that 'all was lost', as part of a memorial to whoever might eventually listen to his recording after he is dead. It's the 'letter in the jar' idea, which we witness in real screen time at the end of the film. The title of the film is a line from a farewell letter that the Redford character writes, echoing literary classics like Hemmingway's *The Old Man and the Sea*, alongside for instance Joshua Slocum's seminal seafaring narrative *Sailing Alone Around the World,* both of which are less about conquering nature than harnessing wind and water and being part of nature. Nonetheless this ostensibly one-note storyline remains unimaginable except as a film experience.[11]

Such first-person engagement with 'wild nature' is by all accounts exhilarating, even if more frequently consumed by new-generational audiences as a vicarious video game experience.[12] But here replicating the real-life experience and the appeals to survival in nature in this primal storyline, we are also shown the high price exacted if one does not appreciate, much less learn, how to cope

FIGURE 2.1   *All is Lost*, 2013, written and directed by J.C. Chandor

with the various secrets of wild nature, including unpredictable high winds and expansive waterways, with its effervescent deep ecological web of meanings.

Furthermore, when we watch the Redford character climb up on top of the boat's mast, rather than simply enjoying the view and recording his prowess over the elements, he quickly recognises a very large storm approaching and must take immediate remedial action. Farmers to a lesser extent, and sailors more particularly, can intuitively read such climatic conditions and decode the prospect of turbulent conditions with great accuracy. The persona of Redford in this film has both the technical skills to respond in navigational terms and the scientific knowledge to use his equipment to good advantage. In any case, instrumental, technical and intuitive knowledge goes hand in hand in this struggle for survival.

For a mainstream film to have no dialogue to anchor the storyline – reminiscent of the long introduction sequence in *Wall-E* discussed above – much less maintaining the narrative nerve and creative confidence to still make it work effectively as a commercial cinematic experience, is by all accounts amazing. Such a lack of dialogue, albeit heightened by a diegetic soundscape that captures the authentic reality of the inclement environment, while foregrounding an individual's struggle for survival, with no need for any psychological back-story to underpin his dilemma, is reminiscent of numerous nature documentaries where filmic time and space is given over to a real-time experience of valorising images of nature and human/animal struggles for survival. Recalling most clearly to my mind Robert Flaherty's cinematic oeuvre, including *Nanook of the North* and *Man of Aran* which effectively created tangible and poetic tensions from creatively examining and documenting human's elemental and primal struggle with and in nature.

Earlier, asleep in his cabin, the Redford character is suddenly woken up by water cascading on to the floor of his well-furnished yacht. On investigation he discovers a randomly floating massive steel industrial cargo container, painted deep red, which just happened to collide with and subsequently puncture his boat. This presents a clear signifier of random fate so prevalent across the long history of classic narrative structures and most particularly for this study, playing off the ever-present dilemma and precariousness of human survival, induced by global environmental risk on the high seas. One presumes only a very small number of such containers have become dislodged from their moorings and are constantly floating around the seas, causing various levels of pollution and danger to such unsuspected pleasure-seeking boats, floating upon an otherwise pristine seascape.[13]

On climbing up onto the container and traversing its full length, he discovers that it is leaking its otherwise benign cargo of canvas footwear. Many of these now damaged goods are seeping out into the open sea. *The New Yorker* review most notably picks up on the ecological significance of this incidence of pollution, signalling how it's a 'small staple of consumerism impinging on a solitary man in the middle of nowhere' and follows up with how apart from Redford, 'water is the major actor here, sloshing, slopping, pouring, swelling, cascading'. As a general rule-of-thumb in environmental film scholarship, explicitly and extensively emphasising ing any of the primary elements – namely earth, air, fire and water – tends to signal the privileging of nature and issues around the environment and call to mind an exploration of some specific aspect of ecological values.

Allegorically, like for example in *Castaway* (see eco-reading by Brereton in Le Juez and Springer 2015), this container and its inauspicious cargo represents and brings immediate attention to the detritus and flotsam of Western society and displays concrete evidence of erstwhile wasteful conspicuous consumption, while at the same time serving as a necessary *deus-ex-machina* to drive the narrative in a particular direction. Later in the film, we witness sightings of huge cargo ships full to the brim with similar container traffic – which is also evident in and plays off an implicit theme of *Captain Phillips* to be discussed presently – thereby maximising Fordist production and distribution models. But like all global commercially driven systems and standardised modes of industrial distribution, the individual human remains insignificant and their innate struggle for survival are by all accounts ignored. Allegorically, the purely functional busy shipping lanes don't encourage or facilitate lateral vision, or even recognise the indigenous sealife, much less the incidence of a lone figure on his lifeboat as he tries to call attention to his plight from the passing container ships. With their strict deadlines, no time can be lost, as most specifically exemplified later in discussions around another successful cargo-ship film, namely *Captain Phillips*, with a skeleton crew conscripted to transport a range of cargo to Africa.

Cinematic re-framing from nature's point of view

As his boat is about to sink, the Redford character surveys all his belongings, while instinctively working off his conceptualisation of environmental risk analysis, as he mentally decides what he has to – Robinson Crusoe-like – take with him for survival in his lifeboat.[14] The sailor's environmental plight is dramatised throughout the film by continuous shots re-framing and re-constituting his dilemma from a broadly environmental and holistic ethical point of view. In particular by showing his precarious situation, either from high up in the sky, looking down on the expanse of the sea and his own insignificance, or alternatively from deep under water and looking up to the surface of the sea, all the while documenting the various sealife moving around, totally impervious to his situation and most particularly from an environmental ethical and aesthetic perspective, re-positioning the storyline as part of a bigger and more expansive series of eco-systems. All of which is reminiscent of a nature documentary and its contrasting modes of address. Essentially, this narrative trajectory is re-framed and re-sized several times within the diegesis of the film, particularly at moments when the camera intermittently goes under water and surveys his fragile eco-system with small fish or other sea creatures making his raft part of their habitat. Alternatively when his precious yellow life-raft is viewed from high above in the sky, the audience is left with a very different impression. At these two extremes, one could argue, humans essentially have become part *of* nature rather than outside or above nature. Such a paradigm shift calls attention to and correlates with a deep ecological agenda.

Documentary elements can certainly be recognised in dramatising the macro versus the micro aspects of all the nature events in this fictional film. As already signalled above, by witnessing the unmediated camera travelling very high in the sky and framing the boat below, and later observing the life-boat as diminutive *vis-à-vis* the huge expanse of water, this very conscious camera movement simulates the nature documentary-style format of reframing from various perspectives and at the same time recalling the effective use of dramatic point of view that is repeated several times throughout the film at key moments in the drama. The audience is treated to fantastic nature shots of shoals of fish swimming in unison under the vessel, documenting species who are in turn completely at one with nature and part of the cycle of life. As witnessed in many nature documentaries, only man in this narrative is out of his usually prescribed natural environment. The sublime sight of fish or birds flying in unison is incidentally echoed as a key motif in several other films explored in this volume, such as the flying bats in *Take Shelter* or the birds flying in *The Tree of Life* or those witnessing murder in *The Constant Gardener*.

Nevertheless, filmed from overhead, I would also suggest the boat itself is presented as out of place, especially as the later life-raft is perceived as a particularly temporary structure and somewhat unnatural looking with its strange colour palette. The very different temporal and spatial time scales and natural habitat of the open sea is counterpointed with the life-raft, designed specifically not to blend into the environment and therefore become more visible. This narrative habitat is very much called attention to and effectively dramatised in contrast with the (minuscule) troubles and preoccupations of humans who are literally and environmentally 'out of place' and 'out of time'. At least allegorically such radical imbalance and re-framing of human ontological identity (reminiscent of feminist cyborg theory helping to reframe what it means to be human(e)) helps to reconstitute the awesome power of nature in the true romantic, sensory sense of the word and recalling its very different environmental trajectory. Like literary classics, such as *Old Man and the Sea* and *Moby Dick* for earlier generations, or most specifically for nautical insiders, *Sailing Alone Around the World*, these filmic seafaring allegories and tales speak to new generations around environmental concerns, while at the same time calling dramatic and imaginative attention to perennial preoccupations and metaphors concerning humans struggling with the elements. Such tensions explicitly bring environmental concerns and ethical debates to attention.

Like in a nature documentary, we also observe other bigger fish and the rich habitat of interconnecting sea creatures that become more threatening as we instantly recognise large sharks swarming underneath. The human's precarious struggle for survival is slowly exposed and witnessed as part of the 'great chain of life and nature'. Thankfully, however, the seasoned sailor does not see beneath the water surface, but certainly recognises the effects of trying to fish, using his small hand-made line. All of which symbolically at least recalls and references classics like *Moby Dick* with the heroic struggle of Ahab against the Leviathan. The ethics of survival cannot get more elemental than this story and feeds into a long-cherished romantic evocation of struggle with the elements.

A fascinating essay by Nicole Starosielski, 'Beyond Fluidity: A Cultural History of Cinema Under Water' (in Rust *et al.* 2013: 149), suggests,

> [U]nder sea environments are typically defined in opposition to terrestrial human environments: they are timeless spaces of 'anti-civilisation'. Diving into the ocean, whether via scuba or cinematic technologies, is seen as an escape from the social and cultural processes that characterise everyday life: the constraints of the nation, the progression of history, and racial and territorial conflict. Like many frontiers, these environments are often depicted as subversive spaces where it is possible to challenge and reorient existing social conventions. Authors, artists and filmmakers, perceiving undersea environments in terms of their fluidity (their ability to shift, reorient, and de-stabilise), have turned to them to experiment with new forms of representation.

In *All is Lost*, this rich evocation of the wild ocean can at a stretch be also read as signalling a new progressive environmental agenda as we have moved beyond the polarising binaries of the exotic and the otherness of humans versus nature.

As water begins seeping into his life-raft – again viewed from beneath the sea – his temporary boat is (re)presented like a big jelly fish or a massive amoeba. But even worse is to come for our lone survivor. A most violent storm is witnessed from above, while the solitary protagonist has to cover both his ears to fight the pain and physical shock of the impact. Music is played very loud on the sound track, effectively conveying the brutal shock and awe of wild nature in extremis. Incidentally, he gets particularly annoyed when he later discovers his big fresh-water container is rancid and emotes a very gutteral 'fuck' – the only word emitted on screen in the film. Yet such personal woes are effectively counterpointed by the absolute beauty of a shoal of fish swimming in perfect rhythm, affirming the grace and power of natural life, almost Borg-like in harmony within their habitat, essentially reaffirming and reimagining the otherwise alien nature of the sea for most humans.

Reminiscent of attempts to desalinate seawater also explored in 1970s Hollywood classics like *Chinatown*, the sailor is very effective in using plastic and heat from the sun to create drinking water. But again, hidden underneath the sea, we witness a beautiful shoal of fish being attacked by bigger fish, recalling the Darwinian principle of nature in perpetual motion and most specifically dramatising the core principle around the survival of the fittest.

The final act of the narrative and the denouement of his journey/pilgrimage foregrounds darkness and a beautiful romantic seascape transition, while recording time change as he spies yet another ship in the vicinity. To be seen in the dark, he proceeds to cut up paper and start a fire, which quickly gets out of control and his raft catches fire. Now in the sea with no life support available and totally at the mercy of the elements, the hapless victim appears to go beneath the sea almost purposefully, as he is apparently losing the will to live. But looking up for the first time viewing the surface of the sea, like the unmotivated camera earlier and recalling the experiences of shoals of various species of fish nearby – a ring of fire frames his vision – a sublime image of magical hope. Lights are coming towards the burnt-out raft and a searchlight is shining down into the sea. He rises up through the deep water (encapsulating a Jungian metaphor one might suspect) and catches the hand of his unseen rescuer. The in-nature odyssey has been almost magically ended as he is finally rescued by a welcome hand (of God!). Is this all a dream/fantasy like the closing of *Gravity* and others explored in this volume, or most usefully I suggest serving as a cautionary survival tale concerning the reimagining of humans and their erstwhile inhospitable ocean habitat.

Environmental ethical lessons explored

By all accounts this ecological analysis of the narrative's space/place creatively reimagines a difficult habitat to survive, while witnessing the hi-tech and high-speed cargo ships passing by, all of which are impervious to our individual hero's solitary calls and futile attempts to signal for assistance. The sea-lanes, as already asserted, are artificially imposed on the sea and primarily function as an efficient, albeit inhuman mode of transport, designed simply to move products from one place to another on the planet in the shortest time possible. Such a forceful trajectory has no regard for the authentic life-giving environment being navigated, much less recognising or having cognisance of the local flora/fauna in its path – even if this happens to be a stranded human in need of assistance, floating aimlessly on the tide on a flimsy life-raft. Such an allegorical replay of an age old (mythical) story of a solitary human who has been forced to literally slow down and try to exist at the mercy of the elements, while dramatising if only in the background the global inequitable distribution system, does not at first display any Levisanian care for the other, much less any ethical responsibility for an open commons or the wild environment. Nevertheless, these ethical issues are at least brought to the surface for contemporary audiences. By all accounts this remains a provocative modern day environmental allegory, whose ethical values are fleshed out more specifically in *Captain Phillips* discussed below, and certainly replay the pervasive power and narrative attraction of classical nautical tales like *Moby Dick* or *The Old Man and the Sea* for previous generations.

Earlier, as his boat was being pulled apart and the Redford character forced to abandon ship, it could be suggested that he adapted to the exigencies of 'nature' and the experience of accepting (our) human lack of control, (much less understanding or appreciating wild nature's awe-inspiring power). All of which served to teach the adventurer and by extension the audience that they must pay great heed to the 'rules of nature'. Most specifically in struggling for survival, the human victim dreams of a form of active humility, which includes respect rather than hubris in being able to control and mobilise the forces of nature. At least it would appear by the end of the film that the driven Western sailor has also reaffirmed a deep appreciation of the ethics around humans' complex relationship with and in nature in all its varying moods and manifestations. He has learned one suspects a greater appreciation of the intrinsic connectivity of the earth's eco-systems and humans' need to recognise the big picture around nature's evolving relationships with all sentient creatures.

The apparent epiphany and closure at the end of the film reads and feels like a nature documentary, recounting a deep environmental and ethical homily. Surviving enormous odds and at the same time embracing and calling attention to various survival myths, while enduring so much down time, alongside co-opting various fictional devices to help keep mass audiences engaged, creates a seamless interconnection between nature documentary fact and fiction. Recalling synthetic performances that have become so prevalent for instance in Robinson Crusoe-type reality television shows, while at the same time revering in an anti-human habitat which is here sustained and recalibrated for a much more noble cause, ensures the narrative holds our attention to the end. Nature's rules and varying bonds and logics, including observing at close quarters the various habitats of fish and their prey, alongside recognising the mega-habitat of a magnificent seascape from high above in the sky, all help to situate and at the same time highlight how insubstantial the human unfolding tragedy really is. Meanwhile, the interconnectivity of all life forms is effectively dramatised for audiences to actively engage with.

Such a perfect therapeutic and environmentally satisfying ending. This of course could be just a dream focused around a Jungian wish-fulfilling and ecological fantasy, which also incidentally echoes the utopian ending of the science fiction fantasy *Gravity* discussed in a later chapter. While *All is Lost* remains small scale and focuses on individual survival, it is certainly effective in signalling, if not fully revealing, what ethical recalibration and transformations are needed to enable the protagonist to face up to the primal and elemental struggle for life and basic survival. *Captain Phillips,* on the other hand, which we now turn to, is constructed across a much larger canvas, while also focusing on survival, in this case against human pirates. These pirates want a share of the spoils of the aforementioned global transport system, using the ocean's natural commons. Both films explore contemporary ethical concerns around the tragedy of the commons, as manifested on the high seas, as the protagonists face life-threatening situations for a predominantly Western audience, who often regard nature-in-extremis simply as a vicarious experience, packaged by professional environmentalists who communicate the experience, albeit second-hand. In contrast, I suggest such narratives illustrate how profound change and transformation is needed to enable such protagonists to face up to the elemental struggle for life and survival. Mother Nature's potency serves as an ethical cautionary tale for such survivors. These tales effectively demonstrate and illustrate the innate power, complexity and inter-connectivity of so-called 'Mother Nature' in extremis, as against human individuals who are essentially fighting to survive and thereby need to acquire a necessary sense of humility and most certainly question their pre-determined and often myopic environmental and ethical values.

Captain Phillips: *global capitalism, tragedy of the commons and third word justice*

In *Captain Phillips* the large Western cargo ship is randomly targeted for attack by local African mercenaries who refuse to let its journey continue in such an anonymous and regulated manner and who justify their unethical activities by expecting payment for using the sea (or what can usefully be characterised in the context of this study as the 'commons'), recalling their apparent ethical rights and jurisdiction to 'tax' all forms of movement around their native coastlines.

The dominant Western ethic legitimating pleasure cruising in *All is Lost* and the free movement of goods is certainly replicated and most dramatically featured in *Captain Phillips*. But when the rules of commerce and free movement of goods are put in jeopardy, then of course the full might of the American navy and airforce, together with sophisticated Western intelligence is brought to bear to crush any local resistance, much less recognising individual rights concerning the high seas as an 'open commons', which in turn expects humans to take clear responsibility for its overall sustainability.

Mark Kermode, writing in *The Observer* (Sunday 20 October 2013), loved the film 'for all its action aesthetics and nail-biting, gut-wrenching tension'. This reading will however focus on how the film can also be examined (if somewhat 'against the grain') as a 'lifeboat ethics' parable, while ostensibly framed around the tension of advanced globalisation and what happens when the paths of the very poor of the Third World and the very rich from the West intersect in the crossfire of world economic values and belief systems.

Captain Phillips opens with the date March 2009, framing a true-life story from the period. Phillips (Tom Hanks) is getting ready for another sailing mission and is shown driving across some anonymous American city to the airport with his wife, while discussing their children's prospects, framed against everyday issues and concerns. He recalls how the 'world is moving so fast' and how it's 'not going to be easy for our kids'. There is so much 'competition out there', you have 'got to be strong to survive'. Dialogue and parental worries one hears all the time, and this everyday interaction is rounded off with concerns that employers and 'companies wanting things faster and cheaper'. Such allusions certainly also call to mind the Darwinian 'survival of the fittest' perennial theme, together with what can be considered the antithesis around issues of environmental injustice, by emphaszing ng the various ethical imbalances between the 'haves' and 'have nots' achieving the so-called 'good life'. Certainly, such expositionary allusions remain hypocritical, when we finally witness the skeleton crew on the tanker at the start of the journey and who are later rightly disgruntled in not being paid to be also fighting soldiers with the prospect of attacks during the voyage, while ostensibly being regular crew members trying to simply do a labouring job of work. No wonder there are not enough eyes to see on look-out duties for a small boat, trying to catch their attention, as exemplified earlier in *All is Lost*.

In classic Hollywood story-telling grammar, the film then cuts to an unnamed tribe in Somalia with young black men sporting guns, recalling a pervasive image of Third World gangster stereotypes outlined in films like *Tsotsi*, as a number of trucks arrive at a village, all heavily armed and whooping for blood. The locals are goaded to go back to 'work' as pirates, and informed that when they capture a big ship, 'you will all be paid'. Worker productivity bonuses have very different ethical meanings for such nascent pirates – incidentally a long way also from the light comic Hollywood pastiche of *The Pirates of the Caribbean* franchise. Reflecting their lowly status, these pirates have very poor equipment and boats to carry out such a bold attack and are certainly characterised as minnows, compared to the big super-tanker (whale-like) prey they are hunting.

Third World eco-ethics: conventional closure!

When these two worlds collide – revealing differing environmental ethical and other values – Barkhad Abdi, who grows into the part of pirate ringleader

Abduwali Muse, responds to Captain Phillip's query regarding his suspect choice of work and illegal income, while alluding to alternative and more ethical paths of subsistence: 'Maybe in America, Irish, [the nickname he gives the Captain when he discovers his nationality] maybe in America'. This conflictual story is all the more tragic, while offering a clear opportunity to explore the film's local Third World politics *vis à vis* global capital's 'prime directive': to transport goods efficiently using the 'international commons' of the high seas, with no impediment being put in the way.

In particular this environmental reading will focus on the much contested jingoistic conclusion of the film. Raphael Hall (in *The Quietus* www.thequietus. com review from 22 January 2014) is most critical of the film's conclusion and its supposed lack of any critique of Western 'political representation' by recalling its environmental ethical lesson. The film concerns a sea captain who is reminiscent of a modern Ulysses at the helm of an endangered cargo charter. A band of impoverished pirates invades the colossal logistics vessel as it strays perilously close to the coast of Somalia – 'a country notorious among seafarers for its breeding of cloak and dagger piracy, and Tom Hanks, a suitably prosaic pawn for the American cause, exhibits a herculean performance as the titular sea farer' (Hall 2014).

One could suggest that the well-regarded director Paul Greengrass seems to be evading the big issue around environmental and postcolonial justice. But I would counter-argue, as also evident in a reading of his 9/11 story *United 93* (see Brereton 2012), that the film suggests a more progressive political and environmental agenda than one initially detects from the filmic diegesis, which is evident mainly through the use of narrative framing and employment of understatement.

In the case of the 'pirates', this working out of local politics involves upholding social interests (pleasing a trigger-happy gangster-like middle man) and personal interests (subsidising the loss of income from evaporating fishing opportunities). Most critics particularly point to how the film in the end 'fails to show a similar regard for the well-being of the four teenage Somalis who subsequently 'find themselves staring down the gargantuan barrels of Uncle Sam's unquestionable might and power' (Hall 2014). But this lack and inequality in representation, I would suggest, is the dramatic point of it all; namely calling attention to the huge imbalance in power and resources of the American navy and its hi-tech commercial infrastructure, as opposed to the paltry resources of these four teenage Somalis. The representational imbalance between the ostensible might of the Wes and the pirates, serves to further highlight the gross injustice and inequality of it all. There is consequently little need to afford explicit agency and further representational weight to the African's 'just cause' by the end of the film. The efficient use of understatement helps get the core political and ethical message across more sharply The outsiders remain othered, even after Phillips had to coexist with his captors on the precarious lifeboat throughout the preceding struggle for survival.

This aspect is echoed in an interesting paper on representations of pirates in *Film Comment* when Chris Norris (2014) argues how the ending of *Captain Phillips* is reminiscent of *United 93,* which 'almost had a spiritual dimension with all performing their assigned roles perfectly'. While the 'package' – the erstwhile kidnapped Captain is escorted into a hastily constructed sickbay – his attackers on the other hand are quickly dispatched, both in temporal and dramatic terms. 'Meanwhile a female navy corps man (played by an actual navy corps man)' checks Phillips' vitals, records his injuries, noting 'a four centimeter laceration to the upper right eyebrow', while asking him simple and soothing questions, as she runs through a standard operating procedure. Finally the medic mumbles 'You're OK, your're safe' and Captain Phillips shows us 'something new in his performance, as he breaks down before our eyes', which certainly in a very different and emotive dramatic fashion counterpoints Robert Redford's understated and more stoical emotive performance in *All is Lost.*

'Acting is truth telling', Greengrass suggests in a talk at the Lincoln Centre, New York, and that's in that scene: 'this shocking sense of humanity. It's a hijacking's best case outcome and something you wouldn't wish on our worst enemy'(Norris 2014). Everyone is brutalised by the violent encounter and there are no winners or losers in the end.[15]

The residue of primal environmental injustice is set up at an allegorical level throughout the narrative. It can be read as the intruders take on a 'dominant' (Western US) hostage, with everyone in the end being brutalised by proceedings. Ultimately performances of power might get in the way of 'doing the right thing' and taking the appropriate ethical response. One does not have to explicitly nod to the particular geo-politics that are being displayed. Certainly for some critics the film appeared to explicitly feature a jingoistic celebration of American might, while for many others it most certainly spoke to the awesome injustice of the colonial power conflict on display.

Nevertheless, according to further analysis by Hall (2014), the tragedy lies once again with the lack of subtlety shown to these competing factions of the story and especially by the film's ending. Indications of the Somalis' impoverished existence and the few choices they are left with in order to make ends meet, from the establishing scenes of a raucous pirate camp based on the coast to the clearly distressed expressions on their faces as they try to negotiate an escape. Ironically, this is in stark contrast to a relaxed Hanks once he discovers the likelihood of their true fate. Yet there is strong evidence of a deep sense of foreboding, as we experience the grand panoramas Greengrass exhibits of the US warships and helicopters sent to the rescue of Captain Phillips and crew (Hall 2014: 3).

While certainly having sympathy with this reading, ostensibly such a conclusion speaks to the pervasive ideological domination of the West.[16] But at another level, one could argue, using a more opaque ecological lens, that such a scene also signals the primal injustice and ethical deficit embedded within Third World politics. These pirates are agents – hunters – who are predestined to fail in their quest and have been doomed from the start. The natives' ethical logic of fighting for their rights and what they consider as their 'commons' – namely the seas around their land – certainly does not mesh with the more established common-law legal Western beliefs and rules of engagement on the high seas.

The apex of these juxtapositions rests on the immense and extraordinary delusions of the film's final shot.

> After we follow Phillips into an emotional vacuum of release and closure within the ship's nursing ward, Greengrass decides to pull the curtain on the film with an explicit huge chest-beating landscape shot of the three Navy warships and their entourage sprawling towards the horizon.
>
> (Hall 2014: 3)

Knowing and admiring Greengrass's work, I would have to take issue with such an *obvious* jingoistic reading. Alternatively, drawing on the more proactive apect of the director's oeuvre, he consciously calls attention to the psychic trauma of Hanks, thus embodying his archetypical role as 'everyman'. This is certainly reminiscent of a common trope of Hollywood heroic narratives and appears to consciously ignore the more serious plight and ethical injustice in the punishment meted out to the indigenous pirates. Their otherness is not finally valorised, much less legitimised. Again this over-burdening of one side of the story in this dramatic ending, simply in itself calls immediate attention to this gross inequity.

A more radical alternative and even proto-environmental reading would suggest that the film is literally 'playing with the audience's minds' and their relatively fixed ideological and ethical expectations. This recalls in some measure feminist 'screen theory' fixation with 1950s melodrama and its attempt to recuperate erstwhile patriarchal hegemonic storylines for more radical agendas in the 1970s by revealing discrepancies between form and content. Here also, the affirmation of a surface hegemonic glorification of American imperialism can certainly be seen as explicitly calling into question, if not actively critiquing. The use of the formal structuring device of the film certainly gives less extensive time and space to exploring the other's psyche and motivation.

The lack of screen time afforded to the othered Somalis at the climax and conclusion of the film explicitly calls even more attention to their plight and most certainly to their inherent and primal sense of injustice. Their story arc is simply cut short and all but ignored at the end, probably to encourage audiences to appreciate the ethical injustices of the storyline, having got to know and experience the Somailis' actions throughout the film. We spend so much time with them in the small escape boat until then and suddenly they are simply expunged from the story. One could further propose that this deliberate narrative strategy helps to re-frame – simply by their dramatic absence – their legitimate ecological and political plight as struggling Third World citizens trying to fight an alien Western capitalist system.

By not simply preaching to audiences using a teacherly message about environmental justice and sharing scarce resources – which is often regarded as ineffective – audiences are instead encouraged to actively and strategically join the dots. As in a conventional horror movie, what is *not* shown often creates more of a visceral engagement for audiences, than what is actually shown on screen. Perhaps, in turn, eco-film scholarship can also adapt and more fruitfully learn from the dramatic power of a range of well-developed generic narrative techniques, by drawing from the long history of film-making and scholarship, including avant-garde as well as more mainstream modes of address.

All these different movies – from the very overtly ecological polemic of *An Inconvenient Truth,* to the more oblique environmental tales on the high seas that have come to our screens in the last few years – certainly cannot be synthesised from an ecological and ethical perspective. Instead they serve to highlight a range of possibilities which eco-textual analysis can take on board as the corpus of environmental film expands to include both explicit and canonical eco-narratives, like *Wall-E* and *The Day after Tomorrow*, and more documentary environmental cautionary tales, like *An Inconvenient Truth*. The two closely related final readings in this chapter of extreme survival allegories, as protagonists face danger on the high seas, serve to call attention to a number of lifeboat environmental and ethical concerns. These tales tend to signal a range of contentious ethical dilemmas, while in subsequent chapters we will focus on more defined thematic concerns and continue to flesh out a broad range of contemporary mainstream films, using an environmental–ethical lens.

Notes

1 Ceremonies of innocence are needed to 'restore the natural core of belief, in the world, in the country, and in the self' (Whitley in Weik von Mossner 2014: 145–6).

2 Spoiler alert: it is assumed readers have seen most of the films discussed in this study, as it retraces and often reframes the outline narrative trajectory of these storylines. For those readers not fully versed in filmic textual analysis see basic strategy in the appendix to paper titled 'Screening not Greening: An Ecological Reading of the Greatest Business Movies' (McDonagh and Brereton 2010).

3 See for instance work of Canadian climatologist Michael Mann who popularised the science of climate change using the image of the 'hockey stick' to signal the radical trend of CO_2 emissions into the atmosphere and graphically signalled for global audiences the serious challenge facing the globe – as evidenced in studies such as *The Hockey Stick and the Climate Wars* (Mann 2012).

4 Brentin Mock's blog in www.grist.org, for instance, provides a useful ecological re-reading of the Spike Lee classic study of race tensions *Do the Right Thing* (1989), set in New York during a blistering hot summer. For instance Lee's character Mookie is warned not to work too hard or he might 'fall out from the heat'. In particular the destruction in the movie's conclusion 'is an apt metaphor for what will happen if the earth's temperature rises under climate change'. Recording the three old men sitting around talking, brings issues of climate change into direct public consciousness; MI tells his friends 'Well gentlemen, the way I see it, if the hot weather continues, it's going to melt the polar caps and the whole wide world'.

5 Scientists, of course, rightly point out the numerous factual inaccuracies with regards to our knowledge around climate science.

6 Greg Smith's 'associative model' (2003), for instance, usefully accounts for how different aesthetic registers work together to construct a film's meaning for the viewer – a process that involves cognitive, emotional as well as affective aspects. Affect essentially is a visceral, bodily response to a film, whereas emotion also includes a cognitive element.

7 Risk research has also demonstrated that the experiential system can have powerful influences on risk perception, decision making and behaviour. Antony Leiserowitz, 'Climate Change, Vicarious Experience and the Social Amplification of Risk' http://environment.yale.edu/leiserowitz/climatechange/TDAT.html.

8 See Bob Mellin 'White Flights and the Environmental Minstrel in Wall-E' paper presented at Film and History Conference 'Film & Science: Fictions, Documentaries, and Beyond', Chicago, 31 October–2 November 2008.

9 Because of space considerations, extensive readings of *Promised Land* on fracking and classics like *Chinatown* and *There Will be Blood* which explore the ethics of varying extractive energy solutions will not be treated here.

10 Hardin incidentally rejected Bouldings's analogy of the earth as a spaceship, for this implies sharing resources without assigning individual responsibility, which he considered a prescription for disaster. He further affirmed that such sharing ethics leads to the 'tragedy of the commons' (Jamieson 2012: 193). Hardin goes on to also critique the related notions of lifeboat ethics, which serves to create an unregulated commons, providing benefits to individuals without imposing responsibilities.

11 The audience's only sense of his psychology and trauma is displayed in his interior monologue and tone of voice. We get no back story around why, how he came to this place, or who he is, neither are we afforded any clues to his motivation. Consequently he remains enigmatic, or at best an everyman, while at the same time intertextually being invoked as a clearly recognisable icon of the golden age of cinema, recalling for instance a free-wheeling *Butch Cassidy and the Sundance Kid,* when he and his co-star Paul Newman were at the height of their celebrity status. Now of course Redford is a grandee and major player/producer in the indie scene, having set up the world renowned Sundance film festival. His aged face and wrinkled hands are effectively used to evoke a complex narrative of engagement and struggle.

12 The narrative as suggested above contains lots of enticing acting business, as Redford tries to protect his boat as a life source. All of this activity displays the sailor's resilience, tenacity and doggedness in adversity. Most specifically it reminds me of the austere, romantic, stoic and primitivist tales like Robert Flaherty's *Man of Aran* (1932) with its deep ecological survival narrative alluded to elsewhere. In both narratives the main protagonist or 'everyman' is literally positioned in an alien and hostile environment, while ostensibly trying to survive against all the odds. This primal struggle foregrounds a number of philosophical, environmental and ethical concerns, most especially how humans can learn to coexist with other life forms on the planet, which of course remains the primary deep ecological ethical dilemma.

13 For instance a recent Twitter picture from the summer of 2014 shows a whole shipload of container traffic going overboard into the sea.

14 On hearing that the radio transmitter is working, he broadcasts: 'This is Virginia Jean with an SOS call', reminiscent of the symbolic, yet also ironic, 'Mayday' sequence, discussed in *Gravity* and set in another more alienated space for humans at least.

15 This 'success story' is dramatically reversed in the latest television series of HBO's *Homeland.*

16 With the successful mission – the US navy clap their hands in delight – it's just a mission for them, like a video game, while Skinny is read his rights and told that his fellow pirates have all been killed.

Bibliography

Braudy, L (1998) 'The Genre of Nature' in N. Browne (ed) *Reflecting American Film Genre Theory and History*. Berkeley, CA: University of California Press.

Brereton, Pat (2012) *Smart Cinema: DVD Add-ons and New Audience Pleasures*. Basingstoke: Palgrave.

Brereton, Pat and Hong, Pat (2013) 'Irish Eco-cinema and Audiences'. *Interactions: Studies in Culture and Communications* 4(2): 191–99. Special issue on eco-cinema, editor Pietari Kääpä.

Cubitt, S. (2005) *Ecocinema*. Amsterdam: Rodophi Press.

Hall, Raphael (2014) 'Star-Striped Tragedy: *Phillips* Reassessed'. *The Quietus*. http://thequietus.com/articles/14306-captain-phillips-analysis

Hardin, Garret (1974) 'Lifeboat Ethics: The Case against Helping the Poor'. *Psychology Today*. http://rintintin.colorado.edu/~vancecd/phil1100/Hardin.pdf

Ivakhiv, Adrian (2013) *Ecologies of the Moving Image: Cinema, Affect, Nature*. Waterloo, Canada: Wilfred Laurier University Press.

Jamieson, Dale (2008) *Ethics and the Environment: An Introduction*. Cambridge: Cambridge University Press.

Jamieson, Dale (2012) 'Living with Climate Change' http://environment.as.nyu.edu/object/dalejamiesonclimatechange.html

Kääpä, Pietari (2013) *Ecology and Contemporary Nordic Cinema*. New York: Continuum.

Keller, David (ed) (2010). *Environmental Ethics*. Oxford: Wiley Blackwell.

Leiserowitz, A. A. (2003) 'Global Warming and the American Mind: The Roles of Affect, Imagery and Worldview in Risk Perception, Policy Preferences and Behaviour'. PHD dissertation, University of Oregon. http://anthonyleiserowitz.com/climatechange/US_assets/SignedDissertation.pdf

Leiserowitz, A. A. (2004) 'Before and After *The Day After Tomorrow*: A U.S. Survey of Climate Change Risk Perception'. *Environment* 46(9): 22–37.

Le Juez, B. and Springer, O. (2015) *Shipwrecks and Islands: Motifs in Literature and the Arts*. Amsterdam: Rodophi.

Leopold, A. (1947) *A Sand Country Almanac*. Oxford: Oxford University Press.

MacIntyre, Alastair (1981) *After Virtue*. Notre Dame, IN: University of Notre Dame Press.

Mann, Michael (2012) *The Hockey Stick and the Climate Wars: Dispatches from the Front Lines*. New York: Columbia University Press.

McDonagh, P. and Brereton, P. (2010) 'Screening not Greening: an Ecological Reading of the Greatest Business Movies'. *Journal of Macromarketing* 30(2): 133–146.

Murray, Robin and Heumann, Joseph (2007) 'Al Gore's *An Inconvenient Truth* and its Skeptics: A case of Environmental Nostalgia'. *JumpCut: A Review of Contemporary Media* 49: 1–13.

Murray, Robin and Heumann, Joseph (2009) *Ecology and Popular Film: Cinema on the Edge*. Albany, NY: State University of New York Press.

Murray, Robin and Heumann, Joseph (2012) *Gunfight at the Eco-Corral: Western Cinema in the Environment*. Norman, OK: University of Oklahoma Press.

Norris, Chris (2014) '*Captain Phillips* and *A Hijacking*'. *Film Comment* 50(2): 46–49.

Rust, Stephen, Monani, Salma and Cubitt, Sean (eds) (2013) *Ecocinema, Theory and Practice*, AFI Film Readers. London: Routledge.

Smith, Greg (2003) *Film Structure and the Emotional System*. Cambridge: Cambridge University Press.

Weik von Mossner, Alexa (ed) (2014) *Moving Environments: Affect, Emotion, Ecology and Film*. Waterloo, Canada:Wilfrid Laurier University Press.

Whitley, D. (2008) *The Idea of Nature in Disney Animation*. Burlington, VT: Ashgate.

Willoquet-Maricondi, Paula (2010) *Framing the World: Explorations in Ecocriticism and Film*. Charlottesville, VA: University of Virginia Press.

3

INDIGENOUS CULTURES AND ETHICAL FOOD CONSUMPTION

From hunter gatherers to *Avatars*

Overview

The primary aim of this chapter is to show how contemporary representations of indigenous cultures and, in some cases, their food consumption, helps break down cross-cultural barriers, while most noticeably obfuscating racial and environmental injustices. Discussion will focus on close readings of *Apocalypto* and *The Road*, alongside the highly influential blockbuster *Avatar*. Most of these mainstream narratives are clearly situated from within a normative white agency, while actively dramatising a wide range of ecological fears and cautionary ethical tales around food and consumption generally. Furthermore, such mainstream Hollywood texts serve to privilege what can loosely be characterised as a form of Western ecological guilt, which in turn highlights growing ethical concerns for our unsustainable planet.[1]

The ecological fears and worldviews of the dominant white Western constituency are dramatically offset in several of these films by indigenous cultures, who frequently have to endure ecocidal destruction. Yet the rhetoric of these constitutionally inscribed humanist and ethical values (in America in particular), as embraced within such storylines, has still to create much radical change in the *real* politics of the world, framed against the increasing evidence of social environmental injustices and poverty.

The readings broadly accept the position that (historical) fictional narratives speak most effectively as populist allegories for contemporary global audiences, expressing their hopes, fears, beliefs and dreams. At least metaphorically, it would appear (contemporary) audiences crave a progressive philosophy of communal agency (see Weik von Mossner 2014; Rust *et al.* 2013), which might in turn overcome feelings of individual, national and global impotence. At the same time such narratives often nostalgically look back into history and myth where the seductive notion of 'communing with nature' and discovering core ethical values around food production and ethical consumption modalities are brought into sharp focus and appear to have been more highly valued than today.

Agriculture and food production remains a defining characteristic of human civilisation. Agriculture's development as a means of providing sustenance marked the transition from a nomadic existence – as evident in *Apocalypto,* discussed later – to a more urban-based consumption-driven lifestyle. No other human activity has transformed so much of the earth's surface as farming. In fact most commentators agree that modern forms of agriculture have become highly industrialised in order to reliably optimise the output of plant and animal product, while minimising labour inputs. Under this productive ecological paradigm, the 'prime directive' is to improve capacity of a select set of plants and animals (Keller 2010: 483). At the outset, this form of land stewardship, simply designed to maximise productivity, is a long way from an erstwhile idyllic wilderness and modes of agriculture where nature appears at least in perfect harmony.

The ethics of food consumption in classic science fiction

Compared with the growing literature around nature and environmental studies, food *per se* surprisingly remains under-theorised from a cultural, much less from an ecological and ethical perspective. As an essential source of life and nourishment, food can be imagined not only as a necessary sustenance for corporeal needs, but also according to Jean P. Retzinger (in a special issue of *Cultural Studies* on the subject), can be read as a 'liminal cultural symbol of life and death, nature and culture, human and non-human', as well as exemplifying various forms of injustice issues. For food

> not only shapes our bodies, but it structures our lives, fashioning daily rituals and helps mark significant rites of passage. Food connects us to others – both directly, through shared meals and culturally through shared 'tastes'.
>
> (Retzinger 2008: 370)

From an ecological and ethical perspective, threats to the food supply chain, together with the search for bodily sustenance at the global and local level, represent a major preoccupation amidst a world of scarcity, while becoming a dominant motif for instance in post-apocalyptic science fiction narratives.[2] This phenomenon is most clearly displayed in a number of fantasies from the 1970s that featured food and its wasteful abuse, as a recurring ecological subtext in their storylines. Notable examples include *Silent Running, Soylent Green* and *Logan's Run*, all of which have white, male protagonists, through whom the audience is introduced into their equally strange futuristic world. Food in particular symbolises the nostalgic world of plenty in *Soylent Green*. When William Simonson, a corporate executive, is murdered, it is the food he leaves behind that gains investigators Thorn and Sol's respect and attention. As eco-scholars Robin Murray and Joseph Heumann articulate, since Sol remembers a better world, 'he creates a *real* meal for himself and Thorn serving it on linen; giving Thorn the one set of authentic silverware with which to enjoy it' (2009: 98, emphasis added).

Meanwhile, another classic, like *Silent Running*, is symbolically set in the year 2001 – adrift in space in a 'Garden of Eden' capsule intended to refurbish an earth devastated by nuclear war. The main character has to cope with many problems and the storyline incidentally has strong echoes of the recent animated feature *Wall-E* discussed in Chapter 2. Bruce Dern refuses to destroy his private world by following direct orders; instead with the help of his robot drones he passionately tends his organic garden and finally at the end of the story 'sends it out into deep space to seed a possible second chance for mankind' (Milne 1998: 789).

Reminiscent of Roman times and the crude strategy of using 'bread and circuses' to keep the masses satiated, the futuristic artificial society visualised in *Logan's Run* is also controlled for pleasure and spectacle, with its inhabitants not required to make any personal decisions, much less forage for food. It echoes in many ways the aforementioned Pixar feature *Wall-E,* with its more contemporary obese animated humans who are drip-fed on synthetic food and thereby become more supine and docile, having all their corporeal needs serviced by a mechanical under-class. In such artificial futuristic environments, the allegory suggests, humans have lost the capacity to appreciate the significance of scarcity, much less the benefits of striving for basic needs and being part of the natural food chain that was historically inscribed in (primitive) hunter-gatherer societies. Many of these threads are further dramatised in contemporary examples such as *Apocalypto,* to be discussed below.[3]

Most pointedly for instance, Spielberg's *AI – Artificial Intelligence* opens with a normative white male voiceover, describing the environmental and social crisis that has reconfigured the earth through 'global warming, cities underwater, people displaced and starved in poorer countries, and strict regulation of pregnancies in richer nations'. This well-trodden dystopic scenario is set up to explain why robots, who are never hungry, became so important as they 'did not consume resources beyond their first manufacture'. Nevertheless, in this provocative cautionary tale, the very life-like and conventionally beautiful white cyborg boy called David becomes 'hungry for love and acceptance', as the Pinocchio-like story develops. Food both blurs and at the same time emphasises distinctions between humans and the machine, as the cyborg body is unable to ingest food and thereby satisfy its desire to feel part of the human community. Alternatively in other recent science fiction fantasies like *In Time*, the fashionable movement of slow food is evoked, with clock-time literally the currency for all human activities.[4]

Indigenous cultures

While American Indians are more usually represented as the hunted prey in classic westerns, such natives within more contemporary and revisionist tales are considered as the 'natural owners' of such a landscape. Being the first to inhabit the landscape and more importantly having helped to build up a complementary rapport within the eco-system, they at least mythically, in spite of some contradictory evidence, are capable of creating a balance and harmony between humans and landscape. Consequently the Hollywood native, at least symbolically, has been co-opted as being more ecologically harmonious within their overall agency, compared to the white colonial hero. Contemporary ecologists and historians narrate how this process is exemplified by new colonial settlers destroying the apparent balance in nature, exemplified by their pervasive symbols of progress such as the locomotive train cutting through an unspoilt landscape, or the even more destructive (Western) notion of property ownership, which enabled land to be fenced off and enclosed, recalling the 'tragedy of the commons'.

For instance, the struggles of the nature-loving Na'vi in *Avatar*, discussed in detail later, as they strive to protect their homeland against the military might of humans who want to mine a precious resource that is more valuable than oil, builds upon such ecologically inspired narrative tropes. Furthermore, ethical allegories like *Apocalypto* and *The Road* testify to how *we* need to rediscover our healthy and pristine love of nature for this planet, not simply as a nostalgic idyll, but rather to appreciate and address contemporary global problems of food consumption and waste, in this instance to actively help fight against all forms of biospheric destruction.[5] As many of these 'fantasies' attest, if the human species is to survive, the nurturing biospheres of planet earth must be actively fought for, to help sustain a bounteous level of food production for all of its citizens. Most particularly food waste of all types, as clearly coded in both of these dystopic fantasies, together with calling to mind a more general unethical abuse of nature and humans – manifested and coded most explicitly through forms of cannibalism and human religious sacrifice – must be faced up to and addressed in an appropriate manner.

Yet by focusing on such large-scale dystopic issues, albeit viewed through the perspective and lens of a small group of individuals, such narratives can often obfuscate more local and equally pertinent injustice issues around class, race and gender, much less effectively situate the range of more complex and nuanced deep ecological discourses. Eco-critics like Adrian Ivakhiv correctly affirm that the real winner in addressing such ecological issues is their commercial success as Hollywood spectacles, with such environmental and ethical agendas often positioned in the background, rather than being posited as their explicit *raison d'être*. Nevertheless, while recognising and appreciating this important caveat, certainly the emphasis on environmental ethics in these two examples help at least to call attention to a broad range of environmental ethical issues and keep them firmly within our public consciousness. For a mass communications medium, scholars should always at least recognise this possibility, while at the same time being careful not to overascribe credit or infer unconditional explicit progressive agency to such narratives. In any event, the growing range of human injustices across the world must constantly be rearticulated and reimagined, as film strives to discover a new grammar, language and creative imaginary to express these complex global (in)justices, alongside more intractable ecological and ethical risks and dilemmas.[6]

Apocalypto: a new liberal white agenda

As evident in earlier research and recalled in the burgeoning of eco-film studies, this broad-stroke environmental representation and criticism can most readily be appreciated and encapsulated through the almost obligatory ritualised and idyllic scenes of native nubile bodies bathing and grooming, as also evidenced in many Western romantic paintings of nature (see Brereton 2005). Old wrinkled bodies are rarely if ever displayed in films of 'primitive' societies, which are linked to the erotic evocation of easy and available sexuality, through the promotion of exotic rites-of-passage, much less through food consumption rituals. Yet this clearly codified romantic convention and trajectory is most firmly subverted in Mel Gibson's historical action-adventure saga *Apocalypto,* with a wide range of bodies on display, alongside surprisingly conventional 'mother-in-law humour'.

Instead of conventional representations of natives, the indigenous settlers have become capable of presenting themselves as whole-heartedly laughing at and with their own families, while playing practical jokes on each other. In other words their ethnicity and pre-defined, even rarefied, ethnographic behaviour patterns are not the *only* measures that define, much less represent them. Within the canon of Hollywood westerns – much less across science fiction fantasies – there are very few comic elements that move outside of the parameters of either exotisation, as opposed to enclosed deference to such othered cultures. Certainly it is more useful and progressive, one could argue, to try to co-opt and adapt a native's point of view and attempt to get 'inside their skin', while creating a more fully fleshed out holistic exposure of a three-dimensional (re)presentation of such an anthropologically rich tribal society. This also encapsulates the *raison d'être* of Cameron's blockbuster *Avatar*.

Fatimah Tobing Ront (1996) usefully reminds us for instance of the 'Rousseauesque study' of remaining 'primitive peoples, which have survived as a taxidermic mode of ethnographic cinema' that began in the early 1920s with Robert Flaherty's *Nanook of the North*. This approach probably remains an initial framing device even for fictional adventures like *Apocalypto* and *Avatar*. Yet in these and other eco-films, like the extremely successful *Dances with Wolves*, at least concessions are made to the native culture's unique, authentic language[7] and customs, with subtitles extensively used. Nonetheless, as many cultural critics assert, even this form of verbalisation can further serve to increase the surfeit evocation of a form of essentialising exoticism. In any case, there appears to be no easy, much less useful formulaic representational method or protocol towards avoiding such polarising (mis)representations between so-called Western 'civilised' and 'primitive' societies, while at the same time representing their ethical mind-set.

The audience is certainly positioned from the start in Gibson's historical epic adventure to actively engage and identify with the freedom and excitement of traversing large environmentally pure spaces. Unlike a dam as the ecological threat to the pristine (emerald) forest, or the exploitative search for a rare and precious metal explored in *Avatar*, here we are presented with an indigenous tribal conflict, coupled with a Mayan religious belief system – all of which at the outset seem very far from any notion of normative environmental ethics. Set in Yucatan, Mexico, during the declining period of an ancient civilisation, *Apocalypto* depicts the journey of a Mesoamerican tribesman who must escape human sacrifice and rescue his family after the capture and destruction of his forest village. The story begins with a defining epigram from Will Durant: 'A great civilisation is not conquered from without, until it has destroyed itself from within'.

While hunting in the jungle in the early sixteenth century, Jaguar Paw (Rudy Youngblood), his father Flint Sky and their fellow tribesmen encounter a procession of traumatised and fearful refugees. Speaking in Yucatee Maya, the procession's leader explains that their lands have been ravaged, and asks for Flint Sky's permission to pass through their jungle. We are informed through expositional voice-over how this hunting tribe have lived in this rich forest for numerous generations and respect its bounteous food. Such exposition is strongly contrasted with the anti-ecological and dystopic landscape to which his people are soon to be transported, as both slaves and sacrificial victims of the brutal alien Mayan culture.

While the massacre of the indigenous tribal village is going on at the start of the movie, Jaguar Paw slips out with his idealised and beautiful pregnant wife Seven (Dalia Hernandez) and his little son Turtles Run, lowering them both on a vine into a deep cave to hide them from the enemy. This universal embodiment of family and striving to protect its 'weaker' members – which transcends time and culture – can be read as celebrating a conservative and even right-wing perspective. At the same time this struggle becomes his motivational strength to survive and reunite with his family, as he faces up to the prospect of horrific torture and death.[8]

Earlier, the film opened with an exciting food hunt for a wild tapir, which is a horse-like animal, as Mel Gibson extols on the voice-over extra features. Apparently it would have been the biggest animal at that time within this primitive forest habitat. Incidentally, the makers also announce that no animal was harmed in the making of the film, as we witness the trap impaling the unfortunate, albeit synthetic creature, whose capture is nonetheless orchestrated primarily for the nourishment of the hunters. There is much written on the intrinsic value of the hunt, including for instance Spanish philosopher José Ortega y Gasset (1986), who celebrated the hunt as involving an authentic relationship between animals: 'It takes people out of the artificial and contingent conditions of their everyday lives and puts them in touch with their animal natures'. While Holmes Rolston has similarly written that hunting can be a sacred way of participating in nature (see Jamieson 2008:142).

This form of hunting solely for food, as also evidenced by the representation of Native American Indians in many Hollywood westerns, is in turn recuperated for white protagonists by eco-revisionists films like *Dances with Wolves*. This ritual can be contrasted with more mercurial agents, who simply hunt for sport, as also evident in several conventional westerns, alongside recent science fiction tales like *Jurassic Park: The Lost World* (1997). But in this tale, food, cannibalism and even forms of religious sacrifice become conflated, as also evident in varying ways through the dystopic futuristic cautionary tale *The Road*, explored later.

The animal's prized heart is taken out with great precision – foreshadowing a subsequent disembowelment for a human sacrifice – and presented to one of the chosen hunters. Finally the least palatable part of the animal, namely its genitals, is presented as a joke to the son-in-law warrior who apparently is infertile. He is initially led to believe in their implied restorative properties and encouraged to eat them raw. This bawdy comic scene specifically calls to mind Lévi-Strauss's semiotic analysis in *The Raw and the Cooked* (1983), with its anthropological and cultural divisions between so-called 'primitive' and 'civilised' cooking protocols and techniques. This display of eating probably results in the crassest olfactory visualisation in the film, calling to mind various food consumption games performed in reality TV shows, set in so-called desert island settings.

Soon, however, this erstwhile benevolent and life-affirming hunting and eating ritual is subverted when this idyllic indigenous tribe, who are clearly 'at one with nature', calling to mind the benevolent image of Native American Indians sitting around camp fires explored in the literature above, are themselves hunted down like 'animals' by vicious 'Mayan' (which, incidentally, does not strictly correspond with historical evidence) man-hunters, who apparently have no sense of natural justice, much less adopt any notion of ethical justice in appeasing their alien gods.

Apocalypto's overarching theme, as highlighted by the epigram at the start of the film, foretells the self-destruction of a long forgotten civilisation, which further signals a form of nostalgic environmentalism. Mel Gibson glibly announcing on the voice-over of the DVD bonus feature that 'malnourishment', alongside 'hygiene issues' may have caused the ancient Mayan civilisation's downfall reinforces this point. The film-makers apparently chose to focus on Mayan culture, because of their immense knowledge of medicine, science, archaeology and engineering, but also as suggested in the audio commentary by scriptwriter Farhad Safinia, because this might also be able to illuminate what some historians have questioned as being 'the brutal undercurrent and ritual savagery that some have practised.'

Unfortunately, more emphasis was placed on such explicit brutality and inhumanity, rather than attempting to explain their culture, affording little sense of this complexity, as evident especially in the *mise-en-scène* through their exotic, yet horror-inspired habitat. The landscape's conventionally beautiful vistas that punctuate the action were captured by a film crew shooting in Costa Rica, who also used digital effects and recorded the most spectacular eclipse of the sun that dramatically serves to break the cycle of ritualistic human sacrifice and also highlights the film's explicit ethical critique through the agency of indigenous cultures.[9]

The dominant (Western) audience can only view with disgust, one presumes, the exotic, green-tinged riches of the high priests with their blood-stained ornate vestments appeasing their alien gods, using fellow human beings from another tribe as sacrificial victims for their 'unnatural', and by any measure, totally unethical religious worship.[10]

Leading up to this violent climax, the captured hunters and their wives pass through a liminal state of 'no-man's land', which is marked by a young girl with a very wizened looking face having unsightly pus marks on her body. The iconic figure prophetically warns them that their civilisation is dying. Finally journey's end – both literally and figuratively – is presented as a dystopian and apocalyptic place, which is totally at odds with the lush and healthy life-affirming Arcadian forest, lovingly displayed through the opening of the film. Baudrillard's notion of 'manufactured catastrophe' comes to mind. This is a place where all the trees and vegetation are brutally destroyed, leaving loose soil washed away, eroding the prospect of any form of productive agriculture involving food production. The harvested trees with no recourse to any form of conservation, much less re-planting, are reminiscent of the criminal contemporary deforestation in many parts of the world, as most recently dramatised in the mythic future-world of *Avatar*. But this is used here instead for more perverse religious customs. Timber is used to help make massive lime quarries and dyes and to help build bigger and more ornate temples that in turn enable the corrupt tribal leaders to carry out a range of even more inhuman and unnatural practices.

Visually of course this iconography serves as classic shorthand of a scene from hell, as evident in many historical adventure epics, while also feeding into and reinforcing conventional stereotypes of ethical abnormality and negative stereotypes around primitive otherness. Meanwhile, Mel Gibson implies on the voice-over for the DVD how this destructive exposition could most particularly be read as the ultimate cautionary ethical tale around conspicuous consumption.[11] Painting their captives' bodies in deep blue dye made from laying waste so much natural forest, presents a strange foreshadowing of the more benevolent digital alien blue *Avatar* creatures, which have dominated world screens of late. The victims are marked off and marched up to the top of architecturally imposing pyramid-like edifices, from where they are butchered and sacrificed in the most horrific way imaginable.[12]

Finally, for the (post-colonial and revisionist) ending, it is little wonder that the heroic indigenous family who finally survive their ordeal are weary of the prospect of a new wave of colonial invaders and do not instinctively recognise them as saviours, either for their environment, much less for their indigenous culture, having encountered unbelievable oppression at the hands of relatively close ethnic tribes in the neighbouring area.[13] Gibson can also of course claim he is far from racist – much less anti-Zionist, as he was accused for his earlier Christian parable – and instead be seen as actively endorsing and embracing all forms of 'otherness', from a more benevolent perspective than is usually presented in commercial cinema. By all accounts the commercial parable raises some very useful insights into so-called primitive societies' environmental ethical values, which are not as naïve or as crude as many other forays into representing indigenous cultures across Hollywood cinema.

Jumping to an even darker worldview, while *Apocalypto* harks back to a mysterious historical past, *The Road* recreates a possible dystopian future where a crude Darwinian form of 'survival of the fittest' mentality, together with a very malign form of anti-environmental ethics has taken hold, foreshadowing the total destruction of the planet.

Dystopic environmental ethics: a reading of *The Road* and the struggle for food

McCarthy is following in the pantheon of Hemmingway, Carver and Falkner in writing such influential and state-of-the-nation cautionary stories for the American continent in particular, and world cultures in general. Every culture can understand and appreciate the concern of a father for his child in times of extreme peril. While the director of the adaptation, John Hillcoat, explicitly talks of the film as calling to mind a combination of references from environmental disasters, ranging from Mount St Helens to Hurricane Katrina. Consequently he explicitly calls on an ecological sub-text to explain the drive of his filmic adaptation that in itself justifies its inclusion in this volume.

The opening shot of total desolation presents a post-apocalyptic world – recalling some catastrophic environmental or man-made disaster. Trees are burned down and stumps left exposed, with no evidence of any (green) nurturing vegetation of any type and this dystopic vision is interspersed later by (sudden) earthquakes and spontaneous fires. Placed within this utterly horrible, anti-bounteous and grey world – not that far removed from the hell explored in *Apocalypto* – is an anonymous father and son who appear craggy and dirty. They have to scavenge for food, like the poorest lower-caste outsiders in India. This journey into darkness is visualised by how they manage their sparse belongings using a disused shopping trolley, which in turn serves to remind us of easy consumption.[14]

Consequently the film can be read as an explicit critique of consumerism and a cautionary tale around environmentalism, while keeping firmly in mind the precarious future of the planet, if we 'don't act now'. Allegorically of course, the narrative trajectory plays off what might happen if 'we' as humans let the

FIGURE 3.1 *The Road*, 2009, written by Joe Penhall, directed by John Hillcoat

world continue to follow a critically unsustainable path. So many dystopic fantasies, including those examined in this and other eco-cinema readers (see Rust *et al.* 2013; Weik von Mossner 2014), target this decisive moment or tipping point of total ecological break-up, to frame their narrative dynamic. Such storylines explicitly use the shorthand of post-nuclear landscapes that follow major world disasters, which in turn pull against the bounteous environmental agency of affirmative life-giving forces, while recalling the ongoing dangers of runaway economic growth. Unlike the historical hunter-gatherer society evidenced in *Apocalypto*, here the 'modern' protagonists have to relearn such 'primitive' coping skills, and go to great lengths to reevaluate what even constitutes food, alongside discovering what is ethically acceptable in this primal struggle for survival.

Furthermore, the protagonists also have to discover and define the ethical tipping point around which human life is not worth preserving. Hence their most precious talisman is a revolver with just two bullets and both of their names on it. This is their only insurance if the horror becomes too much. This narrative scenario recalls the demise of his wife, who could not take it any longer and simply went unprotected into the harsh wilderness to 'face her death'.

The father, played by Viggo Mortensen, whose face according to the director is so full of intense power, emotion and passion, portrays great difficulty in trying to cope with the loss of his screen wife, while still striving to protect their son. He affirms the ultimate 'masculine quest' to save and protect his own flesh and blood, a trope which underpins so many westerns and action adventure narratives. All the while, he espouses a simple (if naïve) ethic focused on a belief that they are 'good people', while recalling their need to be protected from the 'bad people'. This primal preoccupation is somewhat reminiscent of early westerns and the categorisation of various protagonists as either good or bad. This form of polarisation echoes conventional jingoistic western/war movies, where all the characters are forced to be on one side or the other, not having the luxury of reflecting, much less co-opting more nuanced ethical positions.

The Road essentially tells the story of an unnamed man and his son – played by Kodi Smit-McPhee (an Australian child who apparently performed an American accent with no coaching) – as they try to survive both inhospitable habitats and cannibal attacks, traversing the ruined landscape of the American south in order to reach the sea and escape the cold. 'From Coke cans, hammers, birds and plants, to the ideals of truth, goodness and beauty, things and their names are disappearing'; truth-telling language is 'shorn of its referents, and so of its reality'. The epic wreckage depicted in this dystopic novel/film, encapsulates 'the homogenised flatness of surfaces and colourless landscapes, as well as the seemingly pointlessness of the journey to the sea' and reflect McCarthy's comments on life and survival in such a dystopic environment (Carson 2013:175). In the 'post Nietzschean world of *The Road*, the ubiquitous ash covering the earth and floating in the air signifies that all human assurances, including God are gone' (Carson 2013).[15]

Unlike the hopeful journey of a conventional road narrative, which generally retains at least the prospect of reaching a desired destination, in this tale the innocence of the boy becomes the fulcrum of hope for the narrative and, I would suggest, this form of innocence also emphasises a more positive environmental value system. Carson deduces that the man's deepest reminder of grief and loss, the boy himself, is also the last remnant of all that is beautiful and good in the world. In the novel the father looks at the sleeping boy by firelight, and weeps not over 'Death', but over 'Beauty' and 'Goodness'. The film version, however, I suggest finds a way to posit hope and presents a fruitful cautionary tale around the need to discover a useful ethical and environmental trajectory, through an otherwise hopeless worldview.

After the turning point in the film, when the boy's core morality is affirmed, the film turns its attention to ethical values and the possibility of charity towards the other, in this otherwise nihilistic wasteland. All the while the man talks of his struggle to 'carry the fire' and limits his fears and hopes to his own memories of the past and the prospects for the future lying ahead of him, continuously calling to mind the protection of his child. This is the microscopic focus and determination which he can concentrate on to survive in this totally inhospitable habitat. Throughout the remainder of the film, the boy attempts to change this mindset and exhibits a universalising impulse that is not acknowledged by the man until late in the story. The boy acquires a vision that is universal in scope, which in turn, I would suggest, echoes an element of deep ecological philosophising that is beyond the self and can help promote a productive ethical agenda, recalling for instance the pervasive 'myth' of Christianity,[16] together with the need to have faith in the goodness of others, especially when dystopic reality becomes pervasive and malign and his father's fears dominate everything else.

In *The Road*, the boy embodies the truth – there are no separate journeys – he is utterly unable to see the journeys of others on the road as separate from his own and his father's (Luce 2002: 180). This radical transformation of approach calls to mind a deep ecological principle of 'everything being connected' and a rejection of a crude Darwinian 'survival of the fittest' philosophy, where it is every man for himself. Instead the boy helps to create a more eco-centric sensibility, which encourages in turn a form of therapeutic effect, affirming the transcendent possibility where all humans, alongside all other sentient creatures are 'connected' with ethical rights and responsibilities, as opposed to an otherwise Nietzschean and dystopic appreciation of an incoherent eco-system, where food and security are the only triggers for life.

As embedded within many religious beliefs around the world, sometimes resolutely facing evil, loss and suffering in one's life is a precondition towards being transformed and embracing the life-gift of charity. People who have deeply grieved the loss of a loved one, without giving in to despair, often do possess a deeper capacity and sensitivity towards others through this intense loss. This radical transformation of human selfhood or at least its potentiality, can be recognised also in other transformative readings across this volume, such as *The Tree of Life*.

Childhood innocence: embodying deep environmental ethical values

As indicated above, the boy embodies and represents total innocence, yet he also has to learn to become independent – the final major task of any parent – to afford full maturity. Thankfully, such transformation from the liminal state of protected childhood and innocence occurs over a long period of time in Western culture, but here the transformation is most stark and condensed into a very short space of time. The boy radically grows to embody more universal, ethical and environmental frames of consciousness, compared to his father, who selfishly but 'naturally', as in most animal habitats, focussed on doing everything possible to protect his son.

The boy instinctively knows it is right and ethically normative to assist others, even at a cost to themselves and insists most strongly that they go back to where they left a robber who was forced to strip naked. Driven by feelings of remorse, they leave some food and clothes for the robber to hopefully retrieve. The right moral and ethical (including environmental) choice must be made; the diegesis of the film and novel affirms, with humans learning to treat each other humanely and effectively, while sharing scarce resources. The boy further teaches his father to have more ontological respect for the Levinasian notion of the other, such as the old man walking ahead of them.

Alternatively, the protective father, naturally thinking primarily in a Hobbesian state of nature terms, asserts how if you let your guard down for a minute, the 'enemy' will take advantage and attack. Not surprisingly one supposes, knowing the myopic and instinctively selfish behaviour rules of humans trapped in such awful situations, this life-long knowledge and cold-hearted realisation results in him getting an arrow stuck in his leg that eventually kills him. Nature, coupled with a corrupt environment and malevolent indifferent agency of others conspire to disrupt his primal struggle to survive, if only for his son's sake. Nonetheless, he has come a long way and finally successfully equips the child with enough know-how and survival skills, together most importantly with a robust but more open environmental ethical value system to confidentially deal with all the future might bring.

The boy grows into becoming the new ethical fulcrum and radical point-of-view of the narrative. He has to put into action his newfound faith in the benevolence of the other and towards the end of film embraces another anonymous family who is willing to take him in, creating a new surrogate family. This is what a more transcendent form of ethical survival means in an otherwise totally dystopic environment: building trust with others who are willing to take an interest in us.

While the adaptation of *The Road* effectively captures the nihilistic dystopia of a post-apocalyptic world where humans resort to cannibalism to survive, yet even in this literally awesome and unnatural environment there still is evidence of hope when the 'good people' with 'fire in their soul' are able to withstand such temptations for any form of food and face up to their bleak future. This is made possible, as argued in this reading, when the boy takes on the deep ecological and ethically-altruistic role of learning to 'take the fire' and trust others and share their own precious belongings with them in communal solidarity if not hope for the future.

But by all accounts, this remains an extreme and difficult cautionary tale around primal survival, which can be offset by more sustainable notions of resilience and frugality also discussed in Chapter 7, featuring a more local and conventional form of food security, which also involves elemental survival tropes.

Food frugality as an antidote of dystopic environmental nihilism

The traditional romantic poets, who subscribed to the modern doctrine of the pre-eminence of the human mind which could overcome anything put in its way, tended to look upon nature and much less explicitly commercial agriculture, not as anything they might ever have practical dealings with, 'but as a reservoir of symbols' (Jackson in Keller 2010: 477). In a 1905 study titled *The*

Outlook to Nature, Liberty Hyde Bailey argued that a good part of agricultural engagement involves learning how to adapt one's work to nature and to live in a right relation with his natural conditions, 'which is one of the first lessons that a wise farmer or any other wise man learns' (cited in Keller 2010: 477).[17]

As cultural critics suggest, our representation of nature usually reveals as much, if not more, about our inner fears and desires than simply about the environment. Nevertheless the two attributes can be regarded as coterminous, since our inner fears and desires often reflect, or at least constitute in large part, the 'external' environment. For Thoreau and later for Leopold, wilderness was a state of mind as much as a description of a place. Both environmentalists championed 'a land alongside a people' ethic and 'not a land versus people' ethic. Humans are a central environmental force shaping landscapes everywhere, as affirmed in previous readings including *The Road*, while going back into nature, at one extreme, feeds into a more self-sustaining and even frugal state of existence.

Frugality, as McNally suggests, is a term that seems to offer people, communities and society more agency or even self-determination and control over their consumption, rather than simply being considered as restrictive and an escape from capitalism. As an opaque concept, frugality may finally be read as offering a choice between various forms of consumption. Consequently within a sustainable framework, frugality need not be seen simply as puritanical or conservative, but can at a stretch be re-imagined as liberating and supporting a more progressive form of consumption practice.[18]

Yet valorising notions like frugality as a mode of 'progressive' environmental ethics have a long way to evolve from the enforced struggle for food in *Apocalypto* and most significantly in *The Road*, to other more benevolent forms of frugality and food consumption. While in the meantime more mainstream science fiction fantasies like *Avatar* can fill a commercial environmental vacuum and at the same time address such central questions.[19]

Avatar: indigenous food production, hunting and feminist ecology

The story centres around the evocative representations of the inhabitants of Pandora called Na'vi, who literally plug into the exotic, ecologically benign and idyllic flora and fauna, rather than just naturally appearing at one with their habitat, and which is evident in much Hollywood cinema. Adapting a classic narrative framework, Hollywood frequently situates its anti-heroes, like the Native American Indians, within a clearly established environment and portrays them as totally in tune with their habitat, as opposed to the colonising and destructive agency of the white settlers (see for instance Bird *et al.* 1996; Kilpatrick 1999; Elsaesser 2011). As affirmed frequently in film scholarship and discussed above, the western genre has been transformed into a contemporary form of science fiction spectacle, following similar generic and thematic tropes, and this trajectory is especially evidenced in this eco-blockbuster.

Latour suggests:

> If I had an agent, I am sure he would advise me to sue James Cameron over his latest blockbuster, since *Avatar* should really be called Pandora's Hope! Yes, Pandora is the name of the mythical humanoid figure whose box holds all the ills of humanity, but it is also the name of the heavenly body that humans from planet Earth (all members of the typically American military-industrial complex) are exploiting to death without any worry for the fate of its local inhabitants, the Na'vis, and their ecosystem, a superorganism and goddess called Eywa. I am under the impression that this film is the first popular description of what happens when modernist humans meet Gaia. And it's not pretty.
>
> (Latour 2010: 471)

At the same time incidentally Cameron insists on emphasising a gender/sexist embodiment of such aliens. 'Let's focus on things that can create otherness but are not off-putting'. The director is further quoted in *The Huffington Post*, as quipping that his female alien must have breasts – 'She's got to have tits', even though 'that makes no sense because her race, the Na'vi, aren't placental mammals' (in Russell 2013: 213).

Avatar successfully elicits strong 'eco-affects' among many fans, according to a provocative reading by Adrian Ivakhiv, while generating a variety of widespread conversations on socio-ecological topics, yet its potential for bringing about a changed ecological sensibility was hampered by its tight and unoriginal narrative structure.

> If films are to be judged – as I argue they should – both by the extent of 'eco-affects' that they generate and the *depth, resonance,* and *cognitive complexity* of those affects, then *Avatar* did very well on the first criterion and less well on the second. For a Hollywood blockbuster that nevertheless makes it, if not unique, at least somewhat remarkable.
>
> (Ivakhiv in Weik von Mossner 2014: 160)

It has been most successful with its audiences in generating worlds that they enter and engage with, cognitively and affectively. 'Cinema is, in this sense, cosmomorphic: it provides for the morphogenesis, the coming into form, of worlds' (Ivakhiv in Weik von Mossner 2014: 161). While most pointedly, as Salma Monani affirms in the same volume, *Avatar* is simply the 'latest popular rendition of ecological Indians' (Monani in Weik von Mossner 2014: 229).

This hugely successful 3D spectacle follows the journey of Jake Sully (Sam Worthington), a former marine who is paralysed during combat on earth. His twin brother had been working as a scientist for the so-called Avatar programme on Pandora – the well-named planet with the much sought-after energy source, unsubtly called unobtainium. This scientific project constructed genetically engineered machine-human-Na'vi hybrids that enable the humans to control these avatars with their minds, while their own bodies sleep. An avatar, we discover, can only be controlled by a person who shares its unique genetic material; consequently when Jake's twin brother dies, he is asked to join the squad, being the only one who has the appropriate genes to control that particular avatar, but by all accounts remains an unrecuperated patriarchal pawn in the military machine.

After the initial vicarious thrill of being able to freely run around this fantastically rich habitat in his new agile body, Sully faces a major ethical dilemma during his fantasy journey, in being forced to participate in the mechanistic and cosmic Manifest Destiny. This will ultimately lead to the destruction of Pandora and the Na'vi culture, including its magnificent and exotic vegetation under which most of these precious deposits are situated, echoing current concerns around fracking and various other forms of deep mining. Alternatively and more heroically of course, he could choose to embrace its organic and holistic habitat and reject his destructive (masculinist/colonialist) predetermined agency.

> In its luxurious depictions of the Pandoran world, which takes up much of the film's first half, viewers have the option of enjoying this world, finding it beautiful, compelling, and attractive: of failing to enjoy it, finding it fearful or unattractive (it is after all full of horrific creatures).
>
> (Ivakhiv in Weik von Mossner 2014: 165)

In the guise of a tranquil and harmonious interaction with the unknowable otherness of the Na'vi, Sully becomes the audience's eyes, engaging with this alien but idealised eco-utopia. This narrative plays into long-established generic discourses of several indigenous Native cultures portrayed in westerns, alongside more benevolent eco-narratives like Terrence Malick's primal American allegory *The New World* that in turn echoes the ending of *Apocalypto* discussed above. The setting up of this exotic spectacle, using the extreme violence perpetrated by humans in battle, can at an individual level also be viewed as a conflict between the unrecuperated male war-hero Sully and his nurturing love interest embodied by a native princess called Neytiri (Zoe Saldana). In this reading however, I will foreshadow eco-feminist interpretations developed further in a subsequent chapter and focus on representations of Neytiri as an exemplary icon of progressive environmental ethics, as against the female white established military-scientist leader, played by Sigourney Weaver, alongside the representation of the 'Great Mother' figure and feminised (food-producing) 'tree of life' Home Tree. All of these representational elements encapsulate what is benevolent about the non-patriarchal alien culture, together with their hunter-gatherer and native mode of agriculture, which is effectively dramatised in this global eco-blockbuster.

The Na'vi most specifically evoke non-white otherness and stereotypes associated with it (such as primitivism, noble savagery, ecological utopianism), while their re-imagining as catlike, cyan-skinned otherness – which makes it incidentally safer to navigate notions of imaged racial alterity in the twenty-second century – helps to evade the tumultuous reality of race relations and even gender binaries that still dominate contemporary culture.

The image of a nurturing Great Mother protecting the balance of life clearly draws on a pantheistic and deep ecological vision in which energy continuously flows through discrete bodies of organic life. During this and other sequences, Neytiri teaches Jake to behave and think as a Na'vi by 'going native' – a trope eulogised for instance in *Dances with Wolves* (see Brereton 2005: 98–102). *Boston Globe* film critic Wesley Morris and others have mischievously renamed the film 'Dances with Blue People' (see McGowan 2010: 3), to signal the obvious reference to this revisionist western film. Sully records in his video diary that Neytiri is 'always going on about the flow of energy, the spirits of animals', and adds, 'I'm trying to understand this deep connection the people have for the forest'. Further referencing a deep ecological and environmental agenda, Neytiri talks about 'a network of energy that flows through all living things' and affirms how 'all energy is only borrowed and one day you have to give it back'. Such assertions further evoke, I would suggest, a frugal interconnected and sustainable eco-system.

Science fiction representations: defamilarising the familiar

Cameron ostensibly suggests that the primary function of science fiction is to defamiliarise the familiar and he speaks of the need to do this without overtly alienating one's target audience. Like other natural principles of human science such as gravity, as evident in *Gravity*, which feature the weightless vacuum of space and high-speed travel, the conventions of the genre dictate that alien species must assume roughly humanoid form (with enlarged breasts for the female) and other familiar makers of race and gender, so as not to introduce representational realities that would otherwise distract audiences from the narrative, or for that matter so completely alienate them that they would presumably find it too difficult to relate to the storyline in the first place.

On one of his first missions into this alien landscape, Jake wanders off to do some exploring of his own. He is fascinated and delighted with the awesome beauty and life-affirming properties of the planet's life forms. Usually it is only in big-budget nature TV series that features such explicit and focused evocations of environmental habitats and documents their food-producing properties. Jake wanders through the forest absorbed by the breath-taking scenery, exploring the behaviour of the local flora by playfully interacting with it as in a video game. In contrast the scientists demonstrate a different approach to nature, which is narrowly focused on the microstructure of 'samples', from which it pieces together an understanding of the whole. Meanwhile Jake is given over to direct sensuous experience and astonishment. Jake later describes himself to Mo'at, the Na'vi tsahik (the spiritual leader of the clan), 'as an empty cup, signifying in part that his outlook on the world isn't biased by scientific preconceptions' (Lawler in Dunn 2014: 107). Such appetite and endorsement for being totally open to nature's pleasures and richness are often ascribed to the innocence of the child, as explored earlier in *The Road*.

While Jake is naïvely admiring the beauty of Pandora, 'Grace and Norm are sticking syringes into roots and studying images on a computer screen'. It turns out that what they're measuring is the 'signal transduction' between the roots of the trees, which Grace believes constitutes a 'biological mechanism that supplies scientific confirmation for the Na'vi belief in the interconnectedness of life on Pandora' (Lawler in Dunn 2014: 108). Grace eulogises how it has more connections than the human brain. 'Get it? It's a network. It's a network. It's a global network, and the Na'vi can access it.' This eureka life-giving property reminds me of the GMO-like seed supplied by the Deity in the Old Testament story *Noah*.

Furthermore, for the purposes of this study, the precautionary principle and the more obvious danger of 'unintended consequences' would suggest that cutting down indigenous natural forests, much less tampering with holistic eco-systems, might in the long term result in, for instance, not developing medical-scientific breakthroughs from the rich heritage of flora afforded by nature, recounting the great scientific and utilitarian hope and possibility of uncovering solutions to cancer and other diseases examined in films like *The Emerald Forest*. Such explicit justification for instrumental environmental ethics is set up as a rationale for *not* tampering with nature for short-term financial gain, which in turn is often proposed as an important ecological rationale for preserving great swathes of the planet's natural eco-system.

Meanwhile, at a prosaic and common sense level, which echoes the layman's supposed lack of appreciation of such connections, the UN über-male scientific military leader Selfridge retorts: 'what the hell have you people been smoking out there? They're just goddamn trees.' Selfridge sees only the surface image and meaning of vegetation such as the trees, reminding us at another level of abstraction that most audiences and citizens apparently cannot understand much less appreciate how to handle the long-term consequences of climate change. Meanwhile the scientist Grace further perceives 'their recondite molecular structures and the electrical signals through which they communicate, believing these to be the true mechanism of reality.' While Jake as 'innocent' and 'pure' like a child goes on to learn to appreciate the holistic natural beauty and wonder of this alien habitat, becoming much more self-contained within his newfound (deep ecological) holistic eco-system.

Most cogently from Hegel's perspective for example,[20] what is missing from Grace's analysis is 'the unifying principle that binds all these parts together; the Spirit that makes Nature more than just an assortment of separate elements that interact in interesting ways, namely a unified whole in which rocks, plants, and animals are all organically connected parts' (Lawler 2014: 108). Consequently, it is less problematic for the non-scientist and non-environmentalist military leaders to ignore a range of ethical dilemmas, much less construct any deep ecological philosophy in simply exploiting and turning the forests of Pandora into a mining operation' (Lawler 2014: 109). Only following first-hand immersive personal experience, Sully can now fully appreciate the essential ecological truth of this utopian paradise – where environmental and ethical harmony remains in total balance – and clearly recognise the ecocidal disaster that would follow if Home Tree, as primal source of food and sustenance, was destroyed by the military might of humans. General audiences need this first-hand creative imaginary of a Platonic idealised and harmonious environment to fully appreciate what might be lost.

Surprisingly, such an overtly explicitly controlling deep ecological agenda around the interconnectivity of all living things was too much for some eco-critics who found the *mise-en-scène* of the iconic Home Tree as being simply too crude and too obvious. Some dismissed the story as trying too self-consciously to get its didactic message across, which in turn militated against its final achievement in communicating a provocative environmental and ethical message. This point of view is well captured by Adrian Ivakhiv cited above. For a more comprehensive analysis of various other critical and contradictory readings, see also Thomas Elsaesser's (2011) wide-ranging analysis, alongside varying perspectives from a range of scholars cited in Bron Taylor's (2013) reader explicitly dedicated to a critical evaluation of the film,[21] and also see William Irwin and George Dunn's edited volume on the film (2014) that further develops a number of interesting perspectives, as we await future instalments of the franchise over the coming years.

Nevertheless, in spite of scholarly worries and debates, hearing about the network connections which link back to the exotic Home Tree, alongside relating how its non-humanoid inhabitants commune with, rather than abuse their habitat, remains allegorically potent for a whole new generation of cinema-goers and might even help to promote a contemporary form of eco-cinematic literacy. The global importance of this ecological allegory can be appreciated at one level, by recalling how the 3D spectacle banked $2.98 billion within the first two years after its release; 73 per cent of which came from outside of the USA.[22]

Most recently Carolyn Michelle *et al.* (2012) have begun to addresses various audience studies concerns around *Avatar*, where she and others assess the film's influence on environmental awareness. While such small-scale studies highlight the powerful effect the film has had on a range of audiences, such tentative empirical research still remains at a very early stage of methodological development; and much more broad-based evidence is needed to investigate and question the film, like others in the same vein, and take on board their ability to promote pro-environmental messages, particularly around the sacred right of 'nature' to protect itself.

Without question the most provocative critic of *Avatar* remains Slavoj Žižek (2010), who winces over its 'politically correct' themes, supporting 'an array of brutal racist motifs; a paraplegic outcast from earth is good enough to get the hand of a beautiful local princess and to help the natives win the decisive battle.' Rather than promoting a proactive ecological message, he counter-claims, the film teaches us that the 'only choice the Aborigines have is to be saved' by the human beings or to be destroyed by them. In other words, 'they can choose either to be the victim of imperialist reality, or to play their allotted role in the white man's fantasy' (cited in Taylor 2013: 4). In a YouTube video entitled 'Ecology as Religion', Žižek further denounces the film, calling it a mystifying ideology and encapsulating 'the new opium of the masses'. Žižek and other critics of such utopian fantasies, including Renato Rosaldo,[23] cogently claim how we need to love and embrace the real world, not an idealised ecological one (Žižek 2010). Such worries echo long-standing debates concerning Romantic/ Nature literature, art and film studies and how they might inform and not predefine a model of environmental ethics.

Nonetheless, Cameron I would suggest captures a very *real* form of environmental utopian yearning, which needs to be recognised and expressed, even if he and others somewhat less successfully critique the ideologies that fuel its construction. Paradoxically, Cameron's critique of technological excess is accomplished by marshalling the same environmentally destructive technophile and corporatism it attacks. The vast array of computer electronics that allows audiences to share vicariously Sully's experiences of alien fauna and flora as food for the senses is, in itself, evidence of our contemporary inequitable and unjust world and calls to mind the high level of exploitation by multinational corporations in securing 'conflict minerals' for the digital media industry.[24] But unlike *Apocalypo*, the ecological message and allegory of the text is most clearly featured in the film's diegesis.

In any case, its creation of a dazzling alternative ecology, which is also food for the eyes, represents cinematic biomorphism at its best. Through the eyes of its main character, it presents a world that comes alive as ecologically and spiritually *different* and somewhat *more alive* than the world of today's industrial capitalism and fast-food modes of consumption.

Avatar lends a voice to

> the hope that there is a way to turn back the clock, that somehow somewhere there might be a tribe of environmentally correct natives holding out against the pernicious pressures of late-industrial capitalism, including food and energy production and consumption, natives who only needed the white man to come in to marry their princess before they could wage their war against the forces of evil.
>
> (Weik von Mossner 2012: 94)

Bergtaller shows that the movie's effectiveness directly depends on an ethics of dislocation: viewers are yanked out of their comfort zones and thrust into a world – an environment, a place – that is precisely not theirs.

This is in turn a sophisticated critique of Thoreauvian emplacement, one that investigates the desire for action in viewers not by pointing them to a wholeness that they never experienced anyway but by asking them to re-envision themselves as functioning in a world where nothing is ever really in place.

(Weik von Mossner 2012: 95)

Earlier readings of *The Road* and *Apocalypto* explore what happens after such ecocidal events have occurred, leaving no natural resource, much less agency, to help solve human dilemmas. Yet even here there continues to be recourse to their journey being transformed into a pilgrimage, and they begin to recognise the expansive and presumably healthy environmental system, as a natural trajectory for human escape from ecocidal destruction. Similarly in *Avatar* we actively follow Scully from an innocent outsider and 'one of us', towards becoming a deep environmentalist insider, albeit within an alien culture, who in turn realises and learns to embody the core ethics and values of such a rich habitat.[25]

Concluding remarks on ethical food production/ consumption: a polemic

As highlighted in several subsequent chapters, critical commentators rightly question, in particular, how the West can expect the extremely disadvantaged Third World, represented by so-called indigenous cultures addressed in *Avatar* and *Apocalypto*, to give up the possibility of gaining some of the luxuries and benefits which the rich industrialised world enjoys, irrespective of the overall ecological cost to planet earth. Many well-meaning commentators have asserted that global poverty remains too large a problem to be solvable, without destroying *our* way of life, which in turn reinforces Western impotence towards extreme poverty. Astute critics and academics, including Thomas Pogge and Naomi Klein, have effectively demonstrated the inherent fault lines within such a discourse, as discussed later in Chapter 6 dedicated to Third World film production.

Ecological ethics, as Boucher *et al.* (2003) affirm, ought to be explicitly aligned with injustice issues, especially the class struggle to create 'communities of resistance', while engendering real sustainability in the global economy, ostensibly following the lead of indigenous communities. Stopping global ecological disintegration and especially improving structures for food security and redistribution requires massive social change; and the current liberal environmental and regulatory movements can help counter-intuitively almost to prolong, rather than to eradicate, the escalating misery of our growing global population. This is not the agenda of continuing (post)colonial struggles to simply secure scarce natural resources to maintain the hegemonic status quo. Sooner or later this systemic weakness will have to be replaced with a movement for fundamental political engagement and change that seeks to address core global problems, namely the greed and general disregard for the human condition engendered and promoted by rampant (neoliberal) capitalism and conspicuous consumption in particular.

But as André Gorz warns in *Ecology as Politics*, environmentalism is continually being 'commandeered' by the dominant groups in Western society for their own ends. The forces of capitalism are very capable of adapting an 'environmental conscience' to meet the needs of the dominant culture (Gorz 1987: 114–30). Such contradictions and ambiguities must be faced up to and examined, as an environmental education agenda addresses many of the most contentious issues of the planet, particularly global warming, nature management, population growth and food control as explored in this chapter. It remains very difficult however to get consensus on such complex issues, in a world where the West has gained the most from a well developed Industrial Revolution, as against the Third World, which of late wants to acquire equitable levels of wealth creation. Newly developing and economically powerful nations like China and India and the other so-called BRIC countries, will probably determine the future sustainability of our planet, rather than the so-called First World. Food together with energy resource issues will remain the dominant environmental ethical concern, and mainstream film-creative imaginary allegories and cautionary tales can certainly help to foreground and reframe these complex issues as we face even more diverse personal challenges in the future.

Notes

1 Meanwhile more head-on contemporary food narratives like *Food Inc.* and other documentaries, which will be discussed in a future volume, directly address Western preoccupations with cheap fast food and place ethical issues of nutrition and poor food literacy on the public arena. Such fictional/factional narratives help illustrate the growing concern and consequences of food over-consumption, measured against increased levels of poverty and political economic inequities across the food-production chain.

2 When hunger takes a literal rather than a metaphorical form, it propels actions that serve to define what it is to be human – or to be inhuman. Food and water scarcity lead both to brutality and kindness in science fiction films such as *The Omega Man* (1971) or *Mad Max 2* (1982) for instance.

3 In a sepia-toned scene in *Gattaca* (1998) for instance, the eldest son Vincent (Ethan Hawke) reveals his estrangement from his family at the dining room table, while he sits alone, absorbed in a book on space travel.

4 Or recalling another science fiction allegory *In Time*, where the only currency that drives the very inequitable society is literally time itself, as displayed for all to see on the forearms of all inhabitants. The chief protagonist who is gifted a large cachet of frozen time by a very old man – in a young person's body – articulates the desire to die so that others can live. Consequently the now time-rich protagonist seeks revenge for his mother's 'untimely' death. So he ends up in the rich district where everyone literally has lots of time on their hands. The waitress in an upper-class hotel suggests that he is obviously not from around here, because he 'eats so fast'. The so-called 'slow food' movement could probably only flourish in a rich and affluent human environment, where food can acquire a more esoteric and leisurely value.

5 In a recent fascinating study of the classic Australian 'nature film' *Walkabout* (1970), titled 'Rites of Passage, Eco-Indigenes and the Uses of Meat...' in *Senses of Cinema* July 2009, Gregory Stephens asserts how the Aborigine of the film can be read as an 'ecological indigene' whose immediate role is as the man who brings the water back and 'functions to show the Anglo youths' how to live on the land, 'to eat of its fruit and flesh', which starts with knowing 'where the water is kept'.

6 Recalling a purely cynical but commonly held ideological view that escapist and feel-good eco-adventures, alongside dystopic science fiction movies addressed in this study, are simply designed to produce a pleasant sense of being concerned, without costing audiences anything more than the price of admission. Ecological historians like Ivakhiv constantly cite this tendency as suggesting, even validating, a shallow form of ecological exclusivity and environmental ethics, while avoiding having to deal with the root causes of injustices; all the while appeasing Western, white, middle-class guilt and anomie.

Again fully accepting and recognising this important caveat and pervasive truth, I would probably suggest that the movement for ecological justice should not be built up simply on fears of apocalypse and ought instead to be based on achievable struggles for social and environmental justice, as usefully exemplified for instance in the Baudrillard/Beck debate. Here Beck's 'overly pessimistic' and gloomy prognosis regarding the prospect of environmental accidents and disasters can be compared with Baudrillard and his notion of 'manufactured catastrophe', which somehow might be 'deliberate and experimental, triggered by our compulsion to generate something novel and marvellous', something 'which exceeds the nature which we have become so familiar' (Clark 1997: 79). These tensions are most pointedly articulated in *Apocalypto* and are also evident in other science fiction cautionary tales and 'end of the world' climate change spectacles discussed in Chapter 8.

7 In *Apocalypto*, the dialogue is entirely in the Yucatec Maya language, Gibson explains: 'I think hearing a different language allows the audience to completely suspend their own reality and get drawn into the world of the film'.

8 Body torture remains a filmic trope which has preoccupied Gibson in many of his albeit 'right-wing' films; including the Scottish nationalist calling card, *Braveheart* (1995) and of course the highly controversial 'body-porn' Christian foundational story, *The Passion of the Christ* (2004).

9 The fundamental problem with *Apocalypto*'s depiction of Maya culture is that it imposes violence and an apocalyptic world view on the wrong people. Several website reviews affirm how there exists no archaeological, historical or ethno-historic data to suggest that any such mass sacrifices took place in the Mayan world.

10 Jarad Diamond in a chapter titled 'The End of the World as we Know Them' explains how in the year 909 Mayan society experienced a massive cut in population. Most specialists suggest a major factor was environmental degradation by people; deforestation, soil erosion and water management problems, all of which resulted in less food. Those problems were exacerbated by droughts, which were partly caused by humans themselves through deforestation. Chronic warfare made matters worse, as more and more people fought over less and less land and resources (Diamond in Keller 2010: 409) – an accumulation of several tipping points that in turn drive towards total environmental disaster.

11 For instance, one calculation estimates that it would take five tons of jungle forest to make one ton of quicklime.

12 Excessive consumption models of behaviour are signalled by the extravagant costuming of the Mayan leaders with their vast wealth contrasted to the enslaved, sickly and extremely poor indigenous peoples in their charge. Environmental degradation is portrayed both by the exploitation of natural resources, including the over-mining of the land, but also through the treatment of people, families and entire tribes, simply as resources and chattels to be harvested and sold into slavery. *The Washington Post* wrote that the film depicts the Maya as a 'super-cruel, psycho-

sadistic society on the skids, a ghoulscape engaged in widespread slavery, reckless sewage treatment and bad rave dancing, with a real lust for human blood' (Booth 2006). The review goes on to suggest that such 'blood sacrifice' was more typical of the Aztecs than the Maya.

13 With the idealised reassembled family at last secured again 'in nature', the early American settlers can be argued to remain rightly cautious in refusing to acknowledge, much less accept the othered imperialist white invaders arriving in the new world. Who would blame them after what they had gone through?

14 Incidentally, the film director in a bonus feature on the DVD talks of this use of a shopping trolley that contains all their possessions and considers it a key motif for the film. An image that stays and remains linked to real-life disaster.

15 Incidentally, this portrayal is radically different from the positive and therapeutic use of snow for instance in James Joyce's famous short story *The Dead*, which alternatively serves to unify disparate communities and individuals across time and space. While in McCarthy's seminal novel, according to Carson, '[the Man] looked at the sky. A single grey flake sifting down. He caught it in his hand and watched it expire there like the last host of Christendom.' McCarthy's view is 'beautifully embodied in the film, suggesting that the world is utterly indifferent to, and slips out from under human attempts to capture its meaning or become its sovereign' (Carson 2013: 175).

16 See for instance the work of John Caputo (2006), which situates a 'postmodern' theory of religion and Catholicism.

17 Of course this modified utilitarian principle certainly offers no magic philosopher's stone for making difficult choices easy. Instead it forces us to face the question of core purpose: sufficient for what? Needed for what? (in Keller 2003: 524).

18 Frugality could also be applied as a radical new way of re-framing the current hegemonic discourse of 'austerity', as a counter-narrative to redress the material excesses of contemporary Western society and its rampant embracing of conspicuous consumption.

19 Alexa Weik von Mossner suggests at the start of a recent insightful reading of *The Road* and a German film called *Hell*, that 'as a speculative genre, science fiction is in a near-ideal position to explore perceived risks and anxieties regarding large-scale environmental change. Science fiction film, with its ability to visualise and visceralise speculative future worlds, is particularly powerful in this regard' (Weik von Mossner 2012: 42).

20 The Na'vi themselves makes up the body or avatar of a higher consciousness, 'a divine spirit that presides over the entire planet and is known to the Na'vi as the goddess Eywa' (Lawler in Dunn and Irwin 2014: 104).

21 Many observers less worried about creating ecological awareness, highlighted that *Avatar* simply pilfered aspects from films like *The Emerald Forest* (1985), *Ferngully* (1992) or *Pocahontas* (1995). Others complained about Sully's 'white messiah' stereotyping (Elsaesser 2011) and suggested that the film recreated a 'noble savage' narrative, further playing into regressive colonial discourses.

22 The figures would have been significantly higher had not the Chinese government apparently cut short the film's run, reportedly out of fears that it might encourage resistance to development projects and their resettlement schemes.

23 Rosaldo suggests 'Imperialist nostalgia' revolves around a paradox: a person kills somebody, and then mourns the victim – a trope which is also echoed with regards to environmental nostalgia, where people destroy the environment and at the same time ostensibly worship nature (Russell 2013: 212).

24 For instance in the African Congo, essential minerals such as coltan and tantalum which are used for the audio-visual digital industry have been mined, and their increasing exchange value has fuelled conflicts that have despoiled actual environments and claimed the lives of over six million Congolese and displaced millions more since 1996 (Musauuli, Delevigne as cited in Russell 2013: 212).

25 Like so many Hollywood classic narratives, we follow a character from being an innocent outsider towards becoming a deep environmental insider who grows in knowledge with relation to the interconnections of nature and its albeit alien habitat.

Bibliography

Bailey, Liberty Hyde (1905) *The Outlook of Nature*. London: Macmillan.

Bird, E.S. (1996) *Dressing in Feathers: The Construction of the Indian in American Popular Culture*. Boulder, CO: Westview.

Booth, William (2006) 'Culture Schoker'. *The Washington Post*, December 9. http://www.washingtonpost.com/wp-dyn/content/article/2006/12/08/AR2006120801815.html

Boucher, D., Schwatzman, D., Zara, J. and Caplan, P. (2003) 'Another Look at the End of the World'. *Capitalism, Justice Socialism (CNS)* 14(3):123–131.

Brereton, Pat (2005) *Hollywood Utopia: Ecology in Contemporary American Cinema*. Bristol: Intellect Press.

Caputo, John D. (2006) *The Weakness of God: A Theology of the Event*, Indiana Series on the Philosophy of Relgion. Bloomington, IN: University of Indiana Press.

Carson, Nathan (2013) 'Transformation in the Wasteland? Remembrance, Naming and Charitable Action in The Road'. *Film and Philosophy* 17: 173–191.

Clark, N. (1997) 'Panic Ecology: Nature in the Age of Superconductivity'. *Theory Culture and Society* 14(1): 77–96:

Dunn, George A. and Irwin, William (eds) (2014) *Avatar and Philosophy: Learning to See*, Blackwell Philosophy and Pop Culture Series. Oxford: Wiley Blackwell.

Elsaesser, Thomas (2011) 'James Cameron's *Avatar*: Access for All'. *New Review of Film and Television Studies* 9(3): 247–264.

Gorz, A. (1987) *Ecology as Politics*. London: Pluto.

Jamieson, Dale (2008) *Ethics and the Environment: An Introduction*. Cambridge: Cambridge University Press.

Keller, David (ed) (2010) *Environmental Ethics*. Oxford: Wiley Blackwell.

Kilpartick, Neva Jacquelyn (1999) *Celluloid Indians*. Lincoln, NE: University of Nebraska.

Latour, Buno (2010) 'An Attempt at a Compositionist Manifesto'. *New Literary History* 41: 471–490.

Lawler, James (2014) 'They're Not Just Goddam Trees: Hegel's Philosophy of Nature and the Avatar of Spirit' in George A. Dunn (ed) *Avatar and Philosophy: Learning to See*. Chichester: Wiley.

Lévi-Strauss, Claude (1983) *The Raw and the Cooked*. Chicago, IL: University of Chicago Press.

Luce, Dianne C. (2002) 'The Cave of Oblivion: Platonic Mythology in Child of God' in James D. Lilley (ed), *Cormac McCarthy: New Directions*, 171–198. Albuquerque, NM: University of New Mexico Press.

McGowan, Todd (2010) 'Maternity Divided: *Avatar* and the Engagement of Nature'. *JumpCut: Review of Contemporary Media*. http://www.ejumpcut.org/archive/jc52.2010/mcGowanAvatar/

Michelle, C., Davis, C.H. and Florin, V. (2012) 'Understanding Variation in Audience Engagement and Response: An Application of the Composite Model to Receptions of *Avatar* (2009)'. *Communication Review* 15(2): 106–143.

Milne, T. (ed) (1998) *Time Out Film Guide*. London: Time Out.

Murray, Robin and Heumann, Joseph (2009) *Ecology and Popular Film: Cinema on the Edge*. New York: Suny Press.

Ortega y Gasset, José (1986) *Mediations on Hunting*. New York: Scribner Books.

Retzinger, J.P. (2008) 'Speculative Visions of Imaginary Meals: Food and the Environment in (Post-Apocalyptic) Science Fiction Films'. *Cultural Studies* 2(3–4): 269–390.

Ront, Fatimah Tobing (1996) *The Third Eye: Race, Cinema and Ethnographic Spectacle.* Durham NC: Duke University Press.

Russell, John G. (2013) 'Don't it Make my Black Face Blue: Race, Avatar, Albescence and the Transnational Imaginary'. *Popular Culture Journal* 46(1): 192–217.

Rust, S., Monani, S. and Cubitt, S. (eds) (2013) *Ecocinema, Theory and Practice.* AFI Film Readers. London: Routledge.

Stephens, Greg (2009) 'Confining Nature: Rites of Passage, Eco-Indigenes and the Uses of Meat in *Walkabout*'. *Senses of Cinema* Issue 51. http://sensesofcinema.com/2009/towards-an-ecology-of-cinema/walkabout/

Taylor, Bron (ed) (2013) *Avatar and Nature Spirituality.* Waterloo, Canada: Wilfred Laurier University Press.

Weik von Mossner, Alexa (2012) 'Afraid of the Dark and the Light: Visceralizing Ecocide in *The Road* and *Hell*'. *Ecozon@* 3(2): 42–56.

Weik von Mossner, Alexa (ed) (2014) *Moving Environments: Affect, Emotion, Ecology and Film.* Waterloo, Canada: Wilfrid Laurier University Press.

Žižek, Slavoj (2010) Review '*Avatar:* Return of the Natives'. *New Statesman* 4 March.

4

ECO-FEMINISM, ENVIRONMENTAL ETHICS AND ACTIVE ENGAGEMENT IN SCIENCE FICTION FANTASIES

Overview

This chapter will examine a range of science fiction fantasies which privilege female protagonists and in varying ways promote an eco-feminist agenda that in turn addresses environmental ethical concerns. *The Hunger Games* in particular will be closely analysed, concentrating on its main character Katniss who performs the usually male role of hunter and action hero in her struggle to survive within an artificial future games world where she has to literally fight to the death with other contestants.[1] In contrast *Elysium* situates a military leader Delacourt, played by Jodie Foster as the quintessential evil antagonist, who rides roughshod over environmental and other rights of the poor classes, still striving to exist on planet earth. She certainly plays against the more benevolent environmental ethical norms usually embodied by female protagonists, which are constantly associated with nurturing and protection of the innocent. Meanwhile with an Oscar-winning performance by Sandra Bullock who plays scientist and astronaut Ryan Stone, *Gravity* serves as a coda to frame a range of related aspects of eco-feminist discourse, alongside encapsulating a cautionary tale around waste in space.

Eco-feminist and environmental debate

Eco-feminists most notably have developed a pragmatic strategy to actively perceive the ethical dilemma around environmental decay, building upon a well-established and cogently argued body of feminist literature. At its most basic level, one can link questions of gender and race through the lens of eco-feminism, while affirming that 'sexism and the exploitation of the environment are parallel forms of domination' (Warren 1994: i). Karen J. Warren concludes, 'any feminist theory *and* any environmental ethic which fails to take seriously the twin and interconnected dominations of women and nature is at best incomplete and at worst simply inadequate' (Warren 1990: 125).

What all eco-feminists agree about, then, is the way in which the logic of domination has functioned historically within patriarchy to sustain and justify the twin dominations of women and nature. Feminism, as a discourse and a praxis, therefore *must* embrace ecological feminism if it is to end the domination of women, because the domination of women is tied conceptually and historically to the domination of nature (Warren in Keller 2010: 288).

Eco-feminists' certainly criticise the dualistic logic of domination, which pervades much cultural and imperialistic pre-determined discursive debate.

> Environmental problems, whilst they certainly should not be seen in isolation, might seem more amenable to solution if they are disaggregated and instead framed by cosmic apocalyptic narratives that emphasise the provisionality of knowledge, free will, ongoing struggle and a plurality of social groups with differing responsibilities.
>
> (Garrard 2012: 115)

As affirmed throughout this study, environmental ethics in turn deal with the questions of what duties humans have with respect to their environment and the reasons underpinning these obligation. While the image of earth as a 'nurturing mother' that permeates much mainstream cinema carried with it powerful constraints against certain forms of exploitation, the counter-image of nature as a 'wild and a destructive female' who requires control is equally potent across cinematic history. For instance Carolyn Merchant in a piece titled 'Secrets of Nature: the Bacon Debates Revisited' spoke of how Francis Bacon – often considered the father of modern science – advocated extracting nature's secrets from 'her bosom through science and technology' (Merchant 2008: 147). The subjugation of nature as female is argued by many eco-feminists and cultural historians as thus integral to the scientific method; namely power *over* nature. While at the same time other feminist scholars warn against the danger of reifying a form of crude binarisms, clearly coding divisions between nature versus culture. See for instance Val Plumwood's major study *Feminism and the Mastery of Nature* (1993).

Consequently, much of the problem – both for conceptualisations of women and nature – lies in rationalist appreciation of such debates, such as the mechanistic view cited above, with feminists arguing that concern for nature should not be viewed as the completion of a process of (masculine) universalisation, moral abstraction, and disconnection.[2] All of these processes serve to ostensibly discard the self, emotions, and all forms of special ties, much less any spiritual dimensions, which is a long way from the trajectory of a deep feminist agenda.

It is not however that we need to abandon patriarchally conceived ethics or dispense with the universalising ethical approach entirely, although we do need to reassess the centrality of ethics in environmental philosophy (Plumwood in Keller 2010: 304). Deep ecology most specifically locates the key problem area in human–nature relations and specifically within the separation of humans and nature. It provides a solution for this in terms of the 'identification' of self *with* nature (Keller 2010: 305).

At another extreme, some eco-feminists have demonstrated a particular interest in questions of spirituality. This trajectory is alluded to in the final reading of *Gravity*. Greta Gaard most notably argues that spirituality is a central concern for the movement, writing that 'the fundamental principle of eco-feminism is the interconnectedness of all life', the acceptance of which produces 'an awareness of oneness that transcends mere ego identity' (Gaard 1993: 308 cited in Du Coudray 2003: 66).

As noted in Chapter 1, Paul Taylor's *Respect for Nature* has become a seminal text in defending a biocentric (life-centred) ethical theory, which in some ways dovetails with a feminist perspective, by taking into account a person's true human self that includes his or her biological nature (Taylor 1986: 44). Furthermore, Taylor attempts to embed this ethical philosophy within a Kantian framework, which makes strong use of the reason/emotion dichotomy. Thus we are assured that an attitude of respect is a moral one, because essentially it is a universalising and disinterested position. 'It is because moral agents look at animals and plants in this way that they are disposed to pursue the aforementioned ends and purposes' (ibid: 82) and similarly take on board relevant emotions and affective attitudes. Taylor claims that actions do not express moral respect unless they are done as a matter of moral principle and conceived as ethically obligatory, yet not necessarily through a predetermined system of rules (see Plumwood in Keller 2010: 301).[3]

Many scholars seek to assert how environmental ethics remains a commitment to both the moral considerability of nonhuman nature and the elimination of the idolatry around naturism. Particularly as naturism is linked to sexism, according to most eco-feminists, environmental ethics must *de facto* also involve a commitment to eliminate sexism. At one extreme, eco-feminist philosophy rejects both ethical absolutism and ethical relativism, while more generally by privileging gender issues, this approach can *de facto* valorise a skewed, yet nonetheless more altruistic and egalitarian form of anthropomorphic normative ethics.

Warren most noticeably has developed the idea of a metaphor that recalls the concept of a quilt, where the edges or boundaries are determined, but not necessarily the interior conditions. The importance of an 'ethics of care' which underpins the DNA of most female protagonists, is sometimes however dramatically exaggerated and turned on its head within science fiction narratives like *Elysium*. In *Elysium* the female establishment control figure for example – reminiscent in ways of the female antagonist in 1940s film noir – is set up to pull against an erstwhile stereotypical and essentialising 'ethics of care' philosophy, as she plays out a conventional villain persona. This representational reversal in turn can be contrasted with a more normative and almost innate ethics of care philosophy, encapsulated by the teen heroic female figure of Katniss in *The Hunger Games*.

At the outset, J. Baird Callicott remains somewhat dismissive of such strategies that can appear to abstract a coherent eco-feminist and ethical position in the first place, suggesting that 'there is no specific eco-feminist moral philosophy grounding a specific eco-feminist environmental ethic, identifiable as such through its particular theory of intrinsic value in or rights for nature ...' (cited in Warren 2000: 119). Thus, Callicott implies that eco-feminism does not in fact answer the fundamental questions of environmental ethics, namely what duties humans (rather than just the misrepresented female protagonists) have with respect to the environment, and why?

Alternatively, eco-feminism, Warren suggests, addresses head-on Callicott's critique above.[4] While not having a specific rule that is all-encompassing and laying out a code of rules, it can nevertheless provide a framework for ethical environmental decision-making, producing results rather than simply abstract philosophising about various possibilities, which appears more fruitful for environmental ethics that radically needs both a change in thinking, but also and most importantly a dramatic change in behaviour. While not convinced that Warren's high ambitions for eco-feminism has ever been realised, nevertheless these and other tensions will be alluded to within the textual readings.

At least with regards to film, Belmont argues that *Armageddon, Dante's Peak, Asteroid, Volcano* – and I would include many of the science fiction fantasies examined from an ecological perspective in this chapter – remain particularly useful, for eco-feminist scholars and critics ought to take their construction of nature and natural disaster seriously. Such filmic representations of gender, in the specific context of a vision of nature as threatening, remain an abiding trope and their destructive force is usually subdued by authoritative male figures and masculinist institutions which in turn reinforce the ideologies responsible for environmental degradation and social injustice – issues which remain of the utmost importance to eco-feminism (Belmont 2007: 351). In particular, examining major female performances, even if they are constituted as anti-heroes in more contemporary nature/disaster films, can bring to the surface more explicit ethical environmental debates than some conventionally stereotypical male heroes.

Furthermore, the natural disaster film most certainly presents a unique opportunity to examine how 'fear of/desire to conquer nature and fear of/desire to control women are intimately connected' especially in the 'context of nature as a threat to human survival', while to eventually survive is to re-inhabit roles that represent what is safe, familiar, and comforting about 'nature', as it is applied to human relationships, 'which in turn involves repositioning women in ways that are troubling from a feminist perspective' (Belmont 2007: 262).

Discussing the broad relevance of media studies to environmentalism, Jhan Hochman, among others, explains why analysis of representations of nature in film is an important project for green cultural studies. The natural disaster film, in particular, envisions nature not as a mere backdrop, but rather as an active agent – in some cases approaching the level of character as suggested by, for example, *The Day After Tomorrow* – and which in turn is responsible for the (human) drama and also a participant in it. These visions also inform the mastery of nature trope and are worthy of examination, especially by eco-feminists, given that this agency tends to be constructed as female – as 'Mother Nature' (Belmont 2007: 352).

Mother Nature and greening cinema

As Chaia Heller explains, the construction of Mother Nature as 'damsel in distress' (a trope which is often used in environmental representation), has sprung up from 'a romantic tradition' broadly based on a pervasive male fantasy of 'the ideal woman' – a fantasy which leaves women and nature little room to be anything but become 'idealised victims' (Heller 1993: 219 cited in Belmont 2007: 367).

Our dependence on 'Mother Nature' is, of course, based on how we relate to her for our sustenance and survival, but the technological imperative in the context of a 'culture that defines worth, especially masculine worth, in terms of radical autonomy', demands that we try to break the dependency on nature, and when 'she doesn't cooperate with our demands or inexplicably does us harm, we interpret her actions as hostile and unfair' (Gomes *et al.* 1995: 114).[5] Such tensions and pervasive attitudes have major implications for an eco-feminist reading of environmental ethics on film.[6]

The Hunger Games: Katniss as eco-feminist hunter and agent of environmental ethical activism

The Hunger Games was first published in 2008, at the very moment – according to Mark Fisher (2012: 27) – when the financial crisis was pitching the world into panic and confusion. The setting is Panem, the name for North America after a catastrophic civil war, which at least allegorically sets up a cautionary tale around the dangers of not treating the planet in a nurturing manner. Panem is divided into twelve districts, all of which are presided over by the Capital. As a symbolic act of penance for their past rebellions, each district is required to send a young 'tribute' to the annual Hunger Games, a televised tournament in which the competitors are required to fight to the death. Katniss (Jennifer Lawrence) hails from District 12, of which the main industry and function within the system is coal-mining. At District 12's 'reaping' festival, where the names of the tributes are selected by a lottery, Katniss's younger sister, Primrose (Willow Shields), is picked to enter the arena. Katniss volunteers in her place and is joined by the male tribute, Peeta (Josh Hutcherson). The two are transported to the Capital where they are advised by a reluctant mentor

Haymitch (Woody Harrelson) and made over by professional stylists, as well as being interviewed on television before they are rated by the organisers, the Gamemakers (Fisher 2012: 27).

The purpose of the games is to remind the populace of the power of the government, reminiscent of any dictatorship, and to highlight its ability to dispose of any malcontents who dare to defy its rules and regulations. The book's author Suzanne Collins suggests that the system possesses a disturbing capacity to undermine ethical perspectives on the human, the humane and the real. Drawing on Baudrillard's (1981) ideas about simulation and simulacra, as well as Elaine Scarry's (1985) and Susan Sontag's (2003) concerns for media representations of the body in pain, the trilogy heavily references the

> disturbing entertainment of Roman gladiatorial games as well as the immersive nature of computer/video games, the seductive allure of reality television and the distancing effect of mediatised images of war and violence to warn off the sinister uses to which these can be harnessed.
>
> (Muller 2012: 51)

Collins has frequently commented that one of the motivations for writing the trilogy occurred when she was channel switching between reality television shows where young people were competing for money, and footage of the Iraq war in which people were fighting for their lives. This stark juxtaposition highlighted for her the seductive influence of reality television shows and video games, with their leverage of the virtual over the real, their power to not only mute the impact of media representations of adverse and horrifying experiences but also to be established as equivalent 'entertainments' (Muller 2012: 52).

In this reading, however, I would like to focus on how Katniss adapts to her habitat and uses her hunting skills to both survive and develop a more proactive ethics of care for the environment. For instance, the animals the protagonists encounter in the arena are either weird mutations or humans literally transformed into animals. Some

> pockets of semi-wilderness do remain on the outskirts of the districts where Panem's perennially oppressed citizens vegetate, enough to fuel the basic Thoreauvian dream and a return to a better life, a vision of an alternative world, where wonders are still possible. And it is during her wanderings through the woods of her district that Katniss acquires and sharpens the survival skills that will later allow her to stay alive in the strange environment of the arena.
>
> (Weik von Mossner and Irmscher 2012: 91)

The Hunger Games had the third-highest grossing opening weekend in American history and grossed over $400 million domestically, making it the third-highest grossing film of 2012, which of course was built on the huge success of the book franchise. The story of a televised fight to the death, with participants under 24-hour surveillance, immediately calls to mind reality TV (RTV) shows where surveillance works to verify the authenticity of the participants (as consistent with their behaviour). Within this artificial environment there is almost total surveillance, with varying types of cameras observing the contestants' every move. This remains analogous to watching a high-production-values nature programme and where, for instance, 'trip cameras' are set up to photograph wild animals and insects, filming them in real time as they go about their daily life and also recording them at night in their natural habitat. The major difference in this case is the artificially constructed conflict-to-the-death of human protagonists, which is set out in the so-called rules of the games. Similar macro-debates around the ethics of such reality TV story-lines were evident in films like *The Truman Show* (see Brereton 2011). Recalling televisual nature programmes' almost Darwinian 'survival of the fittest' trajectory, the main protagonists have to fight to the death in this spectacle, with nature both literally and metaphorically rigged against the protagonists in their deadly struggle.

Paul Cressey (1938: 519) long ago describing motion picture viewing modalities, asserted that instead of facilitating social interactions, the cinema chiefly serves to set up imaginative states, alongside promoting what is most significant for this volume, a broad range of cautionary tales. In these contemporary narratives, 'imaginative participation takes the place of social participation.' In other words, 'with narratives we simulate social experiences or interactions, rather than participate in them' and the 'social connection between narrative and the real world cuts both ways'. Not only does our social knowledge enable us to make more sense of the narrative, but also there is evidence that, 'as we make sense of the narratives in our lives, we may be increasing our empathy and understanding of people in the real world' (Mar, Oatley and Patterson 2009 in McDonald 2014: 122). These still early stage psychological communication theories help to concentrate on the effectiveness of the creative imaginary of film in promoting an ecological agenda including, for the purposes of this chapter, a specific eco-feminist and ethical framework.

Such technical hypnotising raises a number of audience identification and ethical questions including: do we keep our attitudes, stereotypes, prejudices and knowledge of the world that we have personally experienced, or do we adopt those characteristics that we know are what the character thinks, feels or believes? The picture that is emerging from a range of psychological research is that the former explanation is more likely. It is suggested that audiences retain their ability to step out of the action and back into it at any time. Consequently, we only adopt the goals of the characters to the extent that our real selves see these goals as appropriate within the narrative situation (Magliano *et al.* 1996) and we therefore have an experience of being in the story-world, but still apart from it (McDonald 2014: 126). Particularly with regard to the feminist agency of Katniss, one wonders specifically how these varying questions might be addressed, as we examine the film more closely, focusing on her star persona and appeal to a 'young adult' hyper-mediated audience.

Star persona of Katniss: eco-feminist icon

Katniss's 'performance of non-performing situates her as authentic and true (not wilful or guileful), while at the same time positioning her as the film's hero'(Dubrofsky and Ryalls 2014: 1). Katniss's natural, unaltered white femininity is especially emphasied as producing 'instantiating notions of naturalised embodied feminine whiteness' (Dubrofsky and Ryalls 2014: 1). At the outset, Katniss tells Cinna (a stylist helping out at the games) that she doesn't know how to make people like her. Cinna responds, 'You made me like you'. Katniss retorts, 'I wasn't trying', thereby calling attention to the fact that her actions are unplanned. She behaves instinctively, authentically and without guile.[7]

Remarkably, of course, Katniss wins 'The Games' while at the same time eschewing aggressiveness, codified as a masculine trait, while alternatively showing a prized feminine quality, namely her maternal instincts and what can be characterised as a form of nurturing and embracing a quotient of environmental protection. Katniss's caring for others inspires her bravest and most emotional moments. She attends to her partner Peeta, when he is severely wounded, and unselfconsciously risks her life to retrieve medicine to save him. Most significantly she also inspires the Districts to rebel, protect the weak and fight the good fight (Dubrofsky and Ryalls 2014: 12). But in the end it could also be argued that the first instalment in this franchise at least concludes with an 'ideological reaffirmation of the status quo', as concession is made to the exigencies of the very mainstream adolescent heterosexual narrative, as opposed to the short-term re-alignment of power politics in the system.

By all accounts, the Districts are simply designed to be responsible for the extraction of raw materials and the manufacture of commodities, leaving the citizens of the Capitol to engage in various kinds of service industry, including food preparation, styling and entertainment, not to mention all forms of consumption. This maps across the closely demarked division between urban and rural, where we are invited to contrast the metropolis's almost entirely artificial world, with the coal mines and the pristine woodlands of District 12, where Katniss has honed her unique skills and ability to adapt to (wild) nature. As the daughter of a dead miner, who survives by hunting on the land, Katniss effectively represents and embodies her district's close connection to the environment. Conveyed to the Capitol by high-speed trains,

> it is as if the 19th century is brought face to face with a 21st-century media culture, a disjunction that is pointed up by the garish appearance of the Capitol's citizens, with their grotesque cosmetics, lurid hair dye,

and ornate clothes. But the urban modern versus rural archaic opposition makes for the appearance of anomaly.

(Dubrofsky and Ryalls 2014: 30)

Such a cautionary juxtaposition of urban/rural habitats certainly feeds into growing environmental warnings and ethical challenges for the future.

Katniss is a very proficient hunter – a skill usually reserved in stereotypical representations in films for alpha males. We discover how she could be described as an organic/natural hunter, by her going back into nature and embracing the forbidden forest, a sacred wild space which is normally reserved for the artificial games and which remains a site of spectators' pleasure where a constructed Darwinian 'survival of the fittest' contest is about to be set up. On an environmental and ethical level, the historical hunter-gatherer tradition and mode of engagement with nature has been transformed and abused, reimagined as a public performance and spectacle for the masses, such as reality television shows like *Treasure Island* (see Brereton 2015).

Before the games begin, in her synthetic but luxurious accommodation, she is treated to displays of food in great abundance – reminiscent of *Castaway* and its cautionary critique of food display. Such ostentatious display certainly draws attention to a lack of food resources in the regions and helps dramatise the inequity and injustices with regard to extreme poverty in the real world. Earlier, of course, we witnessed the severe shortage of food in the districts. Her room has a large television with many channels available, including almost still images of her beloved forest landscape displayed in the background. She apparently finds this relaxing and therapeutic, tapping into her nature-based and biophilic sense of connecting with and through nature. (Interestingly, within some more reflexive avant-garde movies like *Funny Games*, this trope of the inherent benefits of 'going back to nature' is very much reversed.[8])

Katniss: taking control and acquiring ethical supremacy

Katniss's major strength, as already stated, is that she can ecologically 'read the forest' like any expert (male) hunter and knows how to secure water and other nutrients to stay alive, as similarly illustrated in *All is Lost* discussed in Chapter 2. She also knows how to build a trap and secure nourishment, as when she hunts, cooks and eats a frog, as well as also knowing how to sleep safely high up in trees, strapped to the branches. In other words, she is especially adaptable in a variety of habitats; recalling Darwin's 'survival of the fittest' or, more fruitfully for this reading, Thoreau's environmental engagement with raw nature in the classic treatise *Waldon*. Therefore from the outset, she appears to have an optimum chance of survival in this otherwise forbidding habitat. Consequently, her persona is used to play out a conventional nature documentary tale, which usually featurs exotic animals and their struggle for survival.

Notwithstanding the suspect environmental ethics of burning forests simply for pleasure, raw nature remains digitally constructed as purely instrumental and not enjoying an innate organic life, much less an essence of its own. In the ensuing dramatic tension, Katniss gets badly injured. Eventually, like an injured animal, she pulls herself up a tree to safety from marauding predators – who in this case are humans. Her injury looks severe and the 'active cameras', as a medical lab, diagnose the extent of her injuries and melodramatically pronounce on this, serving to effectively increase the overall emotional tension. Unlike the Prime Directive of non-interference in science fiction classics like *Star Trek*, which warns against any direct interference from outside the confines of the time-space of the storyline, her survival is aided happily by an extraneous 'help/ gift'. This is somewhat reminiscent of film theorist David Bordwell's (1985) co-opting of Propp's *Morphology of Folk Tales* (1968) to explain core elements evident in all classic narratives, namely the need for some form of 'gift' that finds its way to her and facilitates a positive result. But in this case it is outside of the diegetic worldview of the forest as a real and authentic habitat. This potent magic medicine wafts its way in a strategically flown balloon. Like *Elysium* discussed later, such medicine/technology works as a 'magic bullet', as it heals her wounds almost instantaneously.

Quintessential female innocence and eco-martyring: Rue

Being hunted down – as in *The Lord of the Flies* – when some of the contestants band together, including it would seem her erstwhile boyfriend Peeta, Katniss remains in great peril. But high in the trees she remains safe for the moment. A very young black contestant named Rue performs a benevolent act of kindness in this 'dog eat dog' environment, by placing life-giving leaves around Katniss's skin to protect her from the potent stings of a wasp, after she loses consciousness.[9] Rue reminds Katniss of her sister Prim and serves as an important emotional thread in the film.

Helping to allude to a form of racism, the camera focuses on Katniss's Mocking Jay symbol, which has special significance in Rue's home District and is featured most explicitly later in the series of films. Rue unfortunately becomes trapped in a cage and is accidentally killed by an arrow aimed at Katniss. This builds up to the major melodramatic death sequence of the film. The music swells as Katniss closes the little girl's eyes and picks white flowers to create a rich garland around Rue's body and between her hands in repose. Having a deep respect for the dead and acknowledging the trauma of bereavement remains the mark of a 'civilised' and, ostensibly one could also infer, an environmentally ethical and caring society.

Looking directly at the camera – the nearest such a mainstream film gets to the reflexivity of the ending of *Funny Games* mentioned above – she turns and performs a 'three finger salute' to District 11 where the young Rue hails from. This emotive and iconic revolutionary sign initiates a riot in the murdered girl's home district – reminiscent, for instance, of the emotional playing of the French national anthem in *Casablanca*[10] – a narrative threat which is played out more extensively in subsequent films in the series. Natural justice cannot be ignored or suppressed, as oppressed groups become united when sparked by such incidents, recalling Eisenstein's Russian revolutionary classic *Strike,* for example. Katniss's eulogy and homage at Rue's demise become a touchstone of revolutionary fervour, which in turn serves to affirm the potency of Katniss as a progressive heroic female figure.

The instinctive power of individual agency takes hold as the embodiment of 'free will', recalling the pervasive dilemma of the *Romeo and Juliet* myth.[11] A romantic preoccupation around how we all deserve to have a 'choice' to die and become martyrs for the 'right' reasons is emphasised, as both final contestants consider taking lethal poison, rather than being forced to kill each other. In a world where domination is total, where power has unquestioned command over life and death, then the last recourse for the oppressed is to die on their own terms and use their deaths as symbolic as well as literal weapons. Thus it is Katniss and Peeta's treat of suicide which checkmates the Capital's totalitarian power nexus.[12] But such a selfless heroic and romantic ending cannot be tolerated for the success of the 74th Hunger Games and consequently both contestants are allowed to survive. The narrative provides a full-blown heroine for new generations of audiences who can appreciate the challenge of following a very difficult path. This feeds into a range of environmental ethical precepts including 'doing the right thing' and following a clear value system.

Consequently, realising her potency in the Districts, the establishment handlers and PR specialists suggest to the President that Katniss must be allowed to survive, otherwise there is a danger that the games will create a martyr figure for the oppressed majority. This long-established dilemma around creating revolutionary heroes is verbally teased out, as the President appears to graciously tend his garden – as in *The Constant Gardener* – but he is by no accounts a nurturing agent, much less a steward of the land. Rather the President uses nature, including its human inhabitants, in an instrumental manner, simply to extract the resources he wants. Nonetheless, concessions are made and the regulations are changed so that there now can be two victors from the same district instead of one.

Poignantly, as suggested earlier, the only alternative to the servitude Katniss can imagine at the start of the story is escape into the woods – a form of eco-escape and return to the organic and the local, to a space outside the reach of Empire (Berardi 2009: 30). Finally she has played the game on their terms and has nevertheless been able to keep her dreams and her core ethical values intact. What greater dream can new generations of fans and audiences hope to embrace? This surely encapsulates also a positive ethical role model for developing various forms of environmental praxis. Meanwhile, another less well-known contemporary science fiction fantasy *Elysium* counterpoints such liminal optimism with the agency of a very cynical and otherwise mature female protagonist called Delacourt.

Elysium: science fiction from an eco-feminist perspective

This brief reading will concentrate on the character of Delacour (played by Jodie Foster) who, very much against type and totally different from Katniss in *The Hunger Games,* plays the ball-breaking military leader who breaks every ethical code to get her way and secure her egotistical military power.

American filmmakers have consistently explored 'the theme of wayward/ vengeful nature; latterly Hollywood has outdone itself in bringing natural cataclysm to the big screen.' These films

> appeal to our worst fears about the unpredictability of natural phenomena, the consequences of capitalist greed, and the ramifications of our striving for control over every aspect of nature, from space to the human genome. Specifically they reflect the growing unease plaguing the culture: that we are heading towards the doom of civilisation, and the Earth, if we continue on our current exploitative path.
>
> (Belmont 2007: 349)

Even the period before the financial crisis during the 1990s, as evoked in *12 Monkeys*, presents a tipping point around environmental crisis; environmental mourning that haunts such films as it is woven across several layers. Like *12 Monkeys* or *The Matrix, Elysium* also takes place in a claustrophobic future world, and its characters too are committed to recovering a time when human bodies and ecosystems still existed 'naturally'. To its great credit, *12 Monkeys,* and to a lesser extent *Elysium,* avoids the usual thrills and cheap solutions in its critical examination of (postmodern) environmentalism. It also refuses to dismiss mourning over lost environmental standards, the importance of memory, the depth of feeling that people continue to have even in a besieged and diminished nature, and the integrity and power of the biotic world, as so much postmodern rhetoric often appears to ignore.

Such contextualisation of classic eco-films is fundamental to any discussion of *Elysium*, where the earth is also literally sick: 'its atmosphere is thick, clotted and infectious'. Mars colonisation is

> thus intended at the beginning of Earth's accommodationist-style safety valve: a dumping place for surplus population, a vast new reserve for externalising nature to exploit and strip off valuable resources, and an ideological mouse-hole, a place desperate earth populations can derive hope from and think of escaping to [such spaces. The] gerontological treatments increase those conflicts exponentially. Earth lacks the social system to absorb this new technology, and its arrival serves only to cruelly widen the gap between the elites who can afford the treatments and the vastly more numerous poor who cannot.
>
> (Buell 2004: 276)

This disjunction of resources and ethical values are most clearly present in the gendered lens of the Jodie Foster character portrayed in *Elysium*.

Apocalypse, writes Lawrence Buell (1995: 285), is the single most powerful master metaphor that the contemporary environmental imagination has at its disposal. In post-apocalyptic fiction, the eco-catastrophe of tomorrow is graphically invoked to reflect upon the worsening crisis of today. Climate change, in particular, is envisioned not as a general process of environmental decay and social degeneration, but as an immediate and devastating shattering of cultural norms (Buell 1995: 18).

In most conventional Hollywood cinema, male protagonists battle towards victory over an antagonistic, vindictive nature that threatens to annihilate 'the American way of life'. Heroines, who are initially characterised as 'modern women' – capable, intelligent, and employed – are quickly returned to the domestic sphere and to helpless dependence on masculine physical prowess. The technological know-how of females most aptly emphasises the trouble with nature as being tied to the dissolution of traditional gender roles – as they foster a display of fear while driving to conquer nature. They also 'feed cultural anxiety about women's empowerment and suggest that meekness and passivity are required of women if order is to be restored to a chaotic, unstable world' (Belmont 2007: 350).

As Pepper (1996) points out, at the beginning of the 1970s there was a growing concern about the evident post-war deterioration of the environment which was accompanied by a period of sustained economic expansion. Worried about ecological damage caused by increased consumption, rapidly expanding populations and with use of huge amounts of defoliants by America in the Vietnam War, a heightened awareness of environmental problems emerged (Delveaux 2001: 3). Such tropes continue to play out in significant ways across numerous contemporary science-fiction films like *Elysium*, where it is ideologically easier to critique various forms of capitalism and normative scientific practices set in the future. They can be reappropriated and recontextualised through the lens of an eco-feminist discourse.

The film brings into focus a very common theme around how the wealthy escape from the horribly decayed nature and environment of earth, while the poor are trapped in Third-World ghettos in the near future of 2154. In this stark dystopian world, zero tolerance is afforded by computerised guards who keep the general populace in strict servitude – like the Districts discussed earlier in *The Hunger Games*. Our hero Max (Matt Damon) is ordered to report to a police office following a random check by cyborg officials who leave no margin for any form of discussion or 'banter' which could in turn be construed as disobedience. At the hospital he happens to meet his childhood sweetheart (Alice Braga) who of course has become a conventional nurturing nurse – echoing similar figures across Hollywood films. Female agency in this case is set up as an antidote to the very rigid and authoritarian form of communication evident elsewhere.

The director of *Elysium*, Niall Blomkamp, is pointed out in the bonus features of the DVD as wanting a garish parody of a futuristic real-like world – like Bel

Air in LA, recalling a parody of what space could or would look like. He used the genius of Syd Mead to design the inverse art structures. Blomkamp also speaks of how NASA in the 1970s chose Stanford University for their design of space and subsequently won the prize for best off-space design. The director most specifically wanted to visualise actual mansions in space, as a metaphor for total excess and inexcusable waste. The resultant mix of utopia and dystopia and a self-centred biosphere, by all accounts, remains totally over-the-top. But this is clearly posited within a binary ethical system embodied by the dystopic planet earth in comparison with a pristine terraformed constructed space habitat called Elysium.[13]

The artificial and engineering feat of creating an alternative to the dystopic habitat of earth has long been a dream of science fiction fantasy. As Patrick Murphy affirms in a recent paper, the concept of 'terraforming', the

> engineered transformation of alien planets into habitats sustainable for human settlement has taken on new and concrete meaning in science fiction and contemporary culture, as climate change has indicated that human beings are currently transforming this planet but without a clear plan for sustainable inhabitability.
>
> (Murphy 2009: 54)[14]

Environmental problems have a disproportionate effect on the poor and especially on people from developing countries, and this is clearly evident and alluded to by many science-fiction films such as *Elysium*. The colonial and resource exploitation discourses embodied by Carlyle, the CEO of the huge manufacturing company, is most clearly signalled when, in reporting to the rich bureaucrats and managers up in the terra-formed planet of Elysium, he affirms that he is doing everything possible to make the company profitable with little or no concern for any form of environmental sustainability. 'Do you think I like breathing in this air', he remarks, referring to the impurities brought about by excessive industrial and manipulation of precious natural resources on earth, which in turn serves as a defence against any possible criticism of his management of the company.[15]

There are riots outside in the street and a young girl has an ID burned into her hand so she can get a chance of accessing the best private health care system, which of course happens to be off-planet. The precious digital code is accepted by the shuttle to get her to the 'good life' – a scenario reminiscent of illicit migrant boats from Africa and elsewhere and very much echoed in Blomkamp's earlier science-fiction film *District 9*.

Defence secretary Delacourt (Jodie Foster playing very much against type) is an evil archetype who apparently rejects her erstwhile feminine side and wants total control over the militarisation of the airways between planet earth and Elysium. Observing three illegal airships heading towards Elysium and without showing any ethical scruples, she gives the order to fire at will, not caring about any so-called collateral damage.[16] This shoot-to-kill order is carried out by a highly trained 'implanted' solider called Agent Kruger, based back on earth and somewhat reminiscent of the 2014 real-life shooting down of a passenger aeroplane over Russia. Nonetheless, one of these small planes succeeds in reaching its destination. Through the use of massive machine scanning equipment and the 'magic bullet' of bio-technology, together with other medical innovations, the sick girl gets her health restored almost miraculously, only to be deported immediately back down to earth. This recalls a broad range of what could loosely be construed as environmental and ethical First–Third world conundrums; especially moral panics and fears of migrants coming to the rich West 'in droves' that is also explored in *District 9*.[17]

Back in the factory where the hero Max works, with no health or safety procedures in place, he has to face the consequences of poor medical support. With almost no forms of precautionary principles being adhered to, he is told to enter a dangerous controlled area to sort out a faulty machine. Unfortunately, as a result, he ends up exposed to some form of lethal 'radiation'. On witnessing the result of this horrible accident, Carlyle glibly tells his underling managers to give Max medicine to keep him functioning effectively until he dies. Ethical concerns for human safety are totally disregarded, with workers treated as expendable pawns, like in *The Hunger Games,* and required simply to help maximise production and nothing else. No thought is given to the rights and sanctity of human welfare, much less towards maintaining any level of sustainable environmental ethical values.

Meanwhile the atypical female military controller from Elysium, in defence of her actions to initiate direct military intervention in the first place, calls upon a self-centred logic which does not initially at least pass muster with her bureaucratic over-management team. She expertly calls on the all-encompassing trope of family security and welfare to rhetorically justify her actions. Dramatically pleading in clearly rhetorical fashion, 'do you have children, then [if so] you will act like me'. She continues 'when *they* come for your children … it will not be [PC values] that will save you'. Such emotive and rhetorical appeals to a (Western) notion of protection and defence at all costs, while promoting patriarchal values and framed around family protection, can, in turn, be read as the ultimate, if somewhat perverse test of an ethics of care.

This very compromised logic and faulty ethical strategy is also echoed in an anti-fracking film *Promised Land,* where a female sales agent uses every form of emotional appeal to family values and the need for a good education, to gain support for fracking from the local landowners, recalling an ever-present political debate in the US concerning the escalating cost of a health insurance system being only designed for rich people, as ostensibly dramatised in *Elysium.* By any measure the system remains unethical and othered on every level imaginable. There is no sense of an equitable 'duty of care' regarding health and safety, much less a more basic utilitarian approach around maximising provision for health insurance to cover the greatest majority possible. In this obviously unjust system, a very un-nurturing female commander on Elysium regards (lower-caste) humans as all being expendable, together with workers who are simply treated as pawns in maximising production.

This evocation of a lack of consideration of any form of moral hazard and non-engagement with environmental risk is further developed when Carlyle, the CEO, is asked by the militarily greedy Delacourt to develop an 'over-ride' computer program to afford her total control of Elysium through a computer coup. Notions of accountability and ensuring hierarchies of command and authority to protect individual rights are set against the dangers of corrupting individualisation and pernicious forms of technological control. Consequently Delacourt is determined not to have to answer to process-driven officials, who wish to defend procedures and to maintain some form of ethical framework with robust systems of checks and balances.

As a result of the accident and having only a few days to live, in an attempt to save himself Max agrees to take on an impossible mission, before being physically transformed into a cyborg machine to help him face down their enemies. Max finds his way back into LA, which becomes a no-fly zone after his successful mission and proceeds to the hospital district to find his sweetheart, Frey. She is playing out her nurturing stereotype role by also supporting her very ill daughter, Matilda, who is in the final stages of leukaemia. Frey helps him to her own home to examine his wounds, and Matilda offers the stranger a 'protective story' to help support them all; while Max feels it will not end well for Mircat or Hippo, the magical story-world created by the child in an idealised utopian environment. This becomes the film's final ecological message, realising they can help each other through their difficulties. Max must learn to become a hero of his own life and embrace more communitarian and altruistic ethical values, which in turn are necessary to secure a more healthy and sustainable planet. Recalling various forms of Christian idealisation as the ultimate manifestation of ethical values, this is a trajectory which in turn feeds into many utopian blockbusters like *Terminator 2* (see Brereton 2005). In such narratives the redeemed character has to go beyond being self-consciously egotistical and simply focalising on his own survival or carrying out their mission without counting the cost of destroying human life. Such a hero has to attain a radical transformation in their value system by discovering the 'right thing to do' for the greater good of humanity.

The eureka solution to earth's problems, of course, is a reboot program that can override the whole system and make all humans become full citizens of Elysium. We can save everyone and thereby we can change the course of history. Imagine if this 'simple' but radical solution was expedited for all the environmental problems on earth and political displaced poor migrants across the world. But to activate this egalitarian and utilitarian ethical process, the selfish gene (as popularised by Dawkins) and the pervasive will to live at all cost must always be kept in check: 'I'm not fucking dying', retorts the erstwhile hero with a strong life instinct. The short 19-minute flight time to Elysium echoes both temporally and spatially this radical transformation in Max's ethical value system – reminiscent of the ethical learning process witnessed as the protagonists finally depart from *Jurassic Park* at the end of the first film of the series (see Brereton 2005).

As we expect from our altruistic Hollywood heroes, he has to both save the girl and the family, all the while 'doing the right thing' for *all* humanity, including his dystopian environmental habitat.[18] As Max faces his own demise with dignity and a transformative ethical mindset – echoing Katniss's earlier selflessly ethical decision to commit suicide rather than succumb to murder of her friend – he emotionally speaks on the phone to his sweetheart and nurturing nurse that 'you would not believe what I'm looking at right now'. He has been centrally involved in transforming a very corrupt system of totalitarian control. The renewed (sublime) visual landscape he is now looking at, signals a renewed and more sustained form of environmental agency, as dramatised by its radical transformation. Most pointedly and sentimentally, Max asks her to tell her daughter that he actually loved her naïve 'the child in all of us' stories.

In other words, one could read somewhat 'against the grain' that his nascent nurturing and newly activated 'feminine' side is being effectively dramatised and brought to the fore in the end. The sublime beauty of the rejuvenated planet, as both therapeutic and ethically benevolent, drives the effectiveness of the final resolution. In the end, doing the 'right thing' remains a pervasive environmental trope, I suggest, within many Hollywood narratives, as also explicitly evident in the conclusion of *The Constant Gardener* extensively discussed in Chapter 6.

Reapplying the nature of birth/death as part of an ever-present 'circle of life', while also recalling Christian and other universal myths around rebirth, and also death, our hero offers up his life so that his community survives and the young girl, as foreshadowed earlier, is also medically rejuvenated. Re-atomised and cured – as if further technological proof was needed – in less than a minute, the girl is awarded the all clear from her terminal illness. Her disease has simply vanished, which by any measure remains the ultimate miracle of technology.[19] The erstwhile 'magic bullet' of benign science fiction medicine again comes to the fore. Rather than simply protecting scarce resources and justifying or at worst accepting an unequal and unjust system, which is the norm in Western democracies and political debate at present, the erstwhile environmental and ethical 'logical' solution is carried out. The now-benevolent procedural system of health welfare is re-programmed and kicks into play; once there is a more inclusive and less racist/class-driven definition of 'citizen', all can be cured. The recognition of new citizens in need of medical attention simply results in numerous shuttles being despatched to earth to deal with the 'humanitarian crisis'. Simply and efficiently curing all citizens becomes the order of the day and the *modus operandi* for government apparatchiks. Rather than having to politically decide on the allocation of scarce resources, such an idealised world highlights how all medical and, by extension, environmental problems can be solved relatively easily by simply redefining citizenship. As Max enunciates with his last words, never forget where you come from. This is certainly a clear endorsement of universal, albeit utopian, ethical norms and focusing on the need to be anchored in one's own particular place, which in turn treats all people equally, unlike what was patently an unequal and ethically and environmentally unjust system.

To conclude this chapter we will stay in space and examine a reading of *Gravity* and the prototypical eco-feminist agency of the main character Ryan Stone, played by Sandra Bullock.

Eco-feminism most notably calls attention to a broader, yet less abstract, view of distributive justice that is also evident in other literatures. Given the uneven impact of environmental disasters on poorer communities and on developing countries, redistribution is considered as a core attribute and extension of distributive justice. One could go so far as to argue most convincingly that such a powerful justice argument ought to inform all discussion of progressive environmental ethics, whether in science fiction fantasies or more literally down-to-earth narratives.

Gravity: environmental waste in the sky

Geographers are concerned with perception and response to natural hazards and 'consider popular culture, as expressed in novels and movies, as a potentially significant source of information about disaster' (UCL Department of Geography 2015). *Gravity* has become the largest-grossing science fiction film in the last few years. For the purposes of this study we will begin by examining how it focuses on representations of environmental 'waste' in space. Key questions environmental scholars might pose with regard to the potency of such films include: What image of the environment/nature do people 'obtain' from films? What effect do the images have on the people who consume films, and on society more generally? These open-ended questions are especially interesting for science fiction fantasies like those explored in this chapter. Extensive audience research is however needed to test and evaluate such pertinent questions. Space travel in particular has become a key focus around environmentalism, in setting up the beauty of our pristine planet, as it is viewed from the vantage point of outer space. 'I remember so vividly', said the astronaut Michael Collins,

> what I saw when I looked back on my fragile home – a glistening, inviting beacon, delicate blue and white, a tiny outpost suspended in the black infinity. Earth is to be treasured and nurtured, something precious that must endure.
>
> (Collins 1980: 6)

Earth is certainly a fragile planet, a jewel set in mystery. 'We humans too belong to the planet; it is our home, as much as for all the others'. By all accounts environmental ethics demands the elevation of a number of core concerns around the fragile and precarious nature of planet earth, especially with regards to the pressing concerns around climate change. 'We are searching for an ethics adequate to respect life on this Earth, an Earth ethics. That is the future of environmental ethics' (Rolston in Keller 2010: 572).

Meanwhile, the two behemoths of theoretical physics are Einstein's theory of general relativity and quantum field theory. Both theories are implied and investigated in numerous science fiction fantasies including this one. General relativity describes gravity and the geometry and development of the universe on enormous scales (Zoller Seitz 2013). 'The panorama of astronauts tumbling against starfields and floating through space stations are both informative and lovely', as indicated by the pervasive success of science fiction fantasies in contemporary films, especially since the blockbuster phenomenon that was *Star Wars* in the 1970s. At times, for instance, *Gravity* plays like a high-tension version of 'shipwreck' movies like *All is Lost*, or a wilderness survival story that just happens to take place among the stars. It recalls, for instance, *Castaway*, but here set in stunning exterior views of the big blue planet earth and a particular preoccupation with gravity playing out alongside disaster and environmental (risk) management.

On examining the film, I'm particularly taken with the DVD bonus feature focusing on 'waste in space' as a primary environmental concern. The documentary *Collision Point: The Race to Clear up Space*, begins 'for billions of years the heavens all around the earth were clear and unaffected by mankind. Then in 1957 Sputnik went into space – since then there have been over 4,500 space missions – with millions of pieces of debris. Life on earth grows more dependent on space, [recalling the] danger of having no GPS system, no TV'.

Consequently space can and should be treated as a 'global commons', a natural resource of space. This realisation began with the misconception that space was so vast and it was not possible for anything to collide. But scientist Don Kessler called this assertion into question. (See the so-called Kessler Syndrome which seeks to explain how when two particles collide, so many fragments can end up causing a chain reaction. Some estimate that there is more than 500,000 pieces of space junk currently being tracked around our solar system.) This syndrome has led to 'big sky theory' – drawing an analogy with climate change – which recognises that such growing levels of space debris can exacerbate a catastrophic problem. Dumping all our satellites, simply by turning machines off as they float in space, is not by any measure an environmentally sustainable solution. This in turn causes major environmental risks and may lead to a 'tipping point' with orbital debris getting unpredictable as they career off-course.

The bonus feature documentary particularly 'blames' the Chinese and Russians who are involved in the blowing up of satellites without 'telling the world' and by not following 'agreed protocols' following the 1967 Outer Space Treaty. By all accounts several nations across the planet do not regard outer space as an ethical 'global commons', which in turn needs to be protected and managed. Making the 'polluter pays' a principle of international law reinforces an ethical logic that affirms that the corporation or nation-state which launches the satellite or the space programme is in turn liable for the cost of its destruction. Apparently, it is really problematic if another country's technology 'accidently' hits any piece of equipment in space, as it raises serious concerns regarding who is culpable. All of these ethical dilemmas result in another frontier, this time in outer space to contest, rather than accepting it as a protective open commons, which we might all actively engage with.

Such dangerous and obsolete debris, we are told, travels at over 17,000 mph, which is much faster than a bullet, as they orbit around the earth. Note, for instance, *Men in Black* and other science fiction comedies have been parodying the dangers of such 'waste' for decades, but it was not till the huge success of this 'serious' big-budget blockbuster that the issue has been brought into the mainstream and treated appropriately, being pushed firmly into public consciousness.

Yet as a science fiction fantasy, *Gravity* remains fairly commonplace despite its gadgetry, both in front of and behind the camera. How the Sandra Bullock lead character displays a dedicated and somewhat overwhelmed scientist assigned to fix the Hubble telescope is certainly interesting in itself from a feminist point of view. While she remains somewhat conventional, nevertheless her female persona promotes a rare female characterisation to follow in such a male-dominated action genre.

Such a *modus operandi* and rationale for the film remains somewhat ironical, featuring scientists who perceive the 'solution' to earth's problems as continuing space travel and carrying out even more experiments up in space. Especially as such research and experimentation has caused the problem in the first place. It would appear in such conventionally constructed 'male addressed' genres and science fiction in general, it is normative for male protagonists to simply strive to become a 'master of the universe'. This conventional unidirectional focus is turned on its head, by having the main protagonist a still-grieving mother and by de-centring her persona even further, as reflected in a paratextual short feature that was also designed to be viewed alongside the film. In any case the conventional trajectory of the main feature is somewhat recontextualised by a mini-feature titled *Aningaaq*.

Aningaaq is a short film that the director made as a companion piece to the fictional feature and is designed to be shown before the main feature. It focuses on an Eskimo family of that name living in Greenland. The director, as we are informed on the bonus feature, got the idea from a trip there to source locations on an earlier project and happened upon this fisherman, echoing the super-realism and romantic aesthetic of Robert Flaherty's environmental classic documentary *Nanook of the North*. The short film shows the Eskimo going about his business and answering a call from space on his bulky walkie-talkie, situated in a very desolate snow-filled region of the planet. The scenario of the mini-narrative correlates with a 'lost in translation' situation. We discover that the voice on the other side is our 'heroine' from *Gravity,* shouting 'mayday', as she faces mortal danger in the spaceship miles above in the sky. In many ways this recalls the pervasive trope of deep ecology and dramatises how 'everything is connected', but the fisherman does not understand the protocol, much less the language and thinks the caller's name on the phone is 'mayday'. In patriarchal gendered terms, a woman in distress deep in space creates an even more evocative response than more conventional male heroic types.

Meanwhile the diegetic sounds of dogs barking give solace as the phone-callers simulate the sounds of dogs barking, which is echoed out across space. This cathartic oral mimicry is followed by the sound of a child crying, recalling the trauma of bereavement for our distraught heroine. Nonetheless, this certainly is also human comfort for a mother who has tragically lost her child at the age of four in an unfortunate accident and who now believes is about to lose her own life alone in space. The sounds of the child's voice help to soothe her spirit as she worries that there is nobody out there to 'pray for her', while he mutters incoherently in an alien language that one of his dogs is sick and there is nothing he can do for the poor animal. Unseen by the audience, he proceeds to mercy kill his beloved sick animal.

Such a strange counterpoint and smart paratextual intervention between the feature film and this mini-documentary certainly adds to the total effect, raising numerous environmental and ethical questions around responsibility and empathy between humans, who are so far apart in space. Most specifically, the story speaks to the ethics of mercy-killing animals, alongside responsibility around a 'duty of care' for our fellow creatures. While broadly existential in nature, the need to communicate across space and time calls to mind so many environmental and ethical conundrums.

In particular, the final 'rebirth metaphor' in *Gravity* is especially strong in Alfonso Cuarón's film. The director spoke of how the major point of the film is to suggest a 'form of rebirth'. Facing terminal adversity and at the other extreme, the possibility of rebirth at the same time, helps to promote a new and greater knowledge of ourselves. We have a prototypical mother figure who is drifting metaphorically and literally towards the void. 'A victim of their own inertia. Getting farther and farther away from Earth where life and human connections are. And probably she was like that when she was on planet Earth, before leaving for her mission. It's a character who lives in her own bubble' (Woerner 2013).[20] Essentially she has to shed that skin to start reconnecting with the real world again. 'This is a character who we stick in the ground, again, and learns how to walk' (Woerner 2013).

The director strongly affirms how various forms of rebirth are part of the ontological journey for everybody, not only every human on earth, but it's also the journey of great heroic (fictional) characters. The film firmly focuses on a character who has to reconnect to her inner nurturing side and use this female essence to help her cope with despair and fears of total annihilation. After the horror of the void, there is redemption and rebirth and a particular form of human expression that can revision planet earth in a new more hopeful way.

'So obviously the red rocks and mud that [Sandra] pulls herself up onto [after she lands] was an intentional nod to the rebirth idea'? The director agrees. 'She's in these murky waters almost like an amniotic fluid or a primordial soup in which you see amphibians swimming. She crawls out of the water, not unlike early creatures in evolution. And then she goes on all fours. And after going on all fours, she's a bit curved until she is completely erect. It was the evolution of life in one, quick shot.' Such a primal scene of going back to nature from the excesses of hi-tech space travel, emphasises the strong desire to keep our transient and fragile environment and habitat in check. It again evokes a cautionary tale around environmental sustainability, while reimagining new forms of 'survival'. This visualisation of space also most convincingly calls to mind a major but seldom thought of environmental risk of 'excessive planetary waste' floating around the earth, which initiated the mission in the first place, as they attempt to 'clean up the mess'.[21]

This storyline, more so than others addressed in this chapter, could be compared favourably with Jodie Foster's space travel and specific religious experience in *Contact* (discussed in Brereton 2005) which also displayed some transcendent results, with a female protagonist also in the driving seat. If Ryan's soul is, in fact, detaching and drifting early in the third act, it certainly spends the rest of the movie acting out the way things should have gone.

Mythical dreams of female agency and re-birth remain evocative and help to engender a feel-good sense of environmental and ethical holism. As in the three films discussed in this chapter, female protagonists help to focus on a provocative form of ecological and ethical agency. From the positive representations of Katniss in *The Hunger Games*, to the anti-heroic antics of Delacourt in *Elysium*, and finally the more ethereal maternal quality of Ryan in *Gravity*, all three speak in varying ways to a broad range of environmental and ethical problems in outer space that have resonance for contemporary Western society in particular.

Notes

1 Unfortunately *The Hunger Games* franchise did not continue with the promise the main character Katniss set up in this first instalment.

2 Nonetheless, in spite of this explicit connection set out between women and nature, there remains complex differences and divisions across the field, ranging from liberal feminism, Marxist feminism, radical feminism and socialist feminism, among various other permutations. Most of these avenues tend to start with the proposition that environmental problems are rooted in the rise of capitalist patriarchy and the ideology that the earth and nature can be exploited for human progress through technology (in Keller 2010: 294). This patriarchal position is frequently underpinned by the mechanistic view of nature for instance, developed by seventeenth-century natural philosophers and based on a Western mathematical tradition going back to Plato, which still remains dominant in science today. This view assumes that nature can be divided into parts and rearranged according to a set of rules, based on logical and mathematical operations.

3 New branches of feminist theory – including 'material feminism' (Alaimo and Hekman 2008), alongside 'eco-ontological feminism' (Blair 2008), 'eco-ontological

social/ist feminist thought' (Bauman 2007) – offer a range of strategies for building this approach, based on the key contributions of eco-feminist and environmental justice perspectives. These include the centrality of an interdependent self-identity and the value of embodied knowledge, present in issues of race, class, gender, age and sexuality, alongside privileging environmental health in particular. At the same time feminists must always remain cognisant of the dangers of 'essentialism' that pervade the literature and always speak for a 'feminist politics of the body', founded 'in an affirmation of our dependence on the Earth' (Mann 2006: 129).

4 Warren, on the other hand, is even more provocative and contentious in suggesting that 'viewing nature as morally considerable is like loving one's child. It expresses a groundless attitude … a willingness on our part to see nonhuman animals and nature as subjects, as active participants in our worlds, as not mere things (mere resources, properties, or commodities), as deserving of our care and attention. I suspect that the moral considerability of nature can be explained but not ultimately proven. It is itself groundless' (Warren, *Ecofeminist Philosophy* 1235–38 Kindle edition).

5 *Armageddon* for instance uses (metaphorical) sexual aggression against nature: because the asteroid is a malevolent female entity that challenges humankind, she is 'asking for it' (Belmont 2007: 360).

6 While eco-feminists like Gaard have long been 'sceptical of nature in that ideological sense of natural order, the innovation of queer ecology for instance serves to draw upon scientific evidence to queer nature in the ordering, lay sense. It is a complex movement; subverting the ideological fixation of a hetero-normative natural order, queer ecologists deploy examples from the (queer) natural order, which are then read back into a transformed natural order as always already queer' (see Garrard 2010).

7 'An authentic self of course is one that one does not intentionally perform, or performs without premeditation' (Dubrofsky and Ryalls 2014: 5). On the other hand, unlike natural environments, the rise of online social networks is said to promote all kinds of (inauthentic) performance and the pressure is on to make numerous digital friends.

8 The very evocative Michael Haneke film *Funny Games* serves as a contemporary reprieve of the psychotic horror evident, for instance, in Kubrick's classic *Clockwork Orange*, featuring an apparently wealthy upper-middle-class nuclear family, 'escaping' to the countryside and seeking to enjoy their summer lakehouse residence. The horror ahead is effectively foreshadowed by the sudden transition from relaxing (feminine) classical music on the car radio, which is very much enjoyed by its occupants as they drive into the countryside, to a very sharp transition to a discordant non-diegetic post-punk (male) soundtrack, played as the opening credits roll. The family unfortunately do not pick up the early signals of dissonance, when they call on a neighbour to ask for help to launch their boat onto the lake. Soon after arriving at their holiday home, a 'strange young man' wearing white gloves and sporting all white clothes – a possible homage to Kubrick's masterpiece – enters the house and requests some eggs as part of a neighbourly encounter, recalling a common practice in a tightknit (rural) community. Of course the woman of the house accedes to this request, but when the intruder apparently accidently drops them on the ground and insists on getting more, her suspicions are aroused. Soon his partner in crime arrives and they proceed to intimidate the family. The family's only apparent 'crime' is being rich and desiring the 'good life', away from it all. Essentially they could be said to espouse middle-class environmental ethical credentials.

As a very smart/postmodern tale, the lead villain at several times 'talks directly to the camera' and hence at the audience – a trope which is considered too radical and offputting for more mainstream films, like *The Hunger Games* or *Avatar,* which are the focus of this volume. At one stage he even insists on 'replaying the film' to create a different result, rather than have his partner shot by the family. Such a radical (almost Brechtian) technique displays a form of digital reworking of the rules and conventional logics of cinema, which is rarely evident within analogue or more classic narrative story telling. The denouement is horrific to say the least with all the family dispatched, as the nurturing mother is tied up on a boat, surrounded by beautiful scenery, only to be discarded into the lake with no element of ceremony, while probably avoiding another grossly unethical display of psychic violence. As the pair repeat their 'funny game' with another rich family also situated on the lakeside, again looking directly at the camera with his 'knowing smirk', the audience is left with so many questions to contemplate. Such a reflexive and provocative style and filmic technique is unfortunately not replicated in most mainstream Hollywood narratives including *The Hunger Games*, which always maintain the illusion of a hermetically sealed, if nonetheless, othered environment.

9   We are extra-diegetically informed, as the doubly-coded televisual audience members, that these wasps are in fact 'Tracker Jackers' – genetically engineered wasps, calling to mind various ethical debates around GMOs. The wasps have a powerful hallucinatory effect when they sting and can potentially kill humans.

10   Or more flippantly the closed fist salute of the wolf in *Fantastic Mr Fox* explored later in this volume.

11   The tactics of those with little power are perforce opportunistic, as Michel de Certeau argues, and must be developed 'on the wing' (1984: xix), because they operate within the wider cultural and social environment which 'others' them. Or as Susan Sontag notes, compassion is 'unstable' and 'needs to be translated into action'. Showing 'something at its worst' can often instil the opposite result as explored in *The Road* and other dystopic narratives discussed in this volume, while the 'call to justice' symbolism explored in *The Hunger Games* serves as productively 'didactic' and certainly invites an 'active response' (see Sontag 2003: 81).

12   'Suicide is the decisive political act of our times' claims Franco Berardi (2009: 55).

13   Essentially, the director wanted to continue working on his maverick status, from work carried out on *District 9,* but this time with big budgets and big stars. Most notably, it's the only film where star persona, Jodie Foster, is killed onscreen while playing up and reengineering her gendered anti-heroic status and anti-nurturing ethos.

14   This concept was first coined in the 1930s as part of space exploration literature, and has always meant 'engineered climate changes on other planets in order to make them more like Earth' (Murphy 2009: 55). Murphy questions however if the concept allows for a rethinking of the term. 'Does it mean making other planets more like Earth, or does it mean making over any planet into some imaginary human home, such that Earth itself is undergoing a largely unplanned global engineering project that ought to be labelled terraforming with all of the ethical questions that surround planetary interventions?' (Murphy 2009: 56).

15   On a recent 2014 academic trip to Beijing, I can certainly vouch for the dangers of very poor air quality, while witnessing first hand so many inhabitants walking around with facemasks to protect themselves from extremely polluted air.

16   This is reminiscent of the opening sequence from a later series of the HBO television series *Homeland*, when the chief protagonist Carrie acquires the nickname 'Drone Queen' for her ability to simply carry out orders in shooting down 'enemy' targets with no apparent scruples.

17   This narrative certainly drives such rhetoric and fears around 'the other' and not having enough medicine in quantities to satisfy all human needs. Being somewhat preachy and didactic, these (contemporary) fears and risks in turn drive huge profit margins for private medical care insurance plans particularly in the USA, and at the same time correspond to right-wing political policy around ring-fencing private Medicare only for those who can afford it.

18   A lot to put on the back of individual heroes, nonetheless maybe not surprisingly we seldom if ever perceive a volte-face in systemic change and transformation at

least in such Hollywood fare, without at least first securing a major about-turn by a universally identifiable heroic figure.

19 See also a recent science fiction feature *Transcendence* (2014) that displays a very explicit allegory and cautionary tale around the dangers of developing artificial intelligence to its ultimate degree, which also helps to ensure the radical evolution of nanotechnology and bioscience – but at what cost to human nature.

20 The space suit becomes an objective correlative for feelings about bubbles which are so expansive they take in a whole world. 'I have a bad feeling about this mission', George Clooney says. We all have those feelings at times. Or as Stephanie Wakefield says in an essay on this film: 'the infrastructures that were supposed to have mastered and perfected the world not only cannot, but moreover it is increasingly from within these networked infrastructures themselves that disaster emerges' (in McKenzie Wark 2014: 4).

21 Did *Gravity* really end as it seemed? An alternative theory suggests she did not arrive back on earth – or was it all a dream. There's just enough ambiguity to suggest that Ryan perished somewhere along the way, most likely in the airlock of the Russian Soyuz capsule, moments after she shut down the oxygen supply to hasten what seemed at the time, like her inevitable demise.

Bibliography

Alaimo, Stacy and Hekman, Susan (2008) *Material Feminisms*. Bloomington, IN: Indiana University Press.

Baudrillard, Jean (1981) 'Simulacra and Simulations', in *Selected Writings* ed. Mark Poster. Redwood, CA: Stamford University Press

Bauman, Whitley (2007) 'The Eco-Ontology of Social/ist Feminist Thought'. *Environmental Ethics* 29(3): 279–298.

Belmont, Cynthia (2007) 'Eco-feminism and the Natural Disaster Heroine'. *Women's Studies: An Interdisciplinary Journal* 36(5): 349–372.

Beradi, Franco (2009) *Precarious Rhapsody Semiocapitalism and the Pathologies of the Post-Alpha Generation*. London: Minor Compositions.

Blair, Jennifer (2008) 'Media on Ice'. *Feminist Media Studies* 8(2): 197–223.

Bordwell, David (1985) *Narration in the Fiction Film*. Madison, WI: University of Wisconsin.

Brereton, Pat (2005) *Hollywood Utopia: Ecology in Contemporary American Cinema*. Bristol: Intellect Press.

Brereton, Pat (2011) 'An Ecological Approach to the Cinema of Peter Weir'. *Quarterly Review of Film and Video* 28(2): 120–131.

Brereton, Pat (2015) 'Treasure Island and Reality TV', in Le Juez, B. and Springer, O. (2015) *Shipwrecks and Islands: Motifs in Literature and the Arts*. Amsterdam: Rodophi.

Buell, F. (1995) 'A Short History of Environmental Apocalypse', in S. Skrimshire (ed) *Future Ethics: Climate Change and Apocalyptic Imagination*. London: Continuum.

Buell, Lawrence (2004) *From Apocalypse to Way of Life: Environmental Crisis in the American Century*. London: Routledge.

Collins, Michael (1980) 'Foreword', in Roy A. Gallant, *Our Universe*. Washington, DC: National Geographic Society.

Cressey, Paul (1938) 'The Motion Picture: Experience as Modified and Personality? *American Sociological Review* 3: 515–525.

De Certeau, Michel (1984) *The Practice of Everyday Life*, trans. Steven Rendall. Berkeley, CA: University of California Press.

Delveaux, Martin (2001) 'Transcending Eco-feminism: Alice Walker, Spiritual Ecowomanism and Environmental Ethics'. MA Criticism and Theory, University of Exeter, UK.

Dubrofsky, Rachel and Ryalls, Emily (2014) '*The Hunger Games*: Performing Non-Performing to Authenticate Femininity and Whiteness'. *Critical Studies in Media Communication* 31(5): 395–409.

Du Coudray, Chantal Bourgault (2003) 'The Cycle of the Werewolf: Romantic Ecologies of Selfhood in Popular Fantasy'. *Australian Feminist Studies* 18(40): 57–72.

Fisher, Mark (2012) 'Precarious Dystopias: *The Hunger Games, In Time* and *Never Let Me Go*'. *Film Quarterly* 65(4): 27–33.

Gaard, Greta (1993) *Ecofeminism: Women, Animals, Nature*. Philadelphia, PA: Temple University Press.

Garrard, G. (2010) 'How Queer is Green'. *Configurations* 18(1–2): 73–93.

Garrard, G. (2012) *Ecocriticism*. London: Routledge.

Gomes, M., Kanner, A. and Roszak, T. (1995). *Ecopsychology, Restoring the Mind, Healing the Mind*. San Fransisco, CA: Sierra Club Books.

Heller, Chaia (1993) 'For the Love of Nature: Ecology and the Cult of the Romantic', in Greta Gaard (ed) *Ecofeminism: Women, Animals, Nature*. Philadelphia, PA: Temple University Press.

Keller, David (ed) (2010) *Environmental Ethics*. Oxford: Wiley Blackwell.

Magliano, J.P., Taylor, H.A. and Kim, H.J. (2005) 'When Goals Collide: Monitoring the Goals of Multiple Characters'. *Memory and Cognition* 33(8): 1357–1367.

Mann, Bonnie (2006) *Woman's Liberation and the Sublime: Feminism, Postmodernism, Environment*. Oxford: Oxford University Press.

Mar, R.A., Oatley, K. and Patterson, D.B. (2009) 'Exploring the Links Between Reading Fish and Empathy: Ruling Out Individual Differences and Examining Outcomes'. *Communications*, 34: 407–428.

McDonald, Daniel (2014) 'Narrative Research in Communications: Key Principles and Issues', *Review of Communications Research* 2(1): 115–132.

McKenzie, Wark (2014) 'Anthropo{mise-en-s}cene'. *PS Public Seminar Commons*, 10 December http://www.publicseminar.org/2014/12/anthropomise-en-scene/#. VXP7dWRViko

Merchant, Carolyn (2008) 'Secrets of Nature: The Baconian Debates Revisited'. *Journal of the History of Ideas* 69(1): 147–162.

Muller, Vivienne (2012) 'Virtually Real: Suzanne Collins's *The Hunger Games* Trilogy'. *International Journal of Children's Literature* 5(1): 51–63.

Murphy, Patrick D. (2009) 'Engineering Planets, Engineering Ourselves: The Ethics of Terraforming and Areoforming in an Age of Climate Change'. http://citeseerx.ist.psu.edu/viewdoc/download?doi=10.1.1.467.9554&rep=rep1&type=pdf

Pepper, D. (1996) *Modern Environmentalism: An Introduction*. London: Routledge.

Plumwood, Val (1993) *Feminism and the Mastery of Nature*. London: Routledge.

Propp, V. (1968) *Morphology of Folk Tales*. Austin, TX: University of Texas Press.

Proyect, Louis (2013) 'Gravity: All is lost'. The Unrepentant Marxist blog, 17 October http://louisproyect.org/2013/10/

Scarry, Elaine (1985) *The Body in Pain: The Making and Unmaking of the World*. Oxford: Oxford University Press.

Sontag, Susan (2003) *Regarding the Pain of Others*. New York: Farrar, Straus and Giroux.

Taylor, Paul (1986) *Respect for Nature: A Theory of Environmental Ethics*. Princeton, NY: Princeton University Press.

UCL Department of Geography (2015) 'GEOGG030 Natural Hazards'. http://www.geog.ucl.ac.uk/admissions/masters/msc-modules/geogg030-natural-hazards

Warren, K. (1990) 'The Power and the Promise of Ecological Feminism'. *Environmental Ethics* 12(2): 125–133.

Warren, K. (1994) *Ecological Feminism*. London: Routledge.

Warren, K. (2000) *Eco-feminist Philosophy: A Western Perspective on What It Is and Why It Matters*. Boulder, CO: Rowman and Littlefield.

Weik von Mossner, Alexa and Irmscher, Christoph (2012) 'Dislocations and Ecologies: An Introduction'. *European Journal of English Studies* 16(2): 91–97.

Woerner, Meridith (2013) '*Gravity's* ending holds a deeper meaning, says Alfonso Cuaron'. http://io9.com/gravitys-ending-holds-a-deeper-meaning-says-alfonso-c-1442690788

Zoller Seitz, Matt (2013) 'Gravity'. http://www.rogerebert.com/reviews/gravity-2013

5

SOCIAL RESPONSIBILITY AND ANTHROPOMORPHISING ANIMALS

Overview: anthropomorphising animals

This chapter will focus on how the representation of animals in film reveals a range of normative and sometimes exemplary ethical ideals for humans to emulate, beginning with readings of recent blockbusters such as *Dawn of the Planet of the Apes* and its preoccupation with the ontological relationship between apes and humans, before extending and critiquing ethical values in dealing with animals through readings of *Fantastic Mr Fox* and *Grizzly Man*, before concluding with a discussion of the allegorical power of animals to sustain a spiritual and even transcendental critique of human nature in *Noah* and *Life of Pi*.

Peter Singer most often appears in the literature highlighting the ethical rights of animals, drawing from his revolutionary book *Animal Liberation* (1975), where he suggests that cruelty to animals is analogous to slavery, recalling the philosophical work of Jeremy Bentham in the seventeenth century. Incidentally, Singer also coined the term 'speciesism', to explain the irrational prejudice that Bentham originally identified as the basis of our radically different treatment of animals and humans. Because of its mimetic and realistic features, film, above all the arts, most explicitly foregrounds and dramatises animal–human interrelationships and their environmental and ethical implications.

Cinematic representation of animals rarely, if ever, go as far as Singer's treatise however, and most frequently affirms a more human-centric and utility-based appreciation of animals. This is evident in early Hollywood classics like *The Yearling* (see Brereton 2005), together with recent studies of animals on film and documentaries reviewed in the 2014 eco-film reader *Moving Environments* (Weik von Mossner 2014). Less extreme animal-rights scholars and activists tend to agree with Mary Midgley who in *'Animals and Why they Matter'* (1983), suggests that *we* are at least sometimes right to prefer the interests of our human kind.

While Donna Haraway suggests that 'animals make us human in a continual process of reshaping, just as we affect the evolution of both domesticated and wild species' (in Garrard 2012: 151).

The dominant characteristics and representations of animals in cinema emanates from the extensive back-catalogue of Disney and its explicit evocation and celebration of a deep anthropocentric mindset, which features humans', and specifically children's, apparently innate love and empathy for (at least cuddly and big eyed) animals. This is evidenced through classics like *Bambi*, up through a wide range of animal stories visualised in numerous animated and live action films over the years. According to Garrard (2012: 152), this phenomenon plays into the need for human identification with animals through a form of 'neoteny' – the set of characteristics we instinctively associate with infants. Such explicitly anthropomorphic representations have also been pushed to an extreme in normativising the notion of a nuclear family in films such as *March of the Penguins,* while defining strict codes of behaviour – environmental and otherwise – for audiences to follow.

The anthropomorphisation of animals is traditionally defined as a one-way projection of uniquely human emotions and characteristics into non-human beings conceived of as radically 'other', while in turn this position and worldview was attacked by scholars and scientists, as a 'dangerous pit' or even at another extreme, as a kind of mental disorder.

In any case, anthropomorphic animal narratives are frequently denigrated as 'childish', thereby associating a dispassionate, even alienated, perspective on animal representation with maturity (Garrard 2012: 155). This latter approach most clearly corresponds with the complexity of *Grizzly Man*, in which the main character Treadwell oscillates between romantic dramatisation of the 'personal risks he ran in living among dangerous animals, and a crudely anthropomorphic sentimentality distraught by evidence of predation and death' (Garrard 2012: 156).

Of course, at the same time there has also been a growing thread and thematic preoccupation in film towards a more so-called 'realistic' evocation of animals. This is especially evident in the proliferation and expediential growth of documenting nature and animals in their natural habitat on television programmes, alongside major big-budget nature film projects, to a more reflexive evocation of animals and their ethical rights *vis-à-vis* human responsibility, as evoked in *Grizzly Man*.

The issue of power alongside ethical and environmental justice remains particularly pertinent when taking into account the treatment of animals. Using a somewhat glib example, you can't secure 'informed consent' from animals for their portrayal in a documentary, much less in a fictional film. More cogently, how do you address the possible abuse of invasive filmmaking techniques designed specifically to provoke reactions in animals? Such ethical dilemmas are often more relevant for documentary formats, which are often criticised for voyeuristic dramatisation of predation and sexual congress as the only behavioural activities worth filming. Because of space considerations, the varying aspects of environmental ethics and its implications for nature documentaries will be examined in future publications that are being developed. In any case, the rules of presenting strictly factual evidence or for that matter constructing narratives and telling fabricated stories, remain even more vague and ethically challenging in wildlife or nature-focused fiction films, while probably at the same time far less inhibiting and less aesthetically restrictive than in more traditional documentary filmmaking modalities.

In his seminal 1977 essay 'Why Look at Animals', John Berger treats the massive proliferation of anthropomorphic representations of animals in the modern era, not as a *compensation* for the disappearance of wild and domesticated animals from the daily lives of most Westerners, but paradoxically, as an integral part of their disappearance (Welling in Weik von Mossner 2014: 81).

In cartoons, for instance, we must face up to the fact that there is nothing so human as identification across species. Anthropomorphism, writes John Berger most provocatively, 'was the residue of the continuous use of animal metaphor. In the last two centuries, animals have gradually disappeared. Today we live without them. And in this new solitude, anthropomorphism makes us doubly uneasy' (Berger 1980: 9).

The anthropomorphic residue described by Berger nonetheless retains its power, through the ecological (re)presentation of various species (as most effectively demonstrated in modern classics such as *Antz, A Bug's Life* and *Finding Nemo*) which are less like furry toys today – and most especially like Nemo contain a very explicit moral fable against removing reef fish from their habitat. Animation as an aesthetic format visually imposes a human face on the animal world.

But what we feel when we watch wildlife films, according to some eco-film scholars, does not simply depend on techniques employed by filmmakers to promote a superficial form of anthropomorphism, much less to tap into our innate drive to make sense of the world by comparing animal physiology and behaviour to our own. Rather, it is claimed 'that wildlife films can (intentionally in some cases, unintentionally in others) provide viewers with heavily mediated but potentially transformative modes of access to the emotional lives of our non-human kin' (Welling in Weik von Mossner 2014: 82).

Furthermore, a biocultural and critically anthropomorphic approach can, for instance, go a long way towards explaining what Werner Herzog in *Grizzly Man* calls the 'inexplicable magic of cinema' and how this 'can be ascribed to the basic unpredictability of the world, especially where wild animals are involved' (Welling in Weik von Mossner 2014: 85). Such forms of 'magic' certainly serve to foreground and even explain various contentious environmental ethical dilemmas.

It is, however, an anthropocentric fallacy, according to Welling, to assume that 'pleasure, annoyance, fear, anger, and so on, are strictly speaking *human* emotions at all, and interpreting other sentient creatures' emotions correctly can be a life-or-death matter for wildlife filmmakers and the animals with whom they work with, as much as it is for elephants and their mahouts for instance' (Welling in Weik von Mossner 2014: 88). Such judgements, ethical or otherwise, are most particularly ascribed to the varying explorations of *Grizzly Man* examined in this chapter.

From a more psychological level of engagement with nature and animals, analogies can also be made with Emmanuel Levinas's very influential concept of the 'face'. Levinas argues that the face is the vital medium through which all (un)ethical interaction between humans occurs. By extension, therefore, on an aesthetic level at least, nonhumans in possession of the characteristic of a human face will by all accounts trigger more concern and proactive forms of empathy. This certainly corresponds to the *raison d'être* of the Disney *oeuvre* and its preoccupation with animals in particular.

Animals remain a staple component especially within popular animation, where they appear in anthropomorphic forms, and allegorical narratives play on and affirm familiar human emotions (Lorimer 2010: 245). For example Dumbo's 'weeping and gazing eyes (and uncommonly expressive eyebrows) and his prehensile touching trunk foreground basic human anatomical features which have been identified by phenomenologists like Heidegger (the hand) and Levinas (the face), as triggers for human affection and ethical concern' (Lorimer 2010: 246). Meanwhile, the eyes of the bears in *Grizzly Man* or the monster's eyes represented in a close-up in *Godzilla* are far removed from such early forms of anthropomorphic representation.

Interestingly, as Sean Cubitt affirms,

> we carry in us the biology of mammals and our symbiotes and parasites. To distinguish humans from animals is thus also to establish a fluctuating frontier somewhere within the human, between angel and brute, mind and body, instinct and drive, nature and nurture, sex and gender.
>
> (Cubitt 2005: 25)

While most significantly he continues,

> after Freud and Darwin, it is difficult to say where being animal stops and being human begins. The religious distinction has provided humankind with souls but left the animals without, has faded in the secular light of science, and even the religious find it hard to accept unnecessary cruelty to animals. But then, where do we draw the line?
>
> (Cubitt 2005: 25)

Such ever-present ethical and ontological debates in understanding between humans and animals have of course fundamental implications for framing levels of environmental ethics appreciation, as most explicitly dramatised in the *Planet of the Apes* franchise discussed later.[1]

Most audiences would accept the proposition that the natural and animal world is, by and large, beautiful. Some would go further. Gaston Bachelard, for example, somewhat strangely proposes that a 'need to animalise' is at 'the origin of imagination. The first function of imagination is to create animal forms' (cited in Cubitt 2005: 40). Art historians cite the historical cave paintings which symbolise man's long and close connection with animals for hunting as well as other nurturing properties. So by any measure, the use of animals on film remains a complex phenomenon and has evolved over time, aided by new technology and more enlightened attitudes towards non-human creatures.

Filmic power to represent and shape animal environmental ethics

As Nigel Thrift and others have noted, much of the world lives in the 'age of the screen', enmeshed in 'extensive and skilful assemblages dedicated to the production, circulation and consumption of moving imagery' (in Lorimer 2010: 237–258). While Michael Shapiro suggests that we now live in an audiovisual, rather than a literary, age in which moving images have

> become the primary media through which we make sense of the world and the boundaries between image and [that] which we imagine are increasingly blurred.
>
> (Lorimer 2010: 237–58)

Of course Neil Postman in *Amusing Ourselves to Death* has argued similarly many decades ago. As a film scholar, one is almost preconditioned to endorse such assertions regarding the social and cultural importance of film in contemporary society. Nevertheless, extensive empirical studies are needed to fine-tune and objectively test and evaluate such deeply felt assertions concerning the power of cinema and media generally.

Of late there have been a number of studies framed around ecological psychology and film cognition that in turn explore how film as 'an emotive machine' helps elicit emotional responses from audiences. For instance Totora argues that we should understand cinema as

> the ultimate synaesthetic art, incorporating sound, voice, music, colour, movement, narrative, mimesis and collage in a fashion so visceral and emotive that it can frequently move spectators to think and feel beyond the sensorial limits of sight and sound.
>
> (Totora 2002)

Meanwhile for film scholars like Laura Marks (2000) and Vivian Sobchack (1982), it is most especially the 'haptic visuality' or 'affective materiality' of moving images, and for the purposes of this chapter the representation of animals that give them their allure and evocative power (Lorimer 2010: 240). Playful representations of domesticated cats and dogs most notably continue to be the most popular with massive global audiences, as evident through YouTube material and the various 'best of' funny animal clip shows on television.

Animals as food and as experiments in living

Animals, including human animals of course, also signify simply by living. The efflorescence of nature's aesthetic loveliness, or its sheer sensuousness of touch, taste, smell as well as sound and vision, may or may not be entirely predetermined by human perception, and may or may not, as Alan Bleakley idealistically argues, effectively teach us a moral fable.

> It is the animals themselves who will surely lead us to reformulate the ecological crisis, as we respond to their intentions, for the animal already shows that they do not want an anaesthetic life, a life of numbing insensitivity, a half-life. Rather they will awaken us through their sensitivities, their aesthetic presence, to our self-imposed numbness to the world.
>
> (Bleakley 2000: 37)

This aspect of getting inside the minds and understanding emotions of the animal remains a dominant thesis and rationale for the *Planet of the Apes* franchise, alongside many other so-called animal narratives addressed in this chapter.

While, at the other extreme, the economic reality of factory farming (Rollins 2004) and the ill treatment of domestic and wild animals remain a particularly caustic and cautionary (documentary) tale, as evidenced for instance by some agricultural statistics from America.[2] Ethical concerns around factory farming of food to meet the growing needs of increasing human populations and the drive towards ever-reduced costs across all categories is shocking to say the least. Basically slaughtering animals for human consumption remains the core environmental ethical dilemma.

That's not to say that farmers generally don't have any respect for their livestock – see for example various cautionary documentary tales like *Food Inc.* etc. (although factory farmers like those represented in *Fantastic Mr Fox* would be hard pressed to show that they do), but their relationship with these domesticated creatures lacks the deep respect that the Na'vi for instance represented in *Avatar* show to their prey.[3]

Furthermore, a process of 'white-washing' of authentic animal behaviour is often seen in film, helping in turn to downplay the stark realities of the global desire for vegetarianism and maintaining a 'them–us' polarity – even if this is sentimentally romanticised, as evident in Michael Apted's biopic about Dian Fossey's work with mountain gorillas in east Africa titled *Gorillas in the Mist*. For instance, David Ingram is most pointed in comparing the gorillas, which Fossey describes in her book as practising 'infanticide, masturbation, incest, fellatio and cannibalism' (1983), to the animals represented in the movie version, who are 'idealised figures possessing the redemptive innocence typical of the Hollywood wild animal movies' (Ingram 2000: 135–6).

Historically, after World War Two, many scholars point to the apparent 'natural contract' between animals and humans being broken. See, for example, a contemporary recreation of this phenomenon in Spielberg's *Warhorse*, where the beautiful horses represented have outlived their technological usefulness.[4] While at a macro level the need to apply industrial and machine methods of agriculture to increase efficiency and productivity and to provide the public with cheap and plentiful food supply was brought to the fore in America following the so-called Dust Bowl environmental disaster during the 1930s. Nature could no longer be taken for granted as simply affording an ever-present bounteous harvest. Instead a growing reliance was placed on a scientifically based industrial and mechanised system of production and harvesting to help maximise crop yields, alongside equally intensive factory farming of animals for human consumption.

The huge scale of industrialised agriculture and ever-reducing profit margins per acre or per animal unit, militate against the sort of individual attention and level of husbandry that typified much traditional (organic) agriculture. For instance, it is suggested in traditional milk dairies, say 50 years ago, a farmer could make a good living out of a herd of 50 cows. Today, in America, one needs thousands to survive economically and many herds are over 6000 milking cows. Consequently mass production in agriculture with its inherent risks has become the *de facto* norm, as further illustrated by a growing output of cautionary food documentaries.

Animal care theory and environmental ethics

Care theory can most specifically be applied to the handling of animals, while remaining an important branch of contemporary feminist theory, as originally articulated by Carol Gilligan (1982). Such care is very different from the masculine-driven care of the protagonist, evident for example by Treadwell in *Grizzly Man*. Implicit, for instance, in 'feminist' animal care theory is the notion of

> listening to animal communications and constructing a human ethic in conversation with the animals, rather than imposing on them a rationalistic, calculative grid of human's own monological construction.
>
> (Donovan 2006: 2)

This phenomenon is evident in classic filmic tales like *Doctor Doolittle* and more recently in *We Bought a Zoo*.

Kant argued for instance that sympathy is an unstable base for moral decision-making because, first of all the 'feeling is volatile; second, the capacity for sympathy is not evenly distributed in the population; and third, sympathy is therefore not universalisable' (quoted by Raju 2013). Instead, Kant proposed that 'one should act ethically out of a sense of duty and that one's sense of what is ethical be determined by imagining what would happen if one's actions were universalised' (cited in Donovan 2006: 3). One wonders however whether such 'sympathy' less evident, much less expected and normative with regards to care for animals.

Meanwhile, Tom Regan's primary objection (1991) to such universal notions of care theory with regards to animals is more prosaic, re-affirming Mary Midgley's earlier assertion, suggesting that: '[M]ost people do not care very much what happens to [non-human] animals'… Their care seems to be limited to 'pet' animals, or to cuddly or rare specimens of wildlife. 'What then becomes of the animals towards whom people are indifferent' (Midgley cited in Reagan 1991: 96)? This chapter specifically calls attention to and examines non-cuddly animals like foxes (*Fantastic Mr Fox*) and bears (*Grizzly Man*), in explaining how such 'animal' protagonists effectively problematise these binary assumptions and assertions.

For instance, at an extreme margin of utilitarianism, Singer and Dawn's 'When Slaughter Makes Sense' (2004) argues that the slaughter of 25 million ducks and chickens was ethically justified in order to halt the spread of avian flu. This extreme form of skewed utilitarianism was similarly applied to cows to control 'mad cow' disease and to cats with respect to SARS. The obvious speciesism of their arguments is of course apparent if one considers that 'the slaughter of 25 million humans to prevent the spread of some disease would be considered outrageously evil' (Donovan 2006: 8). Such juxtaposition is most clearly dramatised in cautionary tales around disease prevention in *Contagion* and other cautionary environmental tales, together with the recent proliferation of various forms of zombie movies.

Also connecting the plight of animals to human concerns around racism and slavery serves as cautionary contextual framework. 'Those critters ain't like white folks you know', while, 'one trader remarks of a black woman's misery over a child of hers being sold at auction; *they* [emphasis added] get over things'. As Marjorie Spiegel further points out, '[I]n the eyes of white slaveholders', black people were 'just animals', who could soon get over separation from a child or other loved person (Spiegel 1988: 43).[5]

For these and other reasons, several theorists have urged that humans need to learn to read the languages of the natural world and apply this to a broad conceptualisation of human-ethical values. Jonathan Bate for instance has proposed that we learn the syntax of the land, not seeing it through our own 'prison-house of language', in order to develop appropriate environmental understandings (Bate 1998: 65). Similarly, Patrick Murphy has, for instance, called for 'eco-feminist dialogues' in which humans learn to read the dialects of animals. 'Nonhuman others' he claims, 'can be constituted as speaking subjects rather than merely objects of our speaking' (Murphy 1991: 50). This affirmation of animals' specific agency is something film can help to develop.

No longer must our relationship with animals be that of 'conquest of an alien object', Rosemary Radford Ruether notes, but instead 'the conversation of two subjects'. We must recognise that 'the other has a nature of her own that needs to be respected and with which one must enter into conversation' (Ruether 1975: 195–6). On that basis and in reflecting upon the complex political context, a dialogical ethic for the treatment of animals may be established, according to Donovan (Donovan 2006: 19). This radical transition towards the ethical treatment of animals as part of a more broad-based quotient of environmental ethical concerns is evident in the *Planet of the Apes* franchise, which remains the most populist and pervasive, albeit crudely fictional evocation of human–animal dynamics.

Dawn of the Planet of the Apes

This latest instalment in the globally successful franchise presents a clear allegorical double-take on the on-going 'terrorist', religious and ethnic wars – where divisions are so polarised and divisive, both sides might as well be 'animal' as against 'human' – with atrocities carried out on all sides. The ape storyline somewhat fatalistically feeds into the inevitability of war/conflict, in spite of 'good men/animals' doing their best to avert such disaster. The ending of the film in particular rehearses this trope with Caesar (the chief ape played by Andy Serkis) rising from the dead, aided by the 'good humans' and eventually defeating the 'bad ape' Koba (Toby Kebbell), who was simply fixated on revenge and could perceive no other way out. This heroic ape finally unites his 'tribe' in total submission, as the tribe 'bow to his majesty'. This final *mise-en-scene* is choreographed and dramatised by moving into an extreme close-up of the eyes of the ape as super-hero – from the trappings of his body to his interior soul. This halting image evokes the ultimate in an anthropomorphic gaze, as we witness his pupils dilate and his rising blood vessels, as he braces himself for the upcoming battle and presumably one suspects a film sequel.

Both main protagonists throughout the narrative – human and animal – valorise family values above all else. Such a preoccupation is common across many Hollywood films explored in this volume and in turn this helps to maintain their 'humane' and ethical trajectory, while at the same time affording the protagonists the confidence of knowing what is the 'right thing to do'.

The apes are particularly shocked at the start by all types of guns and weapons, insisting such instruments of destruction are destroyed before they can cause more damage. In the opening sequence – a traditional hunt similar to that explored in *Apocalypto* – we see Caesar's 'side-kick' (but later his arch-enemy) killing a big grizzly with a timber spear, thereby saving the leader's son from attack. Alternatively, the apes display clear evidence of a benevolent human-centric tradition and culture, in witnessing their home camp, which is also reminiscent of the exotic but benevolent nature of Home Tree in *Avatar*. We observe a large orang-utan as teacher and steward of their culture and tradition, feeding the new generation the core principle ethics of apes, around not killing other apes, together one suspects with re-affirming their deep respect for nature.

Meanwhile on the human side of the equation, the opening pre-credits' expositionary sequence provides a historical context for the animal–human conflict, namely recounting some form of epidemic. Later, we are informed of the back-story of this futuristic conflict through a stereotypical female nurse and partner to our main human hero Ellie (Keri Russell). She subsequently ends up medically assisting Caesar's partner when injured. Maybe not surprisingly in this conventional male-centred action genre, Ellie is afforded no other active role or agency in the narrative. This representation is however reversed in a number of science fiction narratives explored in the previous chapter. Caesar's nemesis, Koba, as seen in previous instalments of the franchise *Rise of the Planet of the Apes*, was 'tortured' by humans, thereby explaining why he always wants revenge and cannot trust humans. Meanwhile Caesar, again recalling the nature–nurture debate, remains more sanguine towards the human species, as we discover through a videotape. The ape's relationship to man is consequentially predetermined by how they were treated as infants and noting how for instance he learned English from a 'good man' who treated him well. This human–animal/non-human division is most effectively choreographed in *Avatar*.

Avatar: the most successful ecological cautionary tale

People for the Ethical Treatment of Animals (PETA) surprisingly honoured *Avatar* which is predominantly made up of CGI and special effects, with a Proggy award, signifying progress in the animal rights cause. But as one blogger recounts, 'The Na'vi do not mentally "become one" with the creatures they plug their organic USB in, they literally brainwash them. As a result the creature does everything the rider "tells it to do". Neytiri for instance tells Jake he must choose one of these "ikran" as his own' (quoted in Malamud 2012: 17).[6]

Wayne Yuen affirms how the 'Na'vi truly *see* animals, recognising them as independent beings who have their own needs, desires, and perspectives on the world – and who are therefore worthy of our respect'. We human beings often have trouble seeing other animals in this way and need allegories like *Whale Rider* and many other filmic narratives to remind us of this close relationship. 'Its *just* a dog' or 'It's *just* a cow', someone might say however (Yuen in Dunn 2014: 229), and therefore cannot or should not be treated with the same ethical respect that humans demand.

Meanwhile, Malamud and others counter that the presence of other animals – even in treatment that might seem ecologically enlightened on the surface – invites a critical analysis as to whether the filmmaking industry and its audience are truly becoming more 'concerned about ecosystemic speciesist inequities,

FIGURE 5.1 *Avatar*, 2009, written and directed by James Cameron

or are merely reiterating the same old anthropocentric prejudices under the cover of a fleshy new veneer' (Malamud 2012: 17). One would have to have strong sympathy with this re-stating of the same old values. If ecologically and independently sophisticated representation of animal presence is metaphorically envisioned as the third dimension, then *Avatar* remains mired in the same old flat, two-dimensional rut that has afflicted animals in more conventional visual culture.[7]

Judging from the Avatar-Forums.com website, fans of the movie typically understand *Avatar* as advocating a return to a way of living in harmony with nature including animals and as an incitement to take recuperative environmentalist action.[8] They consider the movie as a critique of imperialistic expansion, exploitation of indigenous peoples, and the depletion of earth's resources.[9] For instance, the film director James Cameron has become openly involved in direct political environmentalist action, as exemplified by his support for the battle against the Belo Monte Dam on the Xingu river in Brazil. He also started the 'Home Tree Initiative' whose goal was to plant one million trees before 2011.[10]

In *Avatar*, the conflict between humans and Na'vi revolves around the dichotomies that continue to divide humans and othered animals, alongside alternative alien species: nature versus technology, indigenous living in harmony with nature versus imperialistic marauderism, earth versus space. These dichotomies are represented in *Avatar* in highly complex ways and have been discussed in Chapter 3. In broad terms, whereas Pandora and the Na'vi represent nature and indigenous beings living in harmony with nature, earthlings represent technology and imperialistic marauderism. Despite the movie's obvious green message, in many ways the nature on Pandora seems to represent a more sophisticated form of technology than actual nature. Somewhat less fantastical in its representations of animals, yet still equally provocative and

FIGURE 5.2 *Avatar*, 2009, written and directed by James Cameron

certainly more playfully ironic, is the rich portrayal of animals in the animated feature *Fantastic Mr Fox*.

Fantastic Mr Fox: DIY anthropomorphism

In an insightful SCMS film conference paper, Elisabeth Walden (2013) argued that *Fantastic Mr Fox* can be read as the ecological inverse of the successful blockbuster *Avatar*. Many critics read this Wes Anderson film as quirky, yet at the same time evident of an imaginative form of DIY cinema, unlike the showy excess of *Avatar*, which is more about the legitimation of professionalism and high-end production processes.

Furthermore, as Paula Willoquet-Marcondi (2010) argues, eco-films can and should 'inspire activism through a rhetoric of optimism and humour that does not sacrifice the seriousness of the message'. Nicole Seymour adds that eco-cinema demands 'unserious' affective modes such as irony, self-parody and playfulness (Seymour in Weik von Mossner 2014: 61). As a mode defined by incongruity, irony is well exemplified by this playful use of animation. This comic attribute is best suited to negotiate 'between the paradoxical desires of eco-cinema audiences: the desire for pleasure as well as information, and the desire to be both entertained and validated as thinkers in their own right' (ibid. 2014: 63). Such playful self-reflexive and ironic humour, as evident in this film, is a long way from the light environmentalism of, for example, children's classic animal films such as *Bambi* or *Finding Nemo*.[11]

Both *Avatar* and *Fantastic Mr Fox* open with depleted nature; while in the former, wild nature is visually created as a moral tale for the camera. As spectators we are often explicitly positioned to enjoy wild nature, while *Fantastic Mr Fox* with its aerial opening shots display cultivated land, rather than a so-called wilderness. Most of the plot of *Fantastic Mr Fox* involves a conflict with big farmers who seek to control the land, rather than recognising it as a commons for the benefit of *all* its inhabitants, including animals. The farmers' energy is focused totally on simply maximising productivity.

The film incidentally also alludes to the dangers of local pollution and its effects on food production. At the same time, the narrative does not embrace the pleasure of innocent identification, as suggested in early Disney fare, with its explicit form of animal anthropomorphism. For instance, from the start the main protagonist Mr Fox is represented as a very 'modern' sophisticated protagonist, with his music headset playing a song about Davy Crockett, who in his time supported the rights of squatters, as highlighted in Walden's reading; while other critics, like Peberdy, have emphasised his deadpan performance. As a very astute and aesthetic fox, most significantly voiced by the star actor George Clooney, he listens to well-chosen and evocative music on his Walkman, while otherwise commenting on his situation and his world. One certainly wonders what diegetic or anthropomorphic world of animals we are entering and what ethical and environmental lesson audiences are being set up to engage with.

Several critics effectively explain the deep semiosis and complex intertextual allusions, which usually only art/smart cinema affords. One could for instance assert that *Avatar* with its big budget narrative heuristic, if only by default, sets up more clearly defined boundaries between civilisation and nature. While in *Fantastic Mr Fox* raw wilderness simply persists as a legend. This is witnessed most succinctly by the iconic black wolf discussed below, which is clearly differentiated from Mr Fox's close-knit community and habitat.

Fantastic Mr Fox opens with the main protagonist holding a cover of the classic Dahl book, affording the film its discrete, yet quirky, literary authenticity (see Dorey 2011 for an analysis of paratextual material on the DVD). He is standing proudly on the mound, with a tree in the foreground – a mock-up of a well-groomed male, with a suave, brown corduroy coat and a 'rustic farming' outdoors elegant sartorial look. The scene evokes many famous romantic paintings of human landowner proudly surveying and controlling his habitat. The image also calls to mind how a vain male fox might want to look; or a quirky filmmaker might want him to look through the eyes of Roland Dahl. In comparison for instance one could examine other children's writers like Beatrix Potter who also promotes a broad range of environmental ethics in their writings (O'Connell in Keyes and McGillicuddy 2014: 31–44).

At the start of the movie, like a 'typical' sentient husband figure, Mr Fox is waiting anxiously for his wife – voiced by Meryl Streep – to come out of the doctor's surgery and is informed that she is pregnant again. He glazes over in total shock, one presumes simulating an accurate response of many fathers of the human variety at least.[12] Nonetheless, he instinctively knows the right thing to say and do, and suggests taking the scenic route home and walk back through the Berk Squab Farm to hunt for some food. The couple as a team have great fun negotiating all the obstacles. Nonetheless, Mr Fox remains too clever by half and in spite of wondering what sort of trap has been set for them by the humans, they still get caught and face mortal danger. She asserts with some trepidation that if they survive this, Mr Fox must promise to take up a new line of work.

Two years later – which is a long period in fox-time – he has stuck to his promise and become a journalist, while later announcing that he does not want to live in a hole any more. As a typical employee on the corporate ladder, he now wants more and strives to escape his mundane lot. On receiving his morning breakfast – several slices of well-burnt toast – he munches his food with no sense of human finesse, essentially displaying his true animal nature. No evidence here of the environmentally valorised 'slow food' movement. Of course this aspect of his animal nature has been masked, if not totally subsumed, by his otherwise sartorial elegance and refined verbal and intellectual (human) wit.

Meanwhile, remaining a fountain of true wisdom and displaying a deep appreciation of the animal–human division, Mrs Fox retorts, 'foxes live in a hole for a reason'. Like some human protagonist fighting against the 'natural' order, he strives to reach beyond his animalistic predispositions, in this allegorical cautionary tale.

Again like many in the human race, Mr Fox strives to become 'upwardly mobile', which remains umbilically embedded within the values of the capitalist system. So he contacts his estate agent, Mr Badger, whose home is a bijou dam across a small stream.[13] Unlike many human financial specialists, the agent warns the fox against moving out and especially taking on the environmental risk of the 'tree house', as it is facing up against three of the worst farming 'magnates', 'capitalists' and 'non-organic' producers of food in the region. By all accounts this scenario clearly highlights a number of environmental ethical concerns and debates addressed in this volume, including issues around moral hazard and the struggle to promote effective environmental and ethical precautionary principles.

The main protagonist asks existential and ethically pertinent questions that are usually reserved for sentient humans, such as: Who am I? Such cognitively loaded questions usually connote higher intellectual activity and are frequently used to differentiate and legitimise animal subjugation by humans. Crudely summarising these divisions, it is implied that animals can't reason or essentially feel emotions, much less engage in the arts and the 'good life' and therefore should not be given the same status as humans. Yet Mr Fox can actively display all of these higher order skills. At the same time, the narrative also celebrates his dualistic animal nature by continuing, 'how can a fox ever be happy without a chicken in its mouth'?[14]

Mr Fox of course has a plan to regain and re-embody his 'true nature' and overcome conventional forms of domestication, and the emasculation process as he sees it, is precipitated by the perennial drive for familial control and the lack of any risk taking, by devising secret attacks on the Bogg's chicken factory. To affirm the old adage, suggested in *Jurassic Park* most notably, namely 'nature finds a way'. In this cautionary tale also, animals *must* actively play out their natural and innate instincts.

Unfortunately, however, in the struggle against the highly malevolent and stereotypical farmers, Mr Fox gets his tail shot off. Since tails don't grow back, this creates a very human feeling of being emasculated. There is a familiar family row scenario between the parent foxes who are paradoxically surrounded by a very rich seam of precious metals shining on the walls, deep below the earth's surface into which they have burrowed. This natural resource has however no use value for the foxes, while being highly prized for its exchange value as a precious metal by humans. The soap-opera style of a somewhat conventional melodramatic (human) romantic row begins: 'Why did you lie to me?' 'Because I'm a wild animal', he retorts. She counters that this story is too predictable. In the end we will all die, she concludes, unless you change. Meanwhile up above the top-soil, the farmers bring in three earth-moving diggers and the extensive siege on the animals securely hidden below begins.

But these three (explicitly overweight) farmers are unable to control the site and ensure their version of 'food security'. 'We can thank them for one thing', the animals assert – recalling the 'war-time Dunkirk spirit' and the communal benefits of having a common enemy, which also encouraged all animals to be more aware of each other. Recalling the pervasive growth of community building, while also intertextually referencing the powerful allegory of the classic *Animal Farm* and its resonance for humans. Having a common enemy certainly facilitates a greater sense of community development and bonding within their close-knit environment. This further calls to mind *The Planet of the Apes* franchise discussed above, regarding the dangers of polarisation between humans and animals and its impact on environmental and ethical values.[15]

Wolf's visitation: iconic mythologising of primal animal nature

The iconic wild animal as quintessential outsider is observed in the distance and most notably witnessed raising a black-power salute, before exiting from the scene and the film. An escape party on a small motorised bike witnesses the epiphany mentioned above of a black wolf in the distance during icy conditions. The wolf is just looking and staring into space; the Fox wonders if he is some kind of Shaman and questions him, 'you think we are in for a hard winter'.[16] While admitting at the outset that he has a major phobia for black wolves, Mr Fox nonetheless gives him due respect and displays the right-arm closed-fist salute, which is immediately replicated by the wolf. This remains an iconic signal of revolution throughout the ages. Re-evaluating such a symbol in this context, it could probably also be read as focusing on how animals ought to stick together, while reaffirming their (animal) version of 'doing the right thing'. This strategy was also witnessed in the cult *Planet of the Apes* franchise.

The concept of wildness not only plays a role in philosophical debates, but also most specifically is played out in representations across popular culture. Wild nature is often seen as a place outside the cultural sphere where one can still encounter instances of transcendence. 'In encounters with the wild and unruly, humans can sometimes experience the misfit between their well-ordered, human-centred, self-created worldview and the otherness of nature', and in doing so face up to, what Plumwood calls, 'the view from outside' (Plumwood 1999: 79). While *Fantastic Mr Fox* remains by all accounts a very light and humorous allegory around animal welfare and their engagement with the natural, a more caustic and reflexive environmental ethical debate is dramatised and foregrounded in Herzog's *Grizzly Man*.

Grizzly Man: reflexive environmental ethics

The very environmentally engaged director Werner Herzog in classics like *Fitzcarraldo* remains preoccupied with driven individuals and dreamers who often move mountains to fulfil their fantasies. The backbone narrative of *Grizzly Man* is constructed from a 'found documentary' made up of original footage, filmed by Timothy Treadwell, an eccentric 'nature lover', who for thirteen summers risked his life living with grizzly bears in Alaska, until eventually being killed by one of the animals he sought to protect. The tagline of the story reads: 'in nature there are boundaries', which also echoes the core ecological message of films like *Into the Wild*.

As Herzog explained,

> [F]or me a true landscape is not just a representation of a desert or a forest. It shows an inner state of mind, literally inner landscapes ... This approach is my real connection to Caspar David Friedrich.
>
> (Cronin 2002: 136)

This attitude is manifested in *Burden of Dreams*, Blank's documentary on Herzog's *Fitzcarraldo*, where the actor Klaus Kinski fulminates against the very nature the director went halfway around the world to find. Just as the 'romantic identifies with nature's unspoilt qualities, its wildness or peace', Herzog 'invents the image, and some decidedly unpretty themes leap out of the German past' (cited in Cronin 2002). Whether Treadwell in *Grizzly Man* reminded Herzog of a former version of the filmmaker himself, is something only Herzog can own up to in any case. Herzog's deadpan irony regarding Treadwell's arrogance and self-importance at face value, even going so far as to refer to the bear who attacked him as his 'murderer' remains a ludicrous designation from an ecological standpoint (Seymour in Weik von Mossner 2014: 69).[17]

The real Timothy Treadwell was an amateur bear expert and filmmaker who lived amongst these creatures in the Alaskan wilderness for ten years.

'Herzog engages in a kind of cinematic dual with what he regards as Treadwell's sentimentalised view of nature', according to a very useful reading by Benjamin Noys; while at the heart of the cinema of Herzog, 'lies the vision of discordant and chaotic nature – the vision of anti-nature. Herzog constantly films nature as hell or as utterly alien. This is not a nature simply corrupted by humanity but a nature inherently "corrupt" in itself' (Noys 2007: 38–9).

'And what haunts me', Herzog confides in a voice-over on the film, is 'that in all the faces of all the bears that Treadwell ever filmed, I discover no kinship, no understanding, no mercy. I see only the overwhelming indifference of nature. To me there is no such thing as a secret world of the bears and this blank stare speaks only of a half-bored interest in food. But for Timothy Treadwell this bear was a friend, a saviour.' This is a long way from the unidirectional anthropomorphism of the Disney and conventional nature documentary *oeuvre*. Since Herzog's films are written to resemble dreams (Cronin 2002: 65), while also critiquing the dominant anthropomorphic representations of nature and animals, it is difficult to mark exactly where the introduction ends and the film proper begins (White 2008: 3).

Critics like John White and others argue that the precarious emergence of the aesthetics of nature in this film lies between the two (competing) views of Herzog and Treadwell. These views compete to impose meaning on nature; at the same time we witness the emergence of nature, without meaning – as something close to Herzog's vision of indifference (White 2008: 44). Later however, Herzog defends Treadwell not as an ecologist, much less on ethical grounds, but rather as a filmmaker.

A good nature programme, Mike Lapinski has noted (Lapinski 2005: 15), requires the following ingredients: a charismatic lead character, an interesting story, and beautiful scenery with wildlife. Herzog certainly has all of these elements and goes back and forth between the Alaskan wilderness to interview people who knew Treadwell in locations as far apart as California and Florida, as he tries to piece the mystery of his death together. One of his first interviewees Sam Egli worked on removing Treadwell and Hugenard's (Treadwell's girlfriend) remains, which gruesomely consisted of four large garbage bags. Later interviewing Marc and Marie Gaede who knew him personally, Marie quotes from one of the last letters she received from Treadwell, where he talks of mutating into a bear, as in some strange form of eco-spiritual experience. Larry Van Daele, a bear biologist, discusses the manner in which Treadwell apparently wanted to become a bear; 'I will die for these animals', somewhat playing off the Christian myth and at the same time embracing a deep eco-centric ethic. Wild, primordial nature was where Treadwell felt truly at home and where he could express his symbiotic human-animal identity.

Sitting beside the carcass of a dead fox, Treadwell emotes to the camera for his homemade documentary: 'I love you and I understand. It's a painful world'. Herzog counters such 'deep' if naïve symbiosis with the director's blank conception of nature: '[H]ere I differ with Treadwell. He seemed to ignore the fact that in nature there are predators. I believe the common denominator of the universe is not harmony, but chaos, hostility and murder'.

Man becoming animal: the ethics of animals and meat as food

Grizzly Man was a big success worldwide, consisting of 100 hours of Treadwell's videotape and fashioned into a most intriguing portrait of the Grizzly Man (Drenthen 2009: 10). Treadwell's fascination with wild nature went so far as to believe that he could live among the bears strictly non-violently and ethically without guns, recalling the fears expressed at the start of *Planet of the Apes* discussed earlier. Treadwell did not even hunt for a living, but brought along his own food from outside.

Treadwell's courage in his quest certainly prompts the viewer's admiration. Does he not live up to the ideal of deep ethical engagement and an environmental ideal of living in harmony with nature, a state that so many in the modern world find appealing (Drenthen 2009: 11)? One of the core problems discussed in this chapter that the movie addresses is Treadwell's far too humanised image of the bears: he gives them pet names like Mr Chocolate, Aunt Melissa and Sergeant Brown and declares his love for them. Treadwell's somewhat paradoxical anthropomorphic view is also reflected in his ideas about communication with wild animals. Yet by all accounts a bear's 'language' will reflect its repertoire of possible actions and anticipations; its 'signals' will mostly signify food, mating and competition etc.

According to Timothy Corrigan (1983: 133), Herzog's contradictory approach to nature in many of his films 'struggle to efface a homocentric perspective'. In fact Herzog's own didactic nature is subverted as hypnotic space gazes out at us, as we too gaze into the 'luminous presence of nature' (Corrigan 1983: 141). Essentially, Treadwell's quest in wanting to be like a bear is criticised as the ultimate form of disrespect, taking into account the holistic integrity of nature and wild animals.

The modern biologist, for instance, resists the siren song of becoming one with the bears merely as a fallacious idea. In contrast, in the native view, the bear represents a sacred realm that transcends our merely human moral code: that's why these worlds should not be conflated. Yes, even this interpretation translates the 'view from the outside' into a 'view from the inside' – to again adopt the phrase of Val Plumwood (n.d.).

Meanwhile Julie Schutten incisively argues that

> the dissonance felt by viewers of the film surrounds a disconfirmation of human faith in the nature–culture binary, and that Treadwell's death is troubling because the predator–prey relationship makes humans 'pieces of meat' and, as such, objects rather than subjects.
>
> (Schutten 2008: 195)

In her book *The Sexual Politics of Meat*, Carol Adams (1990/2003) goes on to discuss the symbolic construction of what it means to be meat. The process of transformation of an animal into meat, she suggests, necessitates the erasure of the subject, that is, the animal. The ethics of food and consumption were discussed in Chapter 3 and become most effective from an ethical standpoint, when humans cross the taboo food chain themselves, as dramatised in *The Road*, for instance, with its portrayal of cannibalism.

But what exactly does *Grizzly Man* bring to bear with regards to environmental ethics? At least one can argue it decentres somewhat conventional views of nature and animals. According to Cronon (1996: 87) 'any way of looking at nature that encourages us to believe we are separate from nature – as wilderness tends to do – is likely to reinforce environmentally irresponsible behaviour'.[18]

Taken together, Treadwell embodies and concretises a deep environmental ethic that includes pieces from a broad range of environmental experts including Leopold (1949), Rolston (2002) and Warren 2000), creating conceptions and illustrating what it might look like for humans to live in a web-of-life mentality. Any ethic that threatens human superiority functions to resist an oppressive paradigm where nature is separate from culture (Schutten 2008: 208).

The environmental teacherly message of a movie like *Grizzly Man* confirms that nature is certainly not in the service of man's desire for escapism or self-actualisation. Nor in spite of persistent urges to escape, is man essentially a solitary animal, but in the end needs both 'family' and 'civilisation' to achieve happiness. At one level, this stark, if well-hewn and conventional message can be read as a regressive–conservative homage to the strictures of home and family. A message which is opposed to individual escape and the desire of the young male – as normally coded in road movies and further evident in earlier readings of *Fantastic Mr Fox* – is to ostensibly wander outside of security and responsibility to 'find themselves'.[19]

The child-like animal lover can help explain the character of Treadwell, rather than simply pique our own sentimental impulses and wishful fantasies towards animals, as *March of the Penguins* and *Happy Feet* do so effectively. Treadwell's rhapsodising about the fox comes across as merely silly, unlike the more self-contained and humorous engagement evident in *Fantastic Mr Fox*. Meanwhile, Treadwell is always moving towards a dominant position in the frame, always from long shot to close-up, he is clearly not concerned with giving nature the last word by pulling back out to a long shot at the end of the scene. In fact Treadwell's missionary persona reflects another American tradition, that of the Puritans who came to the New World to forge a community in the wilderness.[20]

By all accounts *Grizzly Man* sets up a broad range of often conflicting evocations of environmental ethics and representations of animals which is clearly appealing to scholars, but probably less so to mass audiences. Consequently we will round off this chapter with two short readings of very popular and successful films that can be understood as situating animals and environmental ethics within a spiritual and religious dimension, beginning with *Noah*, which is a very old-fashioned cautionary tale recounting an Old Testament treatment of the flood allegory, involving the saving of various species from the ravages of a very ecocidal planet earth.

Noah: lifeboat allegory and the protection of animals

This big-budget allegorical blockbuster, according to the director, can be described as the 'least biblical biblical film ever'. Nonetheless, for the purposes of this study, the blockbuster can also be regarded as an example of 'lifeboat ethics'. In a dismissive review by Mark Kermode in *The Observer* (6 April 2014) titled 'Après moi, le deluge...', he calls it the 'strangest 125 million dollars ever spent by a major studio', nonetheless the film secured 44 million dollars on its American opening weekend. 'Noah is an increasingly deranged extremist, a fundamentalist eco-warrior hell-bent on wiping out mankind.' As discussed later in Chapter 8 in a reading of *The Tree of Life* and its evocation of divine rapture, one wonders how more secular Western audiences read and consume such overtly coded and registered biblical narratives.

Surprisingly from an erstwhile 'smart' director Darren Aronofsky (recalling films like *Lif of Pi* and *Requiem for a Dream*), this contemporary film plays an old-fashioned explicit morality tale very straight, as it explores how so-called 'innocent anmals' have to be protected from the ravages of man, who have abused their power and in turn get 'punished for their sins' by a great flood. This remains an explicit climate-change allegory and cautionary ethical tale if ever there was one.

Yet, unusually I suppose for a modern secular audience, the connection with fears around climate change is not fully explicated in the narrative. Nonetheless, this mythic story remains a potent allegory for the modern age – if narratively and aesthetically undercooked at all levels. I wonder how post-religious, secular audiences actually connect with such evocative and allegorical myth-making. *Noah* serves up a relatively conventional cautionary tale around man's impurity and not managing the gift of the planet, which the 'creator' (God) gave to them.

Furthermore, the tale implies, albeit very tangentially, the need for humans to become vegetarian, to preserve bio-diversity and maintain the existing broad range of animal/plant life. Essentially the tale suggests good people live in harmony with nature including the broad range of animal species, while 'evil ones', led by the King (Ray Winstone), demand total dominion over all creatures, a project which of course remains a recipe for ecological disaster.

Consequently, the global habitat we are introduced to at the start of the film is a truly dystopic one, almost reminiscent of *The Road* discussed in an earlier chapter, with all the trees burned down and the land pillaged, leaving no signs of organic vegetation. Extensive meat eating and even indulging in the ultimate ethical taboo of cannibalism and selling one's own family as slaves for meat, remains the extreme manifestation and marker of anti-ecological values.

Noah has a dream visualising the primary elements of fire and water, cleansing the sins of the 'bad people'. Consequently, in this albeit crude if literal Old-Testament parable, which doubles as a climate-change cautionary tale, all must die for abusing their environment, together with paying for their other sins. Nonetheless, at least he can save some of his flock, including the animals, by building an ark – the ultimate manifestation of environmental 'lifeboat ethics'. Looking for advice from his aged grandfather, 'a wizard-like Methuselah' played by Anthony Hopkins (who incidentally maintains his own Welsh accent and inhabits a distant cave), presents a precious seed taken from the Garden of Eden to his offspring.[21] On planting the seed in the ultra-fertile ground, the very next morning a miracle is created with the 'water of life' emanating from its roots and fresh life-giving liquid filtering across all angles of the landscape running for miles. Sprouting immediately from the now magically ultra-fertile soil are almost instantaneously massive trees and lush vegetation, in turn affording the raw material to construct his ark.

Noah, most notably is played with great confidence by the renowned action actor Russell Crowe (the film being comically nicknamed 'Gladiator in the rain'), who most clearly embodies an Old Testament and unambiguous ethical environmental and deep holistic truth. He remains a firm believer in the literal word of God and journeys on his pilgrimage with his family, while remaining an outsider to the despoilers of the earth. Being taught sound environmental values by his own father at the start of the film, for example he is admonished for plucking flowers from the earth. They are meant to be left growing and undisturbed, he is informed, because of their beneficial environmental role as seed protection of the land. A mini-botany and ecology lesson underpins this cautionary tale around nature and, in turn, permeates the whole film. But the 'bad men', as in so many films in this study, want to 'rape the land' and selfishly extract its goodness with no concern for the 'common good'. Consequently his father is killed without mercy and Noah the son has to run away and take on the environmental legacy of his calling.

This piece of crude exposition is dovetailed against the end of the film, when at last the strangely robust ark – again reminiscent of the 'lifeboat' ethical allegories discussed in this and other chapters – finds land. Noah makes up with his estranged wife (Jennifer Connelly), having earlier threatened to kill his children, following what he believed his God and master demanded. The now-elderly couple adopt and embody a deep environmental and vegetarian code of living in harmony with nature, as they co-mingle their hands while softening the soil to grow plants, creating a new 'more honest and productive' form of land husbandry. By the end of the film, Noah finally completes the ceremony his father began with him at the start, before he was brutally murdered, affirming the lifeline and faith in his grandchildren carrying out the right ethical behaviour.

While *Noah* presents a surprisingly old-fashioned, one-dimensional and essentialising representation of animal husbandry and environmental ethics generally, *Life of Pi* which we finally turn to, calls on a wide range of 'progressive' religious sensibilities from Hindu and Muslim to Christian and even postmodern evocations of animals, that in turn speak to a more contemporary sensibilities.

Life of Pi: religion, animals and lifeboat ethics

Religious teaching on ethics, stewardship, and responsibility has over the years helped to catalyse action among adherents. A recent compilation lists over 32 distinct religion-based organisations, which address climate change for example (Posas, 2007:13).[22] The ethical dimensions of climate change represent a defining critical issue for the modern world and call to mind a range of ingredients to promote continued progress on mitigating and adapting to climate change. Religion, alongside all forms of spirituality in various manifestations, has become a partner in facilitating more wide-reaching recognition and discussion of ethical issues and framing responses to climate change (Posas 2007). When coupled with an engagement with animals, the mixture is very potent indeed, as the novel and film adaptation of *Life of Pi* testifies.

Religion also provides a critical missing link by assigning and instilling a profound sense of individual responsibility, which acts as an antidote to our civilisation's conditioned weakness of conscience for collective acts, such as dealing with greenhouse gas emissions (Posas 2007: 16).[23] The golden rule for instance, suggested by the ethics of reciprocity in world religion, is most clearly encapsulated by Hinduism, which offers many specific guidelines for ethical living, including self-control, restraint, simplicity – recalling earlier discussions of the ethics of frugality – alongside dietary guidelines that are 'respectful of the sanctity of all life' including animals (Millais 2006: 24).

Life of Pi with an estimated production budget of 120 million is built on the back of the international popularity of Yann Martel's novel and stars teen actor Suraj Sharma.[24] Yet the project was still considered as a financial risk, making 'the most expensive art house movie ever', according to Fox UK boss Cameron Saunders. But thankfully the gamble paid off, returning a dividend of over 400 million dollars outside of America.

The main protagonist Piscine Molitor Patel – shortened to Pi – grew up in the former French colony of Pondicherry in India, where his father ran a small zoo in the city's botanical garden. The boy is eccentric and deeply interested in all forms of religion, alongside wishing to understand the ethical norms and values that underpin these global religious value systems.

Norman Holland's (2003) use of the term 'suspension of disbelief' is particularly apt for this narrative, when he talks of the experience of being rapt by fiction (film), which is dependent on our knowledge that what we are experiencing has no immediate empirical consequences in the world outside of the work of art.

FIGURE 5.3 *Life of Pi*, 2012, written by David Magee, directed by Ang Lee

When the narrator meets Francis Adirubasamy at the opening of the film in a Pondicherry coffee house, the latter tells him 'I've a story that will make you believe in God' (Cole 2004: 1x).[25] Pi's zoological odyssey, when compared to the alternative tale of cannibalism and brutality, which he cobbles together to combat his questioner's doubts, leaves no alternative with regards to the question of which is the better story.

When the inquisitive boy tries to get close to the newly arrived tiger in his father's zoo – as in *Grizzly Man* – the father admonishes him: 'animals don't think like we do, people who forget that get themselves killed'. But, of course, the whole tale re-purposes a number of animals, including most specifically a tiger and a hyena, together with various other species in one of the most pointed allegorical tales that privileges a clearly anthropomorphic perspective around the symbolic meaning and agency of these animals. As in nature documentaries, it is easier and safer to show animals in a tale of a 'lifeboat', which privileges a very elemental 'survival of the fittest' scenario, rather than calling attention to the deep horror of human 'animality' in the face of primal adversity.

While the allegorical story develops, the tiger stands in for, and is embodied by, the main protagonist Pi himself, recalling an Eastern notion of yang energy and his 'viagra' (which is the Sanskrit word for tiger). The story recalls a mythical magic-realist tale about baggage and cargo, about the horrors of the world expressed by a dream, while in turn privileging an ethical cautionary tale around animals and their relationship with humans. The tiger in the story, named Richard Parker, is in some ways the same as the mutinous sailor in Edgar Allan Poe's novel *The Narrative of Arthur Gordon Pym of Nantucket*.[26]

Meanwhile the hyena stands in for the nasty and very unhygienic cook on the ship – who has no appreciation of vegetarianism, which is the de facto manifestation of an ethical treatment of animals. Note the director incidentally talks of his fascination with food, which informed his careful casting of the very racist and objectionable ship's cook as the hyena. He chose the powerful persona of Gerard Depardieu, feeding off echoes of *Robinson Crusoe* or even *Moby Dick*, where vicious animals or mammals like giant white whales fulfil primal hunter–hunted narrative trajectories that have mutated and become re-imagined up to the present day. The hyena by all accounts poses the strongest threat to the innocent life of the Indian boy and is quite capable of eating human flesh to stay alive in the days and weeks adrift at sea. Such paradoxical and allegorised animals certainly serve to drive the narrative forward and hint at a broad range of environmental and ethical issues that are unfortunately not fully fleshed out, converging around human's relationship with animals and the need to understand the connection from a religious/spiritual perspective.

In closing such a broad-ranging chapter, from the big emotional effect of animal–human relations in the *Planet of the Apes* franchise, alongside the hugely successful eco-narrative *Avatar*, to the more nuanced reflexive nature of animal–human relations evoked in *Fantastic Mr Fox* and *Grizzly Man*, and finally to the mythic and allegorical primal climate-change narrative around flooding and animal protection in *Noah*, to appreciating again the fear of our own animal nature and spirituality when faced with the ultimate lifeboat scenario in *Life of Pi* – all of these varying storylines serve up a number of interconnecting environmental and ethical hypotheses that certainly add to the growing corpus of eco-cinema and provide future avenues of ethical investigation. By any measure these are all very different filmic examples that speak to varying, often contradictory ethical agendas, which certainly cannot be easily cohered into a concluding synthesis around animals and environmental ethics. Nevertheless they each highlight ways of engaging with film and the representation of animals which deserve much more investigation and debate.

Notes

1 Other notions like zoomorphism that explore the extent to which the child is permitted to be animal-like is usually strictly circumscribed. 'Little angels, little devils, little monsters, children have to be led away from instinct and towards mastery, the mastery of objects, including themselves as bodies, and to that extent mastery over animals as objects' (Cubitt 2005: 30).

2 Note for instance 97 per cent of poultry, 97 per cent of pigs and 61 per cent of cattle raised in the US are raised in factory farms. Animals are crowded into confinement facilities that afford them no opportunity for healthy exercise; they are rarely given access to the world outside; they are mutilated in order to prevent them from injuring each other in the fights that inevitably result from overcrowding; and they are given a constant supply of antibiotics designed to prevent infections caused by their atrocious living conditions (in Dunn 2014: 233).

3 'Perhaps hunting also violates the animal's autonomy, at least at the moment when its life is taken from it without permission. But that's just a moment – not a disrespectful, dominating relationship that lasts a lifetime. We don't need a neural cue to recognise that we owe our fellow creatures much better than that' (Yuen in Dunn 2014: 236).

4 A eulogy to horses which were viciously destroyed by machine technology in the First World War – drawing analogies of course with the way humans were also slaughtered in the trenches.

5 Environmental ethicists such as Callicott classically fall into the naturalistic fallacy when they attempt to justify practices such as hunting by claiming they reaffirm human participation in nature (Callicott 1992: 56).

6 'He will know the ikran he is meant to bond with on sight – and he will know that the ikran chooses him too if the ikran fights back and tries to kill him. It is Jake's duty, while the animal fights him off, to "bond" with the animal by overpowering him, tying him up, climbing on top of him'. Such a relationship with an animal explicitly insinuates a very unjust power regime.

7 'Ever since Muybridge and his zoopraxiscope began the tradition of creating and diffusing novel ways of looking at animals, the human gaze(r) has become more and more vicarious, more and more pleased at its own omnipowerful intrusion into the world of animals ("the wilderness, or nature, or the jungle": however we construe what is ultimately just a backdrop, a set, a tableau, for the dazzling human action that takes place in the foreground)' (Malamud 2012: 18).

8 Bron Taylor who has written extensively about dark-green religion suggests that 'radical environmentalists believe postapocalyptic life will resemble traditional indigenous lifeways' (Erb 2014: 8) and how this might coalesce with the ritual characteristics of deep ecology, recalls the famous 'Council of All Beings' (a ritual devised by Joanna Macy and John Seed) and designed to help participants alter consciousness by assuming the identities of nonhuman beings – imagining their perspective on the environment' (Erb 2014: 10).

9 Furthermore, in *Green Cultural Studies: Nature in Film, Novel and Theory* (1995) Jhan Hochman warns that nature films may render viewers 'separate and superior to film-nature, even as it brings them into apparent proximity. Nature becomes, then, prop(erty) and commodity' (cited in Malamud 2012: 18). But at least one could argue such exposure may stretch the ethical imagination of some of its audiences.

10 The Home Tree Initiative was initiated by Twentieth Century Fox Home Entertainment together with Earth Day Network, see http://www.earthday.org/avatarm, accessed July 26 2011.

11 When viewed in isolation from other cultural factors, other children's classics and environmental animations, like *Finding Nemo,* appear to be more ecologically sound than for instance B*ambi*. According to Brucker 'it distributes environmental responsibility more widely than the earlier film, which places all blame on hunters alone. Yet both films have generated a "syndrome" or "effect", pointing to their cultural impact. The "Bambi effect" is its wholesale indictment of hunting and its sentimental adoration of woodland creatures. The "Nemo syndrome" refers to its promotion of naïve ethical solutions, such as releasing captive nature into the "wild", in this case by flushing the fish down the drain and into the ocean' (Brucker in Willoquet-Maricondi 2010: 188).

12 The role of fathers and the significance of fatherhood is a driving principle in the majority of Anderson's films (see Gooch 2007), particularly fatherhood as a performed social identity (Peberdy 2012: 60).

13 What counts for tampering with nature? A beaver builds a dam and changes the river flow. Is it therefore an environmental terrorist? Of course not. But what if we build dams to generate electricity or protect low-lying regions from floods? See, for instance, Baggini and Fosl (2010).

14 Incidentally so as not to have the kids totally shocked by their innate animal nature, the film never actually shows them killing the chickens. This is the ultimate taboo and not seen as necessary for the anthropomorphically stylish story, unlike the X-rated Zombie killers who have come to dominate our screens of late; they just do it naturally. Consequently there is no need to focus on the explicit violence of hunting for food.

15 The fox as a prototypical stereotypical alpha-male adventurer needs to connect with the excitement and danger of his innate animal nature and consequently outsmarts his human enemies. 'We're all wild animals, I guess', the wife admits. 'I always was', Mr Fox affirms.

16 But despite the long history of animal performers, from *Rescued by Rover* to *Babe*, it is the animated film that animals have come to take their strongest position in the media. Drawn images of animals are among the first records that distinguish the presence of humans (Cubitt 2005: 26).

17 It must be admitted that for all its potential to enable effective, non-elitist political action, irony can also make for inaction, for smug armchair environmentalism or even slacker apathy (Seymour in Weik von Mossner 2014: 74).

18 According to William Cronon (1996: 69), 'for many Americans, wilderness stands as the last remaining place where civilisation, that all too human disease, has not fully infected the earth'. Or as Neil Evernden (1992: 116) points out; 'through our conceptual domestication of nature, we extinguish wild otherness even in the imagination'.

19 Of course there is a whole list of 'anti-establishment' Hollywood films, which this classic calls to mind – none more so than *Fight Club* (1999) with its treatise on anti-establishment and anti-consumer values.

20 See for instance the allegory set up in *Mosquito Coast,* which explicitly plays out such tropes. Dangerous but essential missionary work, together with the missionary zeal to enter the wild was built upon a conception of the New World that sprang from the Old Testament (Henry in Willoquet-Maricondi 2010: 177).

21 A (primitive but very potent) GMO seed organism if ever there was.

22 For instance looking at a graph regarding global penetration of religions across the planet: Christians 33 per cent; Muslims 20 per cent; Hindus 13 per cent; Buddhists 6 per cent; Jews 0.2 percent; atheists 2.4 per cent.

23 Lorne Dawson has distilled some key features of new forms of religion to include 'a pronounced individualism' encapsulating religions of 'intense experience over doctrine and belief'. While notions of dualism are often rejected between West and East – 'focusing on the interconnected nature of spirit and matter' (cited in Erb 2014: 5).

24 The original book was published in 2001 and won the Booker prize in 2002, and considered unfilmable by many critics. In a report from *The Guardian*, 11 December 2012, we discover that Suraj Sharma was only just 17 when filming began and had just learned to swim. Furthermore, as a result of 227 days shoot, he suffered dramatic weight loss.

25 Incidentally, the film is constructed like *All is Lost* explored in Chapter 2, but covers a much longer time period and was filmed in a vast tank of water situated in an abandoned airport in Taiwan.

26 Religious scholar Stewart Elliott Gutherie's study *Faces in the Clouds* speaks of a human 'obsession with putting ourselves at the centre of everything', which is the very foundation of religiosity. See for instance the representation of Richard Parker [the tiger] being the ultimate example of a more reflexive form of anthropomorphism.

Bibliography

Adams C.J. (1990/2003) *The Sexual Politics of Meat: A Feminist-Vegetarian Critical Theory*. New York: Continuum.

Baggini, Julian and Fosl, Peter (2010). *The Philosopher's Toolkit: A Compendium of Philosophical Concepts and Methods*. Oxford: Wiley-Blackwell.

Bate, Jonathan (1998) 'Poetry and Biodiversity', in Richard Kerridge and Neil Sammell (eds), *Writing the Environment: Ecocriticism and Literature*. London: Zed Books.

Berger, John (1977) *Why Look at Animals?* Great Ideas series. London: Penguin.

Berger, John (1980) *About Looking*. London: Pantheon Books.

Bleakley, Alan (2000) *The Animalizing Imagination: Totemism, Textuality and Ecocriticism*. Basingstoke: Palgrave Macmillan.

Bouse, D. (2009) *Wildlife Films*. Philadelphia, PA: University of Pennsylvania Press.

Brereton, Pat (2005) *Hollywood Utopia: Ecology in Contemporary American Cinema*. Bristol: Intellect Press.

Callicott, J. Baird (1992). 'Rolston on Intrinsic Value, a Deconstruction'. *Environmental Ethics* 14: 129–43

Clark, Timothy (2010) 'Towards a Deconstructive Environmental Criticism'. *Oxford Literary Review* 30(1): 44–68.

Cole, Stewart (2004) 'Believing in Tigers: Anthropomorphism and Incredulity in Yann Martel's *Life of Pi*. *Studies in Canadian Literature / Études en littérature canadienne* (29)2 https://journals.lib.unb.ca/index.php/SCL/article/view/12747/13692

Cronin, Paul (2002) *Herzog on Herzog*. London: Faber and Faber.

Cronon, W. (1996) *Uncommon Ground: Rethinking the Human Place in Nature*. New York: Norton.

Cubitt, Sean (2005) *Ecomedia*. Amsterdam: Rodophi.

Donovan, Josephine (2006) 'Feminism and the Treatment of Animals: From Care to Dialogue'. *Signs* 31(2) 305–329.

Donovan, Josephine and Adams, Carol J. (1997). *The Feminist Care Tradition in Animal Education: A Reader*. New York: Columbia University Press.

Dorey, Tom (2011) 'Fantastic Mr Filmmaker: Paratexts and the Positioning of Wes Anderson as Roald Dahl's Cinematic Heir'. *New Review of Film and Television Studies* 10(1): 169–85.

Drenthen, Martin (2009)'Wildness in Contemporary Film'. *Environmental Ethics* 31(3): 297–315.

Dunn, George A. (2014)] *Avatar and Philosophy: Learning to See*. Chichester: John Wiley and Sons.

Erb, Cynthia (2014) 'A Spiritual Blockbuster: *Avatar*, Environmentalism and the New Religion'. *Journal of Film and Video* 66(3): 3–17.

Evernden, Neil (1996) *The Social Creation of Nature*. London: The Johns Hopkins University Press.

Fossey, D. (1983) *Gorillas in the Mist*. Boston, MA: Houghton Mifflin Company.

Garrard, G. (2012) *Ecocriticism*. London: Routledge.

Gilligan, Carol (1982) *In A Different Voice: Psychological Theory and Women's Development*. Cambridge, MA: Harvard University Press.

Gooch, Joshua (2007) 'Making a Go of It: Paternity and Prohibition in the Films of Wes Anderson'. *Cinema Journal* 47(1): 26–48.

Gutherie, S.E. (1993) *Faces in the Clouds: A New Theory of Religion*. New York: Oxford University Press.

Hochman, J. (1995) *Green Cultural Studies: Nature in Film, Novel and Theory*. Moscow, ID: University of Idaho Press.

Holland, Norman N. (2003) 'The Willing Suspension of Disbelief: A Neuro-psychoanalytic View'. *PsyArt* http://www.psyartjournal.com/article/show/n_holland-the_willing_suspension_of_disbelief_a_ne

Ingram, D. (2000) *Green Screen: Environmentalism and Hollywood Cinema*. Exeter: University of Exeter Press.

Keyes, M.T. and McGillicuddy, A. (eds) (2014) *Politics and Ideology in Children's Literature*. Dublin: Four Courts Press.

Lapinski, Mike (2005) *Death in the Grizzly Male: The Timothy Treadwell Story*. Guilford CT: Falcon.

Leopold, Aldo (1949) *A Sand County Almanac and Sketches Here and There*. Oxford: Oxford University Press.

Lorimer, Jamie (2010) 'Moving Image Methodologies for More-Than-Human Geographies'. *Cultural Geographies* 17(2): 237–58.

Malamud, R. (2012) *An Introduction to Animals and Visual Culture*. Palgrave Macmillan.

Marks, Laura (2000) *The Skin in the Game*. Durham NC: Duke University Press.

Midgley, Mary (1983) *Animals and Why they Matter: A Journey Around the Species Barrier*. Harmondsworth: Penguin.

Millais, C. (2006) *Common Belief: Australia's Faith Communities on Climate Change*. Sydney: Climate Institute.

Murphy, Patrick (1991) 'Ground, Pivot, Motion: Ecofeminist Theory, Dialogics and Literary Practice'. *Hypatia* 6(1): 147–61.

Noys, Benamin (2007) 'Antiphusis: Werner Herzog's *Grizzly*' http://www.film-philosophy.com/2007v11n3/noys.pdf

Peberdy, Donna (2012) 'I'm Just a Character in Your Film: Acting and Performance from Autism to Zizzou'. *New Review of Film and Television* 10(1): 4–67.

Plumwood, Val. (1999) 'Being Prey' in D. Rothenberg and M. Ulvaeus (eds) *The New Earth Reader. The Best of Terra Nova*. Cambridge, MA: MIT Press.

Plumwood, Val (n.d.) 'Prey to a Crocodile'. http://www.aislingmagazine.com/aislingmagazine/articles/TAM30/ValPlumwood.htm

Posas, Paula J. (2007) 'Roles of Religion and Ethics in Addressing Climate Change'. *Ethics in Science and Environmental Politics ESEP* 2007: 31–49.

Raju, Trishanya (2013) 'Feminism and the Treatment of Animals'. https://prezi.com/vu-nq2w4kyz4/feminism-and-the-treatment-of-animals/

Reagan, Tom (1991) *The Three Generations: Reflections on the Coming Revolution*. Philadelphia, PA: Temple University Press.

Rollins, E. (2004) 'Animal Agriculture and Emerging Social Ethics for Animals'. *Journal of Animal Science* 82(3): 955–64.

Rolston, H. (1994) 'Winning and Losing in Environmental Ethics', in Frederick Ferre and Peter Hartel (eds) *Ethics and Environmental Policy: Theory meets Practice*. Athens, GA: University of Georgia Press.

Ruether, Rosemary Radford (1975) *New Woman, New Earth*. New York: Seabury Press,

Schutten, Julie Kalil (2008) 'Chewing, *Grizzly Man*: Getting to the Meat of the Matter'. *Environmental Communication* 2(2): 193–211.

Singe, Peter (1975) *Animal Liberation*. New York: Avon Books.

Sobchak, Vivian (1982) *The Address of the Eye: A Phenomenology of Film Experiences*. Princeton NJ: Princeton University Press.

Spiegel, Majorie (1988) *The Dreaded Comparison: Human and Animal Slavery*. Gabriola Island, Canada: Mirror Books.

Taylor, Bron (ed) (2013) *Avatar and Nature Spirituality.* Waterloo, Canada: Wilfrid Laurier University Press.

Totaro, Donata (2002) 'Deleuzian Film Analysis: The Skin of Film'. *OffScreen* 6(6). http://www.horschamp.qc.ca/new_offscreen/skin.html

Weik von Mossner, Alexa (ed) (2014) *Moving Environments: Affect, Emotion, Ecology and Film.* Waterloo, Canada: Wilfrid Laurier University Press.

White, John W. (2008) 'On Werner Herzog's Documentary *Grizzly Man*: Psychoanalysis, Nature and Meaning'. *Fast Capitalism* 4(1). http://www.uta.edu/huma/agger/fastcapitalism/4_1/white.html

Willoquet-Marcondi, Paula (2010) *Framing the World: Explorations in Ecocriticism and Film.* Charlottsville, VA: University of Virginia Press.

6

THIRD WORLD INJUSTICE, ENVIRONMENTAL SUSTAINABILITY AND FRUGALITY

A case study of contemporary Hollywood films set in Africa

Overview

This chapter will frame an analysis of *Koyannsqatsi, Powaqqatsi* alongside *The Constant Gardener* around representations of Africa, while signalling a renewed interest and engagement with environmental justice issues.[1] As Frederick Ferre affirms 'we need to learn in new modes of ethical holism, what organic interconnectedness means for human persons' (in Attfield and Belsey 1994: 237). These readings follow this general lead, while also endorsing and proselytising for the primary environmental ethic around a moral attitude and respect for nature. All the while, critical commentators rightly question how the West can expect the extremely disadvantaged Third World to give up the possibility of acquiring some of the luxuries and benefits which the rich industrialised world enjoy, irrespective of the overall ecological cost to planet earth. While some well-meaning commentators have gone so far as to assert that global poverty is too large a problem to be solvable, without destroying *our* way of life, which in turn reinforces Western impotence towards extreme poverty. Meanwhile, astute critics and academics, including Thomas Pogge and Naomi Klein, have effectively demonstrated the inherent fault-lines within such a thesis. By all accounts these examples have moved a long way from exemplifying crude colonialist and imperialist agendas and speak to a more fruitful post-colonialist and I would add a distinctly environmental and ethical agenda.

Introduction

The language of environmental sustainability is seeping into what would otherwise be considered as establishment thinking and in many ways is beginning to become accepted as part of the common global cultural discourse. The films discussed in this chapter call attention to how Ferre's (1996) notion of 'ethical holism' might apply to the polarising levels of injustice evident in African cinema, all the while endorsing Paul Taylor's (1981) primary environmental ethic of a 'moral attitude of respect for nature'. At the same time, developing countries like those in Africa urgently require more immediate poverty and primary health-care issues to be addressed. The danger of ethical environmental sustainability becoming a somewhat meaningless universal edict, while at the same time appealing to populist, business-driven interpretative notions, around 'universal sustainability' – recalling well-established mantras around 'corporate social responsibility' – is exacerbated, of course, by the conflicting directions and often contradictory objectives evident across the broad-based ecological movement.

Furthermore, appeals to Third World countries *not* to go down the path of exponential economic growth and further promote wasteful values of conspicuous consumption, naturally produces a negative reaction. Indigenous people naturally don't like being denied the prospect of securing a lifestyle and standard of living long enjoyed by the rich First World, even if this is considered unsustainable and harmful, when taking into account the environmental influence of such oil-based wealth on global climate change. Appeals to various forms of austerity and frugality, as the most appropriate long-term strategy to maintain a healthy environment, remain a very difficult proposition to contemplate, much less actively encourage, when the majority of the people in such countries are below the internationally defined poverty line. Feeding off these contradictions and paradoxes, the filmic examples explored in this chapter strive to put flesh on some of these debates and concerns while focusing on ethical and environmental issues.

At the outset, it must be stated, however, that the long-established tradition of Hollywood films set in Africa, use the continent to tell a white and Western story, while also reaffirming, at one extreme, the colonial archetype of Africans not being able to live peacefully, much less achieve economic self-sufficiency, while often wallowing in internecine wars. This chapter signals how a more productive environmental, ethical and even revisionist reading of a number of seminal (Hollywood) African films might be made, beginning with *Koyannsqatsi/Powaqqatsi* and later focusing on *The Constant Gardener*.

Outside the scope of this chapter, there is a growing literature emanating from African scholars around indigenous African-produced films, which capture the complexity of the different socio-political, as well as tribal and cultural influences that have certainly shaped the continent's filmic output.[2] At the same time, however, there is also an increasing number of American and to a lesser extent European-financed 'African' films that have become popular in the West. Inevitably, commentators have often dismissed such Western-facing films as embodying a new form of cultural imperialism, designed to swallow up indigenous production. Nonetheless, even if there was much truth in this proposition, such films at the same time continue to play a significant role in shaping Western attitudes towards Africa.

The range of environmental ethical topics explored in this chapter include: deforestation, medical experimentation and over-population, all of which are reflected and (re)presented within a postcolonial African environment and filmic space. The language of eco-sustainability, for instance, is seeping into what would otherwise be considered as establishment thinkers and in many ways is beginning to become explored as part of the common global culture. Meanwhile, as already asserted, developing countries like those in Africa urgently require more immediate poverty and primary health-care issues to be addressed.

At a more theoretical level and crudely articulated through the literature, many postcolonial theorists have somewhat resisted American-bred environmentalism and eco-criticism with its apparent negation of race and class, while more positively appropriating and valorising [Western] gendered values for instance, as evidenced through the growth of eco-feminism discussed in an earlier chapter. In an African context, phrases like 'sustainable development' often tend to conjure up nineteenth-century colonialist ideologies and fantasies of the 'white man's burden', which in turn are further used to justify exploitation in these former colonies. In essence much of the critical discourse around environmental sustainability and ethics tends to emanate from a rich Western mindset.[3] How to re-formulate or re-fashion such concepts and themes across the world, while addressing more elemental global injustice and poverty concerns, remains a challenge for effective critical analysis.

Ramachandra Guha (1989) for instance has diagnosed this new form of neo-colonialism, which he dubs 'green imperialism', in which First World wilderness preservationists, biologists and deep ecologists have established wildlife preserves in Third World countries, effectively removing and cutting off native inhabitants from vital natural resources. According to Guha, deep ecology, which stresses the interrelationship of humans and nature is an ideological driver of this movement. Guha goes so far as to define deep ecology as a philosophy that elevates 'nature' – itself a human construct – above the human, which could in turn lead to negative social consequences. Furthermore, in *A Critique of Postcolonial Reason*, Spivak criticises notions of sustainable development promoted by global institutions like the World Bank. She asks most pointedly, 'development to sustain what?' (Spivak 1999: 373).

The long-established tradition of Hollywood films set in Africa is similarly critiqued and almost always appears to use the continent to tell a white and Western story. From Compton Bennett and Andrew Marton's *King Solomon's Mines* (1950) to Sydney Pollack's *Out of Africa* (1985), the very conventional evocation of exotic (primitive) landscape is well framed to promote this prospect and is especially evident in this latter multiple Oscar winner. *Out of Africa* begins by affirming its colonial discourse, while also referencing a clear example of environmental sustainability; 'I had a farm in Africa, at the foot of the Ngong Hills' (Blixen 1997: 3), and in Blixon's attempt to find true love, embodied by the big game hunter Hatton, she eventually realises that he, like Africa, is 'impossible to tame' (see Brereton 2013). The pace of this romantic travelogue is rather slow, reflecting Blixen's book and further encapsulated by the line: 'natives dislike speed, as *we* dislike noise'. Meanwhile, more contemporary urban-based narratives like *Tsotsi* certainly cannot be accused of being slow.

First versus second wave eco-criticism

What is often referred to as the 'first wave' of eco-criticism – or as it is sometimes described 'eco-localism'– has in the eyes of many practitioners today, outlived its usefulness (Weik von Mossner and Irmscher 2012). This movement was marked by a concern with place or 'emplacement' and remained heavily focused on literary texts (and mostly Anglophone ones, to boot). In this first wave, critics read such texts for what they contributed towards a decentring of the human subject, for their attentiveness to the pitfalls of anthropocentric thinking. One could argue early forays into the African topography conformed to this first-wave mindset.

The second wave – which by all accounts has not yet become dominant – grew out of dissatisfaction with the first wave's mystification of the human subject and, for that matter, nature. Informed by postcolonialist, feminist and queer studies, as well as most significantly recognising demands for social justice, second wavers have shed the obsession of first wavers with wilderness and substituted for it a concern with 'networks' or systems of relationships that span urban as well as rural spaces, black as well as white selves, women as well as men and in a particularly interesting recent development, children (see Dobrin and Kidd 2004).

Instead of justice for nature, the cherished preoccupation of conservationist first-wavers, the new environmental critics find themselves calling for justice for people *and* nature. This ideological turn remains particularly pertinent when reading Third World filmic narratives, while implying at the outset that the newly formed eco-cinema studies has ridden on the coat-tails of the more well-established literary eco-criticism and thereby remains somewhat underdeveloped. Nonetheless, the trajectory of output around eco-film criticism continues to flit between these two polarities. Furthermore, I would suggest, there is no clear break between the two waves; as 'nature worship' remains a foundational aspect of many eco-film responses, even those calling on more explicit forms of environmental justice concerns, as discussed in this chapter. From the exotic, yet frugal evocation of life and nature in *Koyaanisqatsi*, to more conventional romantic evocations of nature and landscape in *The Constant Gardener*, alongside the dystopic fantasies such as *District 9*; all these narratives are tinged with a pervasive real-life valorising and critique of environmental justice issues, from an African perspective.

As Buell reminds us in *The Future of Environmental Criticism* (2005), 'the factors that define a bioregion are transnational and even global' (Buell 2005: 89). We must keep in mind how these factors have changed as a result of colonial expansion and neoliberal globalisation. Furthermore, in her influential *Sense of Place and Sense of Planet,* Heise points to 'the challenge that deterritorialisation poses for the environmental imagination' (Heise 2008: 10). The global always pervades and informs the local, argues Heise, and we must thus learn to combine more abstract and transnational modes of understanding with traditional and place-based knowledge in ways that are complementary and productive, rather than mutually exclusive. In the case studies that follow, we will signal how the local and the global cross-connect and how such tensions might speak to a more inclusive form of environmental ethics.

Precautionary principle and the valorising of frugality within postcolonial Africa

In a chapter titled 'Carrying Capacity and Ecological Economics', Mark Sagoff (1997) illustrates how early environmentalists such as Henry David Thoreau cited the intrinsic properties of nature rather than its economic benefits, as reasons to preserve it. It was believed that economic activity had outstripped not just its resource base but also its spiritual purpose. John Muir (1988) particularly condemned the 'temple destroyers, devotees of ravaging commercialism', who 'instead of lifting their eyes to the God of the mountains, lift them to the Almighty dollar. This condemnation certainly was not simply a call for improved cost-benefit analysis. Nineteenth-century environmentalists saw nature as full of divinity and regarded its protection less as a prescribed prima facia economic imperative than as a moral test' (Sagoff 1997: 28).

Some contemporary left-leaning environmental economists believe that sources of raw materials and sinks for waste (what are called natural capital) are fixed and therefore limit the potential growth of the global economy. They reject the idea that 'technology and resource substitution (ingenuity), can continuously outrun depletion and pollution'. Growth certainly faces limits, Herman E. Daly has written, and to 'delude ourselves into believing that growth is still possible, if only we label it "sustainable" or colour it "green", will just delay the inevitable transition and make it more painful' (Daly 1997: 28). This economic and environmental debate remains particularly pertinent in many under-developed and resource-depleted Third World countries in Africa.

Sagoff criticises various principles concerning the carrying capacity of the earth, recalling discussions around lifeboat environmental ethics, which is a core theme across several chapters in this overview. 'The first is that entropy limits economic growth. Second, mainstream economists believe, and history confirms, that knowledge, ingenuity, or invention – the formal sources of production – find ways around shortages in raw materials by increasing reserves, substituting between resource flows, or making resources go further.' Finally, Sagoff affirms, ecological economists offer a precautionary principle that 'counsels us to play it safe, but supplying little instruction about what that actually means. As a historical axiom, however, human beings have found it safer to control and manipulate nature than to accept it on its own terms.' This series of propositions certainly are evident on the ground in most Third World countries. The central principle of ecological economics – 'the concept of carrying capacity – however fails to show that economic growth is unsustainable' (Sagoff 1997: 45).

Even if Sagoff's conclusion was accurate, at the same time 'real' economic and social poverty cannot be ignored or forgotten in this global environmental challenge. Some therefore consider the rise of an environmental conservationist discourse as somewhat of a luxury – similar in ways to the proliferation of postmodernist discourses in the Western academy from the 1960s. Thomas W. Pogge in 'A Global Resources Dividend' (1997) strongly contends that the one great challenge to any morally sensitive person today is the extent and severity of global poverty. Hundreds of millions are born into abject poverty and remain poor, dependent and uneducated all their lives (Pogge 1997: 501). It is important therefore to take on board how the rich West bears a heavy responsibility for world poverty, by participating in its unjust perpetuation, while at the same time moving towards embracing more long-term notions of environmental sustainability.

As already asserted, it is often glibly pointed out that global/African poverty is too large a problem to be solvable, without destroying the Western way of life; which in turn serves to reinforce Western impotence towards extreme poverty. There remains a thin line between the ethics of poverty *per se* and the call for environmental ethics, as it relates to various forms of poverty and injustice. But for the purposes of this chapter such divisions are simply unhelpful. Naomi Klein (2007) – and most recently in *This Changes Everything: Capitalism vs The Climate* (2014) – has also effectively demonstrated the inherent faultlines within this thesis. Put most simply, poverty and ecological ethical problems remain a worldwide phenomenon and must be tackled globally as well as locally.

In particular reframing this global dilemma that is represented in this chapter, we must pose the question, where can we position and place the relative environmental resource wealth of postcolonial nations like those of Africa, against the awful economic poverty of many of its citizens? The option of nostalgically reverting back to a prelapsarian, frugal, agricultural-based mono-economy is certainly not a practical, if even a desirable, alternative for many of its people who continue to live in a 'feudal/primitive' rural-based way. Choosing between a poverty-ridden past and present, as against the prospect of accepting the inherent dangers in a (post)colonial and capitalist-driven market economy, appears to be the only option.

At the same time, recognising the paradoxical dangers, I would still pose the questions, how can culture and society use the beneficial attributes embedded within the notion of resilience and 'frugality' (as further outlined in Chapter 7), as a core foundational and ethically just starting point, towards helping to sustain a more progressive model for future environmental development, beyond a continuing fixation with a drive for ever-increasing gross national product

(GNP) and general capital accumulation, as a kneejerk antidote for all human and environmental problems. This preoccupation with frugality and 'going back to nature' to discover the inherent ontological and metaphysical 'truth of life' remains a core back-story for much of the environmental engagement in the narratives discussed in this volume.

Nash (1997) for instance argues in 'On the Subversive Virtue: Frugality', that this notion is one of the most interesting and largely unexamined issues in modern morality, citing the demotion of frugality as a personal and social norm.[4] Essentially, as already suggested, the concept of frugality can be understood as rejecting the popular assumption that humans are insatiable creatures, ceaselessly acquisitive for economic gains and egotistically committed to pleasure maximisation. Such counter-intuitive assertions to the hegemonic Western mindset are seldom expressed outside of a very fundamentalist religious, or alternatively a deep ecological or spiritual, sensibility. Second, according to Nash, frugality serves as a bulwark against, and resistance to, the temptation of consumer promotionalism, particularly the ubiquitous nature of advertising that pressurises us through sophisticated techniques to want more, bigger, better, faster, newer, more attractive, or state-of-the-art products. Third, frugality involves a struggle against the various psychological and sociological dynamics, beyond market promotionalism, that stimulate over-consumption. Fourth, ethically conscious frugality is a rejection of the prevailing ideology of indiscriminate, material economic growth (Nash 1997: 420). The readings that follow call to mind such categories and issues and can be at least tangentially applied to the narratives under discussion.

Ecological sustainability and dealing with extreme poverty

Molly Scott Cato's 2012 paper 'The Freedom to be Frugal' cites Amartya Sen's (2001) *Development as Freedom*, who provides a powerful case for his 'capability approach' to poverty, suggesting that the inability to function in society is the best marker for a clear definition of poverty. 'Poverty' he says 'must be seen as the deprivation of basic capabilities rather than merely as lowness of incomes'. Traditional economists, Cato affirms, perceive the economic system as being like a peach in the Roald Dahl story *James and the Giant Peach,* implying it will simply expand forever, while we sit on its ever-expanding skin, enjoying the sunshine and munching to our hearts' content. Such an analogy evokes a cautionary tale concerning a deep ecological ethic. Meanwhile, the broad church of environmental thinkers remains consistently opposed to much indiscriminate growth, because they recognise that planet earth is a closed system. 'Growth must face the limits imposed by that system, whether they become apparent via resource depletion or the overloading of the natural environment with waste products' (Cato 2012: 48).

As a consequence, we certainly need to challenge assumptions about human happiness and wellbeing being built on expediential economic growth and consumption. If, as Sen suggests, development is about freedom, then we must not forget the Brundtland definition of sustainability and must respect the freedom of future generations to meet their own needs. We must also strive to free ourselves from the advertising industry's view of what constitutes an acceptable level of consumption and be spared its endless cycle of new market creation. Market advertising remains a particular cause for concern in Third World countries like in Africa, as much as in the West, as evident for instance by the proliferation of advertising hoardings in the city space of a film like *Tsotsi*. A strategy and dilemma for so-called 'green marketers' involves trying to grapple with human needs and desires, while at the same time promoting restricted forms of growth and consumption. According to Cato, this would represent a move towards development as emancipation and away from oppressive economic structures and the ideologies that perpetuate them (Cato 2012: 53). Much work is needed however to explore such abstract theorising.

The environmental critique of the concept of growth is defined most clearly by *The Growth Illusion* (1992), where Richard Douthwaite makes the point that excessive growth creates feedback systems that undermine the quality of life that we are seeking to enhance and hence becomes self-defeating. While this may not appear to be a particular problem for the Third World, which is generally at a different stage in its economic cycle of development than those nation-states in the West, nonetheless the pervasive drive towards short-term economic growth, at the expense of other long-term environmental concerns also pervades the majority philosophy of Africa, alongside the West. In a later paper, Douthwaite argues that there are different kinds of growth and lists conditions that economic activity should meet for it to be considered 'good growth'. These include economic activity that does not rely on increased use of energy or raw materials and transport and has a neutral impact on waste production and pollution (Douthwaite 1999).

Most frequently dystopian science fiction fantasies serve up a cautionary tale around what happens if societies are not promoting 'good growth' much less sustainability, by not treating all its inhabitants equitably and not allocating its scarce resources evenly across its inhabitants for the long-term security of the environment. Such a cautionary tale analysis is most specifically explored in *Koyaanisqatsi*.

According to E.F. Schumacher, 'for every activity there is a certain appropriate scale, and the more active and intimate the activity, the smaller the number of people that can take part' (1973: 64). Green economists argue that while a market economy may generate higher levels of output, it will not operate at the appropriate scale in the long term to exist in balance with its environment. This understanding is diametrically opposed to the neoclassical concept of 'economies of scale', which according to green political economists must be subordinated to considerations of environmental impact; otherwise 'economies of scale may increase the scale of the economy beyond which the environment can sustainably support' (Barry 1999).

But while various levels of proselytising and economic theorising are useful to help lay some clear foundations for business and (post)colonial enterprise, real life experiences and representational frameworks posit more conflicted meanings and agendas. These can be framed against the ever-present 'realos versus fundis' debates within the environmental movement, essentially calling on deep divisions between Platonic idealism and pragmatic realism, recalling the dominance of utilitarian ethics. The success of the sustainability movement demands that we in the West, as well as those in the so-called Third World, together with all other very powerful economic and environmental systems of management across the world, change not only our varying modes of behaviour, but also the way we think about nature in all its manifestations, while adapting a more effective stewardship role for humans on the planet. This is a big ask and we are a long way from achieving it, but film as a representative 'creative imaginary' can at least sow the seeds and help point the way. Africa most certainly serves as a laboratory for a range of contested discourses. Godfrey Reggio's powerfully evocative series of films, which we will now turn to, helps to dramatise some of these radical possibilities.

Koyaanisqatsi and *Powaqqatsi*: dramatising First and Third World modalities and environmental ethics

Films that represent Africa have a particular ecological purchase on many of these ethical debates discussed above, as they foreground concerns around sustainability, the precautionary principle and most particularly how best to live a frugal/sustainable life. The avant-garde eco-classic *Koyaanisqatsi* and its sequel *Powaqqatsi* set the scene for some of these ethical agendas and help frame a more in-depth analysis of *The Constant Gardener*; all of these tales help our understanding and engagement with environmental and ethical justice issues, especially as it applied to a Third World society as in Africa.

The growth of civilisation has affected the balance of nature, which has still proved capable of discovering products that would enable nature's original and beneficial intentions to triumph. *Koyaanisqatsi* (1983), meaning a state of life that calls for another way of living, as in the Hopi Indian language, alongside its sequel *Powaqqatsi* (1988), are probably in my opinion the most artistic and explicitly deep ecological provocative discourses captured on film. The opening of the latter begins with a sequence in which a group of Africans struggle to move immense quantities of fine grey dust in sacks. Gibson in a review in *Film Bulletin* recalls the aforementioned tensions between so-called first- and second-wave environmentalism when he asserts:

> The film contrasts scenes of Asia, India, the Middle East and South America with sequences set especially in Paris and Berlin. While the rich west is shot using a 'pointless' speeded up image construction; the

desperate and victimised Third World is nevertheless still represented as strangely graceful, noble and purposeful in its simplicity.

(Gibson 1998)

The director lived an ascetic life until he was 28 as part of a strict religious community and has been mostly lauded for his aesthetic originality. The power of Reggio's imagery, according to MacDonald,

> is a function not so much of his subject matter but of the way in which the imagery is presented. His primary techniques of time-lapse and aerial photography make possible a critique of American culture and of the conventional cinematic depiction of it.
>
> (MacDonald 1993: 139)

While there is always the danger of romanticism and even patronising the exotic Third World environment, the director is well aware of such dangers and concerns. How such strategies are executed on film is most important. The director himself helpfully affirms a clear division between mainstream film and how it keeps nature and the environment in the background:

> one of the obvious things I noticed was that in most films the foreground was where the plot and characterisation took place, where the screenplay came in, and how you directed the photography. Everything was foreground; background (music included) basically supported characterisation and plot. So what I did was to try to eradicate all of the foreground of traditional film and take the background and give that the principle focus. We're not trying to look at buildings, masses of people, transportation, industrialisation as autonomous entities. Same thing with Nature; rather than seeing nature as something bad, something inorganic like a stone, we wanted to see it as having its own life form unanthromorphised, unrelated to human being, ... I was trying to show in nature the presence of a life form.
>
> (cited in MacDonald 1993: 140)

As suggested by MacDonald, Hollywood fictional film is often critiqued for being overly preoccupied with surfaces and the promotion of very clearly defined narrative structures, which call attention to heroic action and serve to de-limit or de-emphasise the representation of the environment in which the action is occurring. Alternatively, the readings in this volume (and earlier in *Hollywood Utopia* 2005) contest such broad aesthetic generalisations and ethical value judgements. It is particularly useful to road test this most provocative audiovisual experience that explicitly provokes a proactive ecological and environmental ethical response, as it creatively juxtaposes extensive 'found' images and scenes from around the world to create a series of montages and 'creative imaginaries' of our planet and its interconnecting habitats. Such sentiments help articulate a very deep ecological aesthetic. Rather than telling a conventional linear story, like in a piece of countrapuntal art, Reggio continuously juxtaposes beautifully composed photographic images, recalling nature documentary capturing found images from around the world, while demonstrating the busy nature of the urban built environment, as against 'raw wild nature', with its more human created beauty.

Koyaanisqatsi translates the three Hopi (eco-mythic and ethical) prophecies, which calls for another way of living, while helping to codify a very deep ecological and ethical agenda and a corresponding cautionary tale and allegorical warning around the dangers of conspicuous consumption. In turn, the valorising of nature is addressed in several of the films discussed in this volume, particularly those that speak to the dangers of natural disaster and extreme climate change discourse. These environmental tensions are directly cited at the end of the film:

- If we dig precious things from the land, we will invite disaster.
- Near the day of purification, there will be cobwebs spun back and forth in the sky.
- A container of ashes might one day be thrown from the sky, which could burn the land and boil the oceans.

Metaphors that evoke the cosmic risk of ecological disaster if humans tamper with the symbiotic balance of nature, particularly abound within the cultural expression of various so-called 'primitive' Indian tribes, and are also explored in Chapter 8 in particular, which examines 'end of the world' narratives. The landscape functions as a mnemonic, alive with particular meanings, upon which native Americans typically hang their sense of collective identity and environmental values. In Reggio's *oeuvre* this speaks for a certain notion of justice that has its own distinctive qualities, integrities and meanings.

Herbert Marcuse remains a champion of ecology and believed that not only did the degradation of nature affect the prospects of human survival, but also diminished human self-identity and worth. He argued for a new relationship between humanity and nature where

> the objective world would no longer be experienced in the context of aggressive acquisition, competition and defensive possession, and furthermore nature would become an environment in which human beings would be free to develop the specifically creative and aesthetic human faculties.
>
> (Marcuse cited in Dobson and Lucardie 1995)

Such radical countercultural ideals have acquired more mature filmic reality towards the end of the twentieth century, as especially projected through contemporary narratives like in Reggio's *oeuvre*.

The music of Philip Glass punctuates the various movements in *Koyaanisqatsi* which are signposted on the cover as: crazy life; life in turmoil; life disintegrating; life out of balance; and finally a state of life that call for another way of living. The non-linear mosaic/narrative begins by observing and framing images of sublime natural outcrops of rocks, water and canyons and then finding counterfunctional elements in the clouds above, as they roll and flow like water. Back on earth human intervention has created a tapestry of many colours and shapes of plants/ crops grown in rigidly symmetrical fields. But such invasive/intensive use of soil is strongly critiqued with the first close-up of a massive machine with the number 6 written in red on its front, which extracts coal or other deposits from the ground, followed by giant steel sculpture-like edifices of electricity pylons mapping the landscape below.

Reviewers tend to agree that Reggio uncovers the beauty and symmetry within such exploitation of the landscape (the nearest mainstream artist who comes closes to him might be Terrence Malick and *The Tree of Life* discussed in Chapter 8). For instance, smoke rising from a power station and other industrial complexes serving as iconic manifestations of industrial growth are largely filmed from above, dramatising its majestic integration into the skyline. Even an exploding atom bomb – the ultimate destructive force of human nature – creates a 'beautiful' organic mushroom shape in the sky. This is further counterpointed with a space shuttle – another more benevolent expression of human ingenuity and evidence of power over nature – blowing up and being slowly pulled back to earth by the force of gravity (as further explored in recent science fictional tales like *Gravity*).

The reality of such global environmental aspects of pollution is cogently dramatised through one of the first representations of humans in the landscape: a mother and child sunbathing. When the camera pulls out of a close-up of the scene, the mediated audience is exposed to the contextual squalor of a shanty type environment, which in turn dwarfs a massive factory complex, belching out its detritus from enormous chimneys and yet romanticised through aesthetic abstractions, a few frames earlier.

The pace and tenor of urban civilisation and the ethics of excessive growth, much critiqued in this volume, is effectively reflected using speeded-up cameras, which capture the abstraction yet alienation of such spatial configuration. For instance, the cars travelling both ways on the freeway at night with conventional streams of white and red lights flowing in opposite directions, are at another abstract level reminiscent of a giant organism with blood-like vessels traversing rhythmically through its expansive body. The earth and all the activity on the planet, including human movement, is reframed to be read like in a coherent holistic ecosystem and an expansive high-production-values nature documentary.

Meanwhile, lacking the visceral sensation of movement, the conspicuous consumption of rows upon rows of neatly ordered new cars – the ultimate manifestation of conspicuous consumption in the environment – are effectively counterpointed with static displays of destructive army tanks serving other more malevolent purposes, alongside the monotony and homogeneity of factory life, servicing a Fordist model of capitalist production. Such a radical montage and counterpointing evocation of the objectification and representation of nature is surprisingly reiterated by cultural critics Kevin Kelly, the West Coast and laissez-faire computer guru who contends that:

> The entire range of living matter on earth, from whales to viruses ... could be regarded as constituting a single living entity, capable of manipulating the earth's atmosphere to suit its overall needs and endowed with facilities and powers far beyond those of its constituent points.
>
> (Kelly 1994: 107)

While welcoming all this esoteric valorisation of Reggio's provocative ecological aesthetic, unfortunately this does not correspond with mass audience tastes and modalities of engagement with audiovisual media that inform the more mainstream selection of films for this volume. Nonetheless, as heretofore argued with regard to the avant-garde in general, such texts can more radically assist in reframing aesthetic possibilities and feed into cross-fertilising new modes of communicating environmental concerns across the mainstream (see Brereton 2012). Most conventional Hollywood output is less frequently so nuanced, or provocative, while also being driven by conventional narratives and nature identification tropes. Surprisingly few commercial films take either the time or the aesthetic risk of explicitly foregrounding nature, much less exploring and situating a range of global environmental and ethical debates. That being said, this volume will demonstrate the recalibration and growing preoccupation with environmental concerns that is happening in the mainstream. Maybe this is occurring simply through happenstance, together with a growing concern for the environment by audiences and citizens, which in turn is feeding into a broader range of narrative concerns, alongside a reframing of creative production practices. Either way, there is certainly a growing recognition, as evident in the narratives discussed – explicitly or implicitly, allegorically or metaphorically – around the need to urgently address and reframe human relations with and in nature and the environment before it is too late.

In particular the evolving language of eco-sustainability, while taking into account the exigencies of the precautionary principle focused around the ethical demands of environmental justice, is seeping into what would otherwise be considered as 'establishment' thinkers and in many ways is beginning to become accepted as part of the common global (Western) culture. These radical sentiments have even begun to seep into the form and content of Hollywood texts, including African-addressed ones like *The Constant Gardener*.

The Constant Gardener: a cautionary tale of Western environmental injustice

Directed by Fernando Meirelles and starring Ralph Fiennes (Justin Quayle), Rachel Weisz (Tessa) and Hubert Kounde (Dr Arlond Bluhm), the film is set in a remote area of northern Kenya, where activist Tessa Quayle is found brutally murdered. Tessa's companion, a doctor, appears to have fled the scene and the evidence points to a crime of passion. Like the director's earlier *City of God* (2002), the story is told using countless tributaries, according to a review by the late Roger Ebert in the *Chicago Sun-Times*, that at all flow together into a mighty narrative stream. This fragmented style is the best way to tell such a complex story – in both novel and movie – as it's not a logical exercise, beginning with mystery and ending in truth, while circling around an elusive conspiracy. 'Understand who the players are and how they are willing to compromise themselves, and you can glimpse cruel outlines beneath the public relations façade' (see Ebert 2005). By all accounts, this is very different from the male lead performances in *Out of Africa*. Justin Quayle essentially represents a bureaucrat who seems at first totally detached from such issues and is presented as the polar opposite of his feisty partner Tessa.

The original book and film clearly expose the dubious ethical practices of 'big pharma' in Africa, which serves as a shorthand for so much colonial exploitation and abuse of indigenous people and their innate natural resources. The fictional plot focuses on a corrupt drug company touting a supposed cure for tuberculosis.[5] Testing drugs on an extremely large and relatively poor African population, which has a much higher mortality rate than the West and presumably a less-developed medical regulatory system, plays into moral panics and abuses of the precautionary principle, where African subjects can be experimented on with less concern or legal culpability, than the erstwhile more litigious Western citizens.

There is a certain familiarity in this notion of the Western character embarking on a reluctant voyage through Africa revealing the darkness of the human soul, as suggested by critics like Alan Britton (2007: 97–99) who recall obvious connections with Marlowe's journey in Joseph Conrad's classic *Heart of Darkness*. Through Justin's eyes we witness the corruption of the pharmaceutical industry and at the same time revealing his wife's innocence. As an activist, Tessa sets out to prove the ethical abuse of power and medical misuse of drug experiments, using the poverty of African people as a ruse. For this she is apparently executed. 'As he re-traces and re-enacts her ultimate fate, Justin's crucial concluding insight is that individual lives matter' (Britton 2007) – a core-deep ethical lesson also learned by the main protagonist in *Tsotsi* that 'action has to take the place of introverted passivity, exemplified by his previous horticultural obsession' (Britton 2007). This rationale is a pervasive dilemma for erstwhile liberal Western heroes who must act on their principles, rather than just emotionally and cognitively engaging with injustice issues. Departing from the ambiguous ending of the book however, the film allows some form of justice and comeuppance to be visited upon the senior UK government official implicated in Tessa's death and neatly legitimates and concludes Justin's investigation, alongside his ethical rehabilitation from a Western imperialistic perspective.

This environmental-ethical reading develops an ontological 'right way of thinking and behaving' for an active and committed environmentalist. I will further draw upon a number of bonus features on the DVD of *The Constant Gardener* to illustrate this point of view and perspective, beginning with an extended scene not fully developed in the final version of the filmic release, but explored in a bonus feature titled, 'Haruma – play in Kibera'. This anthropological side-drama narrates an allegorical tale with three identically dressed native male youths in blue business suits, before going out to work – all talking in unison – while conversing with their mothers, who are equally uniformly attired, but in traditional costume. The subsequent HIV educational drama enacts how they lose their jobs after being tested HIV positive[6] and are about to be doubly victimised by being kicked out by their families for bringing shame and causing a deep stigma by catching this deadly virus.

'If you can't protect your bodies, you don't get my respect', their mothers enunciate in chorus. But the younger children present – who have the education and knowledge – tell their parents and elders not to reject their sons, repeating the educational mantra: 'only blood and unprotected sex can spread the virus'. The on-screen street audience watch in rapt attention and engagement with this health education morality play, self-consciously embedded within this otherwise escapist fictional story. The sequence ends surprisingly with a familiar cut-away motif of birds flying in unison, a trope that suggests a form of ecological connectivity, evident several times in this film and also in other African-American nature films. Humans urgently need to learn from nature and their environments and become cognisant of being part of the broad-based biotic eco-system; which in turn is as true for erstwhile poor and deprived Africans, as it is for so-called rich Westerners.

All the actors stand facing the audience breaking normal Hollywood diegetic modes of verisimiltude and thereby affirming the moral weight of the story. However, in the final broadcast version, this morality tale episode is unfortunately heavily truncated, leaving a more conventional Western-focused identification on the heavily pregnant Western activist Tessa, observing the spectacle as an outsider, while meeting up with her black doctor friend Arlond. The diegetic mini-morality tale, designed explicitly for indigenous audiences, is simply reframed as an exotic background through her sympathetic, albeit Western point of view. In other words the local teacherly register of the episode, which speaks directly to a need to environmentally educate natives around dealing with such a dangerous disease, is somewhat obfuscated for Western audiences and marginalised back into the background of the story, recalling MacDonald's critique of Western cinema through his analysis of Reggio's more progressive *oeuvre* cited earlier in the chapter. Unfortunately such mainstream and commercially-driven cinema is not always willing to compromise its primary narrative logic of producing heroic identification and emphasising active engagement for its primary Western audience. Alternatively, if some more creative risks were taken, the results might speak to a range of other audiences and interests. But at least the full bonus features as paratextual markers enables such dialogical filmic experiences to cross boundaries and take more aesthetic risks in evoking pro-filmic engagement with the material, while at the same time addressing a wider range of environmental and social issues (see Brereton 2012).

Another bonus feature which is equally useful in setting up a potential eco-ethical agenda is one titled 'Embracing Africa: Filming in Kenya'. Kibera, where the film is shot, is we are informed, a real-life suburb covering over 30 per cent of the total population of Nairobi. Apparently when scouting for locations, the crew recall their first visit and the uniqueness and spirit of the place, with statements amounting almost to a form of environmental essentialism. Recalling for instance E.O. Wilson's (1986) benevolent notion of 'biophilia', which suggests that because we evolved from nature, we still carry a part of nature in our hearts. This in turn precipitates our relationship with and ethical responsibilities to nature and our habitat, through the complexity of human–land relations. The feature affirms a particularly close linkage of indigenous people with their habitat, while at the same time valorising its unique touristic evocation of place.

Nonetheless, by using Blue Sky Films – a local Kenyan film company – the outside multinational crew apparently feel able to break down a range of 'cultural imperialist' barriers, all the while acknowledging and embracing the grounded sensitivities of local people. Yet at the same time, the film crew are also able to feature this exotic romantic landscape, especially the mountainous volcanic harsh landscape, described as being the 'end of nowhere'! Again such a useful bonus feature speaks to the erstwhile binarism of local as opposed to global concerns; and at least from a political economy and practical film-making perspective, serves to break down erstwhile postcolonial modes of filmmaking practice and mindsets. All the while such exposition at least implies a more 'bottom-up' and localised form of sustainable environmental ethics in representing Third World 'creative imaginaries', which may not necessarily counter the dominant Western modes of presentation, but at least serves to feed back such values into the mainstream.

For instance, Todd McGowan's provocative feminist reading in *Film-Philosophy.com* (2007) suggests that the film depicts the politicisation of Justin Quayle through a narrative structure that breaks from an everyday or ideological conception of time. Politicisation and ethical learning occurs, the reading implies, through an encounter with 'feminine enjoyment'; an encounter that transforms the subject's relationship to time and facilitates the subject's entrance into a non-ideological temporality, or what one might call a temporality of the real. Justin's romance with Tessa entails navigating her enjoyment with Africa, and the process of doing so alters his sense of time (just as it alters the narrative structure of the film itself) and transforms him into a political being.

Such an argument by McGowan remains pointed, if somewhat crude, in its over-valorising of the 'feminine principle', a concept which was implied in the earlier eco-feminist chapter and its close reading of figures like Katniss for example. Certainly, romance can become the vehicle for political awakening, as also evident more crudely in many Hollywood narratives. But such a shorthand explanation remains simply a generic convention to enable or entice mass audiences to again 'buy into' the exigencies of an exotic African continent. A greater residue of semantic meaning and understanding can be uncovered I suggest, at least for 'smart/active' audiences, who wish to further engage with the material and uncover its ethical complexity and engagement with a range of deep environmental issues. But of course such a positive injunction and hypothesis would require empirical audience analysis to unpack, alongside a range of comparative attitudinal investigations, which again is outside the scope of this textual analysis overview study.

Justin's gardening functions as a mode of avoiding political engagement and adjusting himself to symbolic restrictions. Again, according to McGowan, to be a 'constant gardener', in the sense that the film proposes, is 'to align oneself with the symbolic law and its restrictions. Gardening allows the subject private pleasure, as a compensation for adhering to these restrictions. The gardener works to sustain life, just as Justin works to prop up the British regime. He protects both his plants and the British power structure from possible disruption' (McGowan 2007: 63). A readibly agreeable and well argued reading, nonetheless, I wonder if this gardening metaphor simply helps to ideologically promote the status quo and is fully in tune with the film's overall diegesis and textual dynamics within the storyline. Surprisingly, his gardening prowess is less pronounced in the final film version it must be said, except for his worries regarding the (over)use of pesticide as weed killer, as cued most pointedly by the violent reaction of his wife on hearing such a practice. Like any good utilitarian who has an explicit preoccupation with an ethics of care, he strives to achieve the most effective balance in nature; but his more emotionally driven partner demands a more radical and less rational or considered response to a totally unjust system of values and ethical norms. In the end he must adopt this moderate approach to prove his abiding love for her.

A deeper, more sustained form and typology of ecological gardening is probably being suggested and called upon, which in turn subverts an otherwise conventional ideological reading. For instance, calling to mind the polarising differences between Sunday dabbling through a form of bourgeois gardening (reminiscent of 'Sunday painting'), as against a more deeply felt organic and sustainable form of cultivation of the soil. Recalling the broad differences laid out between a conventional call to allotment gardening in the light romantic comedy *Green Card* (1990), as opposed to that signalled in Hal Ashby's *Being*

There (1979). The latter focuses on an enigmatic character Chance the gardener (Peter Sellers), whose philosophical musings about gardening serve as a touchstone for the fictional public in the film, who sheep-like in turn perceive his enigmatic responses as evidence of genuine deep insights into the ethics of human nature, precisely because the nurturing demands of gardening and plant husbandry appear to serve as a bulwark against the reductive binary structure of bourgeois ideology. Gardening becomes a convenient shorthand in these films to set up a range of ecological and ethical notions around 'doing the right thing', which includes environmental sustainability and non-wasteful forms of frugality discussed at the start of this chapter, while also and at the same time affirming the intrinsic benefits of being ontologically and environmentally 'at one with nature'. These tensions are most clearly explicated by an analysis of Justin's demise in the story.

Martyrdom and the eco-sublime: promoting a nascent form of deep environmental agency

The romantic undertones of Justin's final act obscures its thoroughgoing political nature. Justin can accept death in the way that he does, only because he becomes a politicised subject, according to McGowan's prescriptive Lacanian reading. Justin certainly makes no effort to hide from the henchmen of the guerilla group called KDH, seeking to kill him, and almost welcomes their intervention – reminiscent of T.S. Elliot's historical allegory *Murder in the Cathedral*. It is certainly difficult *not* to read Justin's actions at the end of the film as anything but suicidal.[7] But this would, I believe, be a misreading. While agreeing with McGowan in his general assessment, I would see very different reasons for coming to the same conclusion. According to McGowan, Justin neither tries to die nor tries to survive at the end of the film. He exists here in the jouissance of the drive, and, as Lacan notes, 'jouissance implies precisely the acceptance of death' (1992: 189).

Applying an alternative deep ecological and ethical lens to read the sequence, however, one can reframe such a Lacanian reading to alternatively help to understand and appreciate his spatial and psychological state. He has, one could optimistically suggest, fully learned the deep-ecological and ethical lesson of life and come to realise the true meaning of death as part of a holistic life cycle. His conscious reawakening is driven not simply by psychological realignment, but through political insight and finally recognising the deep ecological and pervasive injustice realities of his newfound African homeland. Of course there is a danger of over-emphasising a transcendent, even a universal individualised sensibility and thereby re-affirming the dilemma of appearing to promote an apolitical stance in such an apparently 'first wave' eco-reading. Nonetheless, it is apparent that Justin's deep spiritual form of ethical stasis can most clearly be fully appreciated by understanding this heightened form of ecological acceptability and connectivity with and over his newly invested habitat. His new-found agency, cognition and affective engagement with his environment is certainly capable of embracing first-wave environmentalism and the unconditional love of nature, as well as connecting with the profound second-wave, trans-cultural justice measures and values and the abiding need to speak to a universal environmental ethic, which at its most profound level serves to bring the diachronic and synchronic elements of environmental engagement together.

Like *Into the Wild*[8] or *The Color Purple*,[9] *The Constant Gardener* adopts provocative and empathetic techniques that help to demonstrate how spaces need not necessarily be represented as static, much less simply therapeutic, but instead become an active process aiding human agency to contemplate and appreciate the big picture around environmental interconnectivity. The erstwhile transient tourist site exemplified in such films can at a stretch become the motor, the philosophical or psychological 'black box' for audiences and protagonists to express their hopes, fears, desires and utopian dreams, rather than simply remaining subsumed within a uni-directional Western-focused romantic gaze.

The film's closure and the visualisation of the death of the main protagonist calls to mind a form of transcendent style, as suggested by Paul Schrader in his 1998 study of film directors like Bresson and others. While a related and equally fruitful means of exploring this death/life wish is evident, I suggest through the prism of deep ecology, which also serves to promote effective strategies to fully recognise, appreciate and address environmental ethical concerns. Provocative but at the same time romanticised cinematic examples like *The Constant Gardener* can ostensibly help audiences construct and call upon fruitful ecological objective correlatives following this experiential, even transcendental, form of pilgrimage/travel.

While this esoteric life–death grand narrative puzzle is being investigated, a more urgent contemporary tribal conflict is being played out. We earlier followed Justin finally putting the pieces of the jigsaw of his wife's murder together, when he accidentally meets Dr Lorbeer (played by the late Pete Postlethwaite). Lorbeer had given Tessa the evidence in the form of a letter which she needed for her to confirm the truth of what occurred, involving nefarious activities of a multinational drug company. As also explored in Chapter 7, multinational companies engaged in fracking and all forms of mining and energy production, together with food and drug companies, alongside others not directly engaged in explicitly harmful ecological prospects – all promote the 'bottom line' of profit and increasing consumption. They do this no matter what their 'corporate social responsibility' charter might speak to, much less recognising and abiding by prescribed precautionary principles, or their so-called 'green marketing' strategy. This letter is finally read out at the memorial service for Justin back in London, after his nemesis Sir Bernard Pellegrin (Bill Nighy) spoke (with a forked tongue) of how Justin was a self-effacing man, who chose to take his own life; a sad reflection of his life while displaying his tormented state of mind. Misquoting a classic aphorism from a Shakespearian drama, the sly British government bureaucrat concludes his fake eulogy, '[N]othing becomes his life like the leaving of it'.

Meanwhile, reaffirming the Western archetype of Africans not being able to live peacefully with its neighbours and wallowing in internecine wars, which in turn plays into conventional ideological stereotypes, we are privy to a slow-motion sequence, as fires are started and horrible deeds executed by marauding tribes – using a perversion of animal-hunting tropes, with suitably cued haunting indigenous music and singing. Again the stereotypical 'white man's burden' to secure universal ethical value is further illustrated, as Justin and his confidante try to bring an orphaned young black girl onto their escaping plane, only to be rebuked by the indigenous pilot. Justin tries to get his way by pleading for an exception: 'it's a child's life'– this is *one* we could help! Justin is firmly rebuked however for such emotional manipulation and using myopic ethical standards and is informed that this is *not* the way things are done here. As they strap themselves into their seats and escape from the horrors, in a further cloying attempt to pull at Western heartstrings, the little girl in question runs alongside the plane.

Different ethical norms and procedures are played out in very stark trajectories. Saving an African child's life is often dramatised in such films – and in numerous charity campaigns for that matter – as evidence of Western benevolence and constructed as a salve to assuage *our* (universal) charity consciousness. But of course these responses at worst can be considered as hollow tokenism and do not systematically address the deep underlying environmental and ethical global problem, which the West is certainly complicit in maintaining, if not promoting.

Nonetheless, our hero Justin does not want to simply escape the horrors and persuades the pilot to land the plane in the exact place Tessa earlier met her death – reminiscent of the lions in *Out of Africa* revering the eco-hero's grave and also going back to the primal site of rupture. As the plane finally flies over this beautiful picturesque scenery for the last time, again a further link is made with birds flying underneath. By all accounts this topography embodies an exotic other-worldly space/place, while displaying a rich natural habitat. As his mechanical mode of transport disappears, Justin is on the final leg of his journey, a journey which has been transformed into a sacred pilgrimage. In this inhospitable, yet beautiful dry lakeshore, he glances at a native appearing in the distance. He is no longer 'othered' and has at last come 'home'. 'I am home', he cries out to his beloved Tessa on the 'other side', echoing the dénouement of an almost Shakespearian drama. At a metaphysical level and taking into account a deep environmental context, this corresponds to also being totally at one with nature.

His off-stage death which the cinema audience is not shown, is again accompanied by the haunting sounds of birds flying, as in the kitsch Western countercultural self-actualisation parable *Jonathan Livingstone Seagull* (see Richard Bach's 40th anniversary edition). Taking off over the sea, the bird's flight is followed by a blank screen. The audience don't need to actually witness his brutal murder by African tribesmen. Instead the more benevolent transcendent vision of birds as 'nature in flight' becomes an appropriate shorthand, articulating his psychological and deep ecological state of newfound oneness with and in nature – the ultimate manifestation of environmental and ethical harmony. Instead of an 'open verdict', as is often the case with suicide, when it can't be completely proved, here moral culpability in his own death is repositioned from a romantic and gendered perspective, as McGowan (2007) affirms. But also it can be added that this can be read more fruitfully from a transcendent and a deep ecological/ spiritual and therapeutic perspective and framework which is very different for instant to a futuristic allegorical fantasy like *District 9*.

Concluding remarks

It is important to re-stress that the main focus of the 'African' race narratives discussed in this chapter is explicitly framed through the lens of a Western cinematic representation of Africa, rather than through the domestic or indigenous African film industry.[10] How Western agency can be actively addressed and hopefully transformed in the process of becoming more sensitive to the exigencies of Third World indigenous notions of environmental justice, together with a deep ecological appreciation of the specificities of the local habitat remains a challenge. From the broad contemporarity of justice and environmental issues in Reggio's *oeuvre*, to more mainstream narrative drivers and heroic identification including total transformation, articulated through the chief protagonist portrayed in *The Constant Gardener,* audiences are encouraged to identify with such characters and in turn learn to appreciate and fully empathise with their othered habitats. Justin learns the deep environmental message of transcendent connectivity with his new African homeland.

All these narratives allegorically play out Western society's relationship to nature in varying forms of *in extremis*. An examination of the textual and narrative cues attempt to reanimate and reframe Hollywood's eco-revisionist take on erstwhile regressive forms of African narratives. In particular the conventional heroic narrative evident in *The Constant Gardener* reflect a healthy engagement with the environmental richness and diversity of African cinema, as a vibrant and often forgotten series of cultural manifestations. Conventional debates and frames of otherness and even regressive stereotypes are turned on their head in such provocative re-workings of mainstream generic tropes within a very contentious (South) African setting.

Notes

1 Because of space I have had to cut comparative readings of *Tsotsi* and *District 9* from this chapter, but they appear in an earlier format in a journal article. In many ways for instance, the grungy science fiction habitat evident in *District 9* is reminiscent of Paul Virilio's notion of 'grey ecology', through its focus on post-industrial degradation and the depth of field of the terrestrial landscape (Virilio 1997: 41).

2 Certainly more indigenous directors than these sampled here, remain intently aware of Africa's unique ecology, and the pervasive need for engaging with local grounded environmental ethics, which is somwhat different from (Western) directors discussed in this chapter. Most notably see Souleymane Cisse's *Finye* (1982), *Yeelen* (1987) and *Waati* (1995), or the films of Jean-Marie Teno, *Afrique, je te plumerai* (1993) and *Clando* (1996) as a small sample of such output.

3 This crude 'Western' colonial discourse is of course complicated with Chinese and other colonial interests of late taking hold across more countries in Africa.

4 Historically, of course, frugality was a prime Christian economic norm and also a Protestant one. While at the outset fully recognising I'm in difficult territory, appearing to endorse if not necessarily embrace a form of ultra-conservative and even historically myopic politics; nevertheless such notions can be repurposed to provide a fruitful, and dare I say progressive, eco-political direction for the future.

5 This has some echoes in a recent real-life lawsuit by the Nigerian government against Pfizer, alleging that an experimental antibiotic to treat meningitis led to death and disability in a group of children.

6 Of course HIV is rife in Africa, but all but forgotten in the West, which has effective drug control of the disease in recent years.

7 Recalling the heroic contemplation of suicide to affirm romantic love and 'beating the system' in *The Hunger Games* as discussed in Chapter 4.

8 As suggested in an eco-reading of the closure of *Into the Wild* (2007) for instance, film theorists can learn a lot from the way 'geographers represent place as the location of direct experience, a sensuous swirl of emotion and perception and myths, which rational analysis can only ignore or destroy' (Rose 1993: 71). 'Instead of classic closure, audiences are presented with an "excess of signification" that allows a metaphysical engagement with spatial identity. This spatial identity is posited as coexisting with a more contemporary psychological and temporal identity' and they have 'potentially at least acquired the ability to co-opt their preconceived notions of place and identity while endorsing an eco-utopian sensibility'.

9 In *The Color Purple*, for instance, it is the white man in Africa who 'annexes' the territory of the native Olinka tribe for rubber exploitation. Celie's sister Nettie describes in her letter that 'the ancient, giant mahogany trees, all the trees, the game, everything in the forest was being destroyed, and the land was forced to lie flat' (Russell 2013: 144).

10 There is already an extensive literature on African-produced films, mainly populated by African scholars, which capture the complexity of the varying socio-political as well as tribal and cultural influences that have shaped this media – see for instance Jacqueline Maingard's *South African National Cinema* (Routledge 2007) alongside classics like Frank Ukadike's *Black African Cinema* (University of California Press 1994), Keyan G. Tomaselli's *Encountering Modernity: Twentieth Century South African Cinemas* (Rozenberg-UNISA Press 2006) or Pietari Kääpä's edited collection *Transnational Econcinemas* among others.

Bibliography

Attfield, R. and Belsey, A. (eds) (1994) *Philosophy and the Natural Environment*. Royal Institute of Philosophy Supplements. Cambridge: Cambridge University Press.

Bach, Richard (1970) *Jonathan Livingstone Seagull*. London: HarperCollins.

Barry, John (1999) *Rethinking Green Politics*. London: Sage.

Blixen, Karen (1992) *Out of Africa*. New York: Penguin.

Brereton, Pat (2012) *Smart Cinema: DVD Add-ons and New Media Pleasures*. Basingstoke: Palgrave.

Brereton, Pat (2013) 'Eco-cinema, Sustainability and Africa: A Reading of *Out of Africa* (1985), *The Constant Gardener* (2005) and *District 9* (2010)'. *Journal of African Cinemas* 5(2) 219–235.

Britton, Alan (2007) 'The Constant Gardener', *Policy and Practice*. www. developmenteducationreview.com/issue5-reviews1

Buell, Lawrence (2005) *The Future of Environmental Criticism: Environmental Crisis and Literary Imagination*. Cambridge: Blackwell.

Cato, Molly Scott (2012) 'The Freedom to be Frugal', *Feasta Review*. http://www.feasta. org/documents/review2/cato.htm

Daly, Herman E. (1997) 'Reply to Mark Sagoff's Carrying Capacity and Ecological Economics' Economics', in David Crocker and Toby Linden (eds) *An Ethics of Consumption: The Good Life, Justice and Global Stewardship*. Lanham, MD: Rowman and Littlefield Publishers.

Dobrin, Sidney and Kidd, Kenneth (eds) (2004) *Wild Things: Children's Literature and Ecocriticism*. Detroit, MI: Wayne State University Press.

Dobson, Andrew and Lucardie, Paul (1995) *The Politics of Nature: Explorations in Green Political Theory*. New York: Routledge.

Douthwaite, Richard (1992) *The Growth Illusion*. Dublin: The Lilliput Press.

Ebert, Rodger (2005) 'The Constant Gardener'. http://www.rogerebert.com/reviews/ the-constant-gardener-2005

Ferre, F. (1996) 'Persons in Nature: Towards an Applicable and Unified Environmental Ethics'. *Ethics and the Environment* 1: 15–25.

Guha, Ramachandra (1989) 'Radical American Environmentalism and Wilderness Preservation: A Third World Critique'. *Environmental Ethics* 11: 71–83.

Heise, Ursula (2008) *Sense of Place and Sense of Planet: The Environmental Imagination of the Global*. Oxford: Oxford University Press.

Kelly, Kevin (1994) *Out of Control: The New Biology of Machines, Social Systems and the Economic World*. Boston, MA: Addison-Wesley.

Klein, Naomi (2007) *The Shock Doctrine: The Rise of Disaster Capitalism*. New York: Knopf.

Klein, Naomi (2014) *This Changes Everything: Capitalism vs the Climate*. New York: Simon & Schuster.

Lacan, Jacques (1992) *The Seminars of Jacques Lacan, Book vii: The Ethics of Psychoanalysis, 1959–1960*. Trans Dennis Porter. New York: Norton.

MacDonald, Scott (1993) *Avant-Garde Film: Motion Studies*. Cambridge: Cambridge University Press.

McGowan, Todd (2007) 'The Temporality of the Real: The Path to Politics in *The Constant Gardener*', *Film Philosophy.com*. http://www.film-philosophy.com/2007v11n3/ mcgowan.pdf

Muir, John (1988) *John Muir in his Own Words: A Book of Quotations* compiled and edited by Peter Browning. Lafayette, CA: Great West Books.

Nash, James A. (1997) 'On the Subversive Virtue: Frugality', in David Crocker and Toby Linden (eds) *An Ethics of Consumption: The Good Life, Justice and Global Stewardship*. Lanham, MD: Rowman and Littlefield Publishers.

Pogge, Thomas W. (1997) 'A Global Resources Dividend', in David Crocker and Toby Linden (eds) *An Ethics of Consumption: The Good Life, Justice and Global Stewardship*. Lanham, MD: Rowman and Littlefield Publishers.

Rose, Gillian (1993) *Feminism and Geography*. Cambridge: Polity.

Russell, John, G. (2013) Don't It Make My Black Face Blue: Race, *Avatar*, Albescence and the Transnational Imaginary'. *Popular Culture Journal* 46(1): 192–217.

Sagoff, Mark (1997) 'Carrying Capacity and Ecological Economics', in David Crocker and Toby Linden (eds) *An Ethics of Consumption: The Good Life, Justice and Global Stewardship*. Lanham, MD: Rowman and Littlefield Publishers.

Schrader, Paul (1998) *Transcendental Style in Film: Ozu, Bresson, Dreyer*. Berkeley, CA: University of California Press.

Schumacher, E.F. (1973) *Small is Beautiful: Economics as if People Mattered*. London: Blond and Briggs Publishers.

Sen, Amartya (2001) *Development as Freedom*. Oxford: University Press.

Spivak, Gayatri Chakrovorty (1999) *A Critique of Postcolonial Reason*. Boston, MA: Harvard Press.

Taylor, Paul (1981)'The Ethics of Respect for Nature'. *Environmental Ethics* 3: 197–213.

Virilo, Paul (1997) *Open Sky*. New York: Verso Press.

Weik von Mossner, Alexa and Irmscher, Christoph (2012) 'Dislocations and Ecologies: An Introduction'. *European Journal of English Studies* 16(2): 91–97.

Wilson, Edward O. (1986) *Biophilia*. Boston, MA: Harvard University Press.

7

BUSINESS ETHICS

Sustainability, frugality and the environment

Overview

The 'smart' contemporary corporate/business parable *Wall Street: Money Never Sleeps* is a well-timed sequel to the 1980s homage to capitalist greed that appears to ironically set up the systemic conflicts within corporate business culture, while at the same time upholding the economic 'bottom line'.[1] More recently the even more provocative parable *The Wolf of Wall Street*, which was a major box office success, speaks to such contentious debates for a new generation.

Concurrently, while the costs of climate change, peak oil and continued economic development are becoming major global issues, the solution posited by utilitarian and more contemporary ecological ethicists and policy-makers revolves around mutual coercion and consenting to a form of sustainable regulation of resources. Finding appropriate solutions to such global problems also has to take into account the dangers of pandering to an environmental agenda, just to appear wholesome, which is often called 'green washing' and the legitimation of new forms of corporate responsibility or some other manifestation of 'universal sustainability'.

Nevertheless, the fundamental flaw with regards to notions of 'sustainable development' is that it continues to regard the Earth and all of nature simply as a resource to be used. In contrast, the underlying conviction in the sustainable biosphere model is that the current trajectory of the industrial, technological, commercial world is generally wrong, because it will inevitably overshoot (Rolston in Keller 2010: 567).

Wall Street's sequel focuses on the new 'clean tech' industry, which appears in the short term at least to create a solution for the energy industry, while in this instance needing a major injection of capital and risk management to get it up and running. This is in contrast to more conventional and unsustainable industries, with their ever-decreasing reserves of carbon-based oil as the primary raw material, which qualifies most certainly as a 'dirty' (non-green) energy source.

The ethical notion of 'moral hazard' is especially brought into focus within business narratives explored in this chapter. Executives who take risky decisions simply to maximise personal profit, while not taking responsibility for the consequences of their actions in the longer term, remain a subject of debate, as currently evidenced by so many real-life bankers and builders – the *bête noire* of 'evil capitalism'. So many businesses have gambled to help maximise their short-term profits, without having to consider the long-term consequences of their actions, much less having regard to the 'common good' for people and the environment. Moral hazard remains a primary ethical concern and is concurrently framed for the purposes of this volume in environmental terms and business's lack of consideration for such dangers.

Essentially, deep ecologists would hypothesise that consumer capitalism transmutes a once-healthy pattern of desires into avarice. With escalating opportunities for consumerism, driven by markets in search of profits, publics in turn need more self-discipline that often does not come naturally. Our self-interested tendencies overshoot, since we love ourselves (egoism) and find it difficult to know when and how to say enough is enough.

In the West especially we have built this egotistical philosophy into our concept of human rights: promoting a right of self-development and ultimately self-realisation. Such a non-egalitarian ethic constitutes a public sense of value that is simply driven to maximise productive consumption and in turn drive an unsustainable world. When everybody *only* focuses on his or her own good, there is a corresponding diminution of communal sustainable and controlled growth, which explicitly speaks to debates around the tragedy of the commons discussed in Chapter 1.

Changing such a dominant mindset remains a major difficultly, but is one that the global challenge of climate change demands. A robust environmental ethical strategy will be required to begin to cope with what is termed in the literature a 'wicked' problem. If environmental ethics can persuade even larger numbers of persons that 'an environment with biodiversity, with wilderness, is a better world in which to live than one without these, then some progress is possible' (Rolston in Keller 2010: 566). The creative imaginary of film this study suggests can help in this primary paradigmatic shift towards supporting a more sustainable environmental worldview.

Most explicitly featured in this study is a critique of neo-liberal capitalism and growing forms of conspicuous consumption that have become a predefined enemy of environmentally sustainable economic development. This position seems explicitly evident when speaking with or about businessmen and marketers – who are often considered the ultimate proponents and the embodiment of a neoliberal form of capitalist enterprise. Yet surprisingly, at the same time, debates around sustainability and environmental ethics are more nuanced and reflexive in a growing area of green marketing, for instance, than one would have expected from such a profit-driven sector, where green-washing and other forms of unethical approaches to the environment might appear to be the default and a dominant strategy to help in turn to maintain a 'business as usual' philosophy.

In this chapter, I will analyse the creative imaginary of what can be loosely categorised as business films, to examine how this might in turn help promote and develop positive business models of practice that serve to protect the environment and promote effective and efficient forms of sustainability.[2] In addition to espousing and promoting various forms of so-called ecological cinema that can hopefully signal new ways to help create an environmentally sustainable future, what is especially needed currently are also visual and eco-critically literate viewers who are able to discern and challenge the ways in which representations of nature, culture, alongside business and marketing paradigms are framed and composited, across a range of Hollywood narratives. This open educational and media literacy approach can hopefully help to offset the dangers of simply reinforcing and reproducing values and worldviews that contribute to the degradation of ecosystems, while at the same time co-creating more productive models for economic sustainability.[3] See McDonagh and Brereton (2010) for a thumbnail survey of the greatest business-environmental films and how they might be repurposed from an environmental perspective, which serves as an initial road test and model for this analysis.

Environmental issues have been of interest to marketers for almost 40 years, however since the 1990s in particular, consumers' concern for the safety and preservation of the environment has been escalating at an exponential rate. But at the same time with increasing populations and heightened levels of conspicuous consumption, there is certainly no sign of decline in environmental damage, resulting from runaway modalities and wasteful processes of production and consumption. While humans as consumers remain significant contributors to environmental problems, in contrast businesses, as an aggregate system of economic development, continue to make an even more substantial contribution to total environmental degradation.

Societal marketing as a discipline questions the implicit assumption of marketing that the collective satisfaction of individual customer's needs and wants are always in the best long-term interests of consumer welfare and society (see Belz and Peattie 2009: 27). While sustainable marketing is also part of a macromarketing concept:

> [I]t embraces the idea of sustainable development, which requires a change in the behaviour of virtually everyone, including both producers and consumers. In addition to this progressive notion of a macromarketing perspective, sustainable marketing emphasises the triple bottom line of ecological, social and economic issues, unlike green marketing, which

tends to focus on environmental problems and the reduction of the environmental burden.

(Belz and Peatttie 2009: 30)

In business and marketing, eco-scholars remain closely aware of the dangers of green-washing and the use of environmentalism simply as a marketing opportunity to ostensibly create further appeal to mass audiences. Many critics believe the so-called greening of business simply serves to promote an old-fashioned 'business as usual' model, rather than a necessary more radical reversal of values in the corporate sphere. While the more established literature on 'corporate social responsibility' serves to put big corporations in a cocooning ethical register with regards to societal needs and responsibilities, the drive towards achieving a low-carbon-based renewable energy economy to replace old and 'dirty' industries remains a more pressing, long-term and global concern. Of course some environmental critics believe big business/marketing is still simply latching onto another business opportunity to help stave off a deep and long-term systemic economic crash, while more optimists accept that a business/technical suite of solutions to the global impact of environmental catastrophe remains the most pragmatic response that ought to be embraced by stakeholders across various sectors.

With regard to the global media industry, one must also ask how can the most superficial material-based film medium – often coupled with the advertising and promotions industry – be capable of developing a counter-business discourse. How can it posit radically new ethical frameworks and modalities, as opposed to the dominant 'business as usual' orthodoxy that implicitly believes in economically predetermined growth, production and consumption cycles. It is, by all accounts, a big ask to expect mega-corporations like the Hollywood studios to even contemplate promoting such a radical ethical and environmental agenda.

Robert Kuttner talks very cogently of the so-called imperialism of the market. In a capitalist economy, he reminds us in *Everything for Sale*, 'the marketplace is only one of several means by which society makes decisions, determines worth, allocates resources, maintains a social fabric and conducts human relations'. As economist Arthur Okun has noted most succinctly, 'the market needs a place, but the market [also] needs to be kept in its place'. Paul Hawken *et al.* goes on to affirm 'markets are only tools. They make a good servant but a bad master and a worse religion' (cited in Speth 2008: 90).[4]

Culturally many critics across various disciplinary boundaries have pointed out that globally inclusive myths have become even more necessary as comfort blankets, as society becomes more destabilised following severe economic depression. While others suggest that, 'the psychic and social structures in which we live have become profoundly anti-ecological, unhealthy and destructive'. Consequently there certainly appears to be a need for 'new forms, (re)emphasising our essential interconnectedness rather than our separateness, evoking the feeling of belonging to each other' (Gablik 1991: 5). As a relatively modern phenomenon however, ecology as a barometer of the common good and recalling for that matter an ethics of sustainability, remains a totalising concept, which is inclusive rather than exclusive.[5]

Early environmentalists, such as Henry David Thoreau, cited the intrinsic and ethical properties of nature, rather than its economic benefits, as reasons to preserve it. They believed that economic activity had outstripped not its resource base but its spiritual purpose. John Muir condemned the 'temple destroyers, devotees of ravaging commercialism' who 'instead of lifting their eyes to the God of the mountains, lift them to the Almighty dollar'. This ethical condemnation was certainly not a call for improved cost-benefit analysis. 'Nineteenth century environmentalists, seeing nature as full of divinity, regarded its protection less as an economic imperative than as a moral test' (Sagoff 1997: 28). In the West at least, business in particular has stayed a long way from this philosophy.

More recently however Andrew Dobson (1992) helps to reconstruct ecologism as a comprehensive ideology in which the philosophical basis (limits to growth) the ethical perspective (ecocentrism), the social vision (a sustainable society), and the political strategy (radical transformation, not reformism) provide a coherent and cohesive ideology (Dobson 1992: 15). Ecologism most certainly provides the core underpinning ethical principles and validates the non-sustainability of scarce natural resources, together with its central premise of human interconnectivity with the rest of the biotic community and even with the cosmos.

Later we will focus on a number of high-finance cautionary business narratives to set out the ethical range of debates addressed by Hollywood and how such narratives speak to very contradictory environmental and ethical trajectories. This can be illustrated with a few classic Hollywood narratives which have a clear business subtext, before moving on to the more explicit critiques and contemporary Western cautionary tales around the excesses of financial capitalism, through a polemical evocation of the ethical dilemma around the pervasive striving for growth through gambling in the very successful film *Wall Street*[6] and its sequel, alongside the more recent *The Wolf of Wall Street*.

Counter ethics to explicit valorising of conspicuous consumption

Drawing on the work of James Nash (1997) and the subversive virtue of frugality explored in Chapter 6 which seeks to reject the popular assumption that humans are insatiable creatures, ceaselessly acquisitive for economic gains and egotistically committed to pleasure maximisation, frugality involves a rejection of the prevailing ideology of indiscriminate, material economic growth that incidentally was at least historically recognised as a Christian economic norm.[7] Embracing this austere form of sustainability appears a long way from the neoliberal mantra involving ostentatious wealth and conspicuous consumption and the fiction of ever-increasing economic growth, addressed if not critiqued in so much Hollywood fare including *Wall Street*, together with the hyper-satire of Scorsese's *The Wolf of Wall Street*.

Furthermore, one could draw contrasting parallels between such rampant consumption with its focus on the individual and resulting atomisation, as against the evocation of frugality drawn from a bygone era that helped us promote a deeper sense of community and egalitarian society. This old-fashioned notion also has echoes across current debates and counter-trends cited in the business literature, calling on various forms of positive psychology and an ever-present desire for holistic wellbeing within society.

It could also be argued that frugality, rather than the more hegemonic notion of austerity, which has become the mantra in dealing with deep financial recessions in the West, might become a more useful concept. Nonetheless, with so many negative connotations, one can't easily imagine the notion gaining traction. Yet frugality seeks to affirm, if not re-create, a more sustainable form of human solidarity and can be read through numerous business films, contrasting with the binary opposites of excess and conspicuous waste. Reading such business stories as allegorical cautionary tales, they signal in contrast the need to reconstitute a radically alternative ethos than those that feed off a green-washed form of business-as-usual.

Green business and representations on film

As argued by McDonagh and Brereton (2010: 33), the 'filmic representations of nature, while multifarious have a tendency to present nature as the resource for business and the market to engage in economic progress.' This is in contradistinction to the belief that characters must always seek to save the planet, recalling a utopian and deep environmental agenda. Perhaps as a consequence, filmic representations of business in general have not yet actively engaged with a green agenda, encapsulated in the pervasive quest for a so-called sustainable consumption model. Gangster 'business' movies like *The Godfather* parts I and II for instance, clearly illustrate how ill-gotten lucre cannot in turn buy happiness, much less support a sustainable environmental community. By all accounts the business movie (a notion which is not foregrounded incidentally in generic film studies) has not privileged any notion of ecology, much less environmental ethics. Rather such films depict 'nature as an economic resource and as a result the business movie seems to perpetuate the dominant social paradigm and the quest for materialism inherent in this' (McDonagh and Brereton 2010: 33).[8]

McDonagh and Brereton have also noted how top-rated 'business' films broadly anthropocentricise nature as simply an easily available resource for humans, as opposed to what might be typified as 'anti-business' films, many of which emphasise ecological biocentrism and harmony with nature. This choice reflects the reality of how top business movies basically appear to uncritically represent, if not validate, the global market. While this chapter will explore how more contemporary films have at least begun to portray and reframe a 'business agenda', alongside an 'ecological one' as a series of contradictory discourses, which in turn makes good drama. As evidenced, for instance, in a reading of an anti-fracking movie *Promised Land*, environmental issues and dilemmas are feeding directly into business representations that promote forms of extractive energy production, using the ever-present benefits of a PR industry to prop up an erstwhile anti-environmental business model. Looking through a number of canonical cinematic texts that can also be read as 'business movies', we can also trace some of the core environmental and ethical themes examined in this chapter.

Citizen Kane remains number one in many critics' lists of top films of all time and is also in the Forbes top 10 business movies list. It incorporates a bravura cinematic tale by Orson Welles and tells the story of William Randolph Hearst, the real-life media mogul who put together an empire of newspapers, radio stations, magazines and news services and in the latter end of his life builds himself the flamboyant monument of San Simeon. As Roger Ebert (1998) affirms in his review in the *Chicago Sun-Times*, Hearst was 'Ted Turner, Rupert Murdoch and Bill Gates rolled up into an enigma'. He became obsessed with success and 'living the American Dream', which ostensibly affirms that anyone can become successful, if they have the requisite tenacity, conviction and the entrepreneurial spirit. Such attributes appear a long way away from the communal and non-competitive spirit embedded in promoting ecological sustainability.

This early cautionary tale exposes the capitalist and heroic dilemma embedded within American business culture before World War Two, which seeks to valorise self-actualisation, while at the same time critiquing 'soulless banking' and crass unadulterated money-making. Such a film can also serve to demonstrate how much has changed with regards to modern methods of financialisation and neoliberal approaches to business which have become the norm in more contemporary films like *Wall Street*. Being endowed with enormous wealth while still a young boy, his parents struck gold with some lucky investments and as a consequence Charles Foster Kane grows up trying to 'find himself'. After many misadventures and world tours, he finally settles on running what he considers a failing newspaper, but which has 'high standards' and broadsheet audience appeal. Through trial and error he moulds his media empire to reflect his own ego and interests, while striving to secure general mass public approval. Later, when accused by his banker guardian of frittering away his wealth, Kane coyly responds that at this rate he will take a lifetime to lose it all. No worries about environmental ethics here, much less any consideration around long-term sustainability.

Yet some ethical interpretations of the film speak of its thematic focus around how surplus wealth becomes the root of all his problems and that this remains an abiding preoccupation within the story. The stuffy world of banking and wealth creation is most certainly shown to be a chimera. 'True happiness' and romanticised self-individualisation, this story-fabula affirms, like the perennial 'feel-good' Christmas classic *It's a Wonderful Life*, only comes from the inside, far away from surface wealth and emanates from a bedrock of deep humanistic and communal values.

This story speaks to a form of business innocence, before the ecological turn hailed in Ulrich Beck's *Risk Society* in the second half of the twentieth century. This innocence embodies a narrative trajectory where wealth creation brought personal angst and personality challenges, while wider ecological questions around growth and sustainability are not directly addressed, perhaps because at this time few contemplated such ecological questions as being relevant. In this respect nature is certainly present, but simply characterised as an economic resource. Furthermore, nature is crudely coded as lost innocence – symbolised by the nostalgic snow scene at the start of the boy's story – when he is forced to give up his family and rural idyll. This loss is specifically symbolised by the boy's sleigh (spoiler alert as the core McGuffin of the story), whose name Rosebud becomes the narrative enigma driving the story, being the last word spoken by the old man. By all accounts, the chief protagonist's 'Great Expectations' in being awarded a huge financial legacy, leaves nature ostensibly conceived as an economic resource for business purposes only.[9] The *Godfather* saga, to which we now turn, remains even more explicit in critiquing the power of money and wealth to negatively motivate and influence human behaviour, from a more suspect business position.

This classic gangster franchise from the 1970s speaks to a particularly latent environmental agenda which, like many films examined in this volume, serves as an allegorical cautionary tale. The gangster genre is often considered in the critical film literature as the 'great no to the American yes' (Warshow 1948) and in ways sets up the polar opposite to the heroic myth making of the western, as reflexively exemplified in *Citizen Kane*. Essentially, in this gritty gangster family drama, we are presented with the underbelly of modern urban America where the dream of poor emigrants is corrupted by their struggle for survival and the ethical choices they make. But also evident in this cautionary tale is a critique of 'official' capitalism, which accurately reflects this conflictual period when corruption such as the Watergate affair eroded the pillars of government and power politics in America. These family-based 'business men', generally coded as gangsters with their highly suspect ethics – environmental or otherwise – try to survive through various nefarious business enterprises and also through controlling public regulation and legislation, which might temper their excesses and thereby serve to protect against all forms of environmental depreciation in particular.

They sink or swim, depending on their cunning, while pushing the boundaries of official business enterprise through their use of violent action to get their own way. This vicarious extension of the 'business ethic' can be seen to be appealing to erstwhile mild-mannered business types who are encouraged to succeed by whatever means, within the 'survival of the fittest' paradigm. There is little space for environmental caution and doing the right thing for the common good and general community. The original story and sequel deal with the transfer of power from father to son and considers how a new generation has lost the somewhat prescribed 'ethics of care' and communal business acumen, as they face bigger challenges around survival into the future. In other words, naked greed takes over, as they relax their ethical norms to include exploiting more high stakes drug-dealing. As a result such gangster iconography present and embody the extreme flip side of 'raw American capitalism' and politics everywhere. Coppola's critical reinterpretation of the gangster genre serves to dramatise and at the same time call attention to the changing social and business underbelly of American life.

Such elemental ethical conflict and tension are articulated most famously in the opening sequence of Coppola's original masterpiece and encapsulated by the: 'and what has America done for me' speech. This monologue by a disaffected emigrant businessman, who simply wants 'justice' for his violated daughter, cues the audience to reflect on an ongoing dramatic struggle around the 'survival of the fittest' model of social development, together with the primacy of the dollar in determining and ensuring a robust American ethical value system. Such measures of social and personal success, through human security and fulfilment are most certainly conflicted by the universal and ever-present ethic of citizenship and legal restraint, which also serves to underpin communitarian/ecological social development.[10]

Wall Street: from business sharks to wizards

More explicit business and finance agency films dominate the rest of this chapter, starting with the original *Wall Street*, which is read as a critique of financial traders and their abuse of human and ethical values in the 1980s, with its prophetic recreation of the chimera of high-risk electronic moneymaking and what can simply be regarded as downright gambling that has dominated world money-markets of late. Precautionary principles of any kind seem to be thrown out of the window. Roger Ebert (1987) begins his review of the film in the *Chicago Sun-Times*: 'How much is enough? The kid keeps asking the millionaire raider and trader. How much money do you want? The trader seems to be thinking hard, but the answer is, he just doesn't know. He's not even sure how to think about the question. He spends all day trying to make as much money as he possibly can, and he cheerfully bends and breaks the law to make even more millions … money is just a way to keep the score.' The millionaire in question is a predator, a corporate raider, a Wall Street shark, called Gordon Gekko – recalling the lizard that feeds off insects and sheds its tail when trapped.

The freezing of the credit markets' sub-prime mortgages, the collapse of behemoth financial firms, and debt problems in the Eurozone mark the global financial crisis of late 2000. But what caused this crisis? Answers to this question are of course complicated, but financial instruments called derivatives seem to be part and parcel of the crisis. Broadly speaking, derivatives are the antidote to any need to uphold a precautionary principle, being instruments for spreading risk, deriving their value from the underlying asset; they are essentially, bets on bets (Gillespie in Levina and Bui 2013: 287). Gillespie most insightfully describes such financial 'entrepreneurs' and risk capitalists as equivalent to 'wizards'.

Stone's radical critique and parody of the capitalist trading mentality suggests that most investors are dupes and that big market killings are made primarily by middlemen and brokers like Gekko, who swoops in and snaps up whole companies out from under the noses of their stockholders. The current global recession has produced an even more Manichean version of such financial wizards and bankers in *The Wolf of Wall Street* discussed later, designed, according to some critics, to scapegoat global financial problems and at the same time reflect the deep-seated distrust of the general populace around the truly awful state of affairs such rampant unregulated financial enterprise has left the world. Essentially, as a counter-force various forms of precautionary principles are urgently needed to protect habitats and environments including the financial ecosystem, from the selfish ravages of individual so-called entrepreneurs, where strong regulation is required to offset the prospect of unethical behaviour.

Roger Ebert's perceptive review further explains how such financial wheeling and dealing seem complicated yet convincing, while 'Gekko's law-breaking would of course be opposed by most people on Wall Street, his larger value system would be applauded' (Ebert 1987). The dominant and controlling ethos of a very reductive form of big business has become a major conundrum also within our current crisis. More holistic ecological models of doing business, which are often simply alluded to by the foregrounding of even more destructive business practices help to highlight an alternative and more benevolent model for which to strive. In all these subsequent readings the pervasive question remains: are the excesses of such dystopic business allegories signalling this need for more sustainable and ecologically based new strategies for business management? Audience research would be required to test such a somewhat counterintuitive hypothesis, but one might suggest that textual analysis at least indicates this reading is possible. *Wall Street* is ostensibly about various forms of injustice, which can in turn be cross-linked to debates around ecological injustice – especially within and between the globalised First and Third World. This contentious debate was also addressed in the previous chapter on Third World cinema, while here the focus is on the centre of Western business.

If business and markets are systemically interested in helping achieve ecological sustainability and promoting a propensity towards environmental and ethical probity, then robust green business agendas ought to be represented and endorsed at the same time. This assertion suggests there is still a way to go and if we want to depict business as a means to avert an increasing 'tragedy of the commons' (Shultz and Holbrook 1999), then we need to show more clearly such an ethical tension on the big screen.

Wall Street: Money Never Sleeps: **financial meltdown**

Blurb: 'Following a lengthy prison term, Gordon Gekko (Michael Douglas) finds himself on the outside looking in at a world he once commanded. Hoping to repair his relationship with his daughter Winnie (Carey Mulligan), Gekko forges an alliance with her fiancé Jake (Shia LaBeouf). But Winnie and Jake learn the hard way that Gekko is still a master manipulator who will stop at nothing to achieve his goals.'

In this broadly ecological reading, I focus on Jake's endorsement of clean environmental technology, by actively supporting a company developing alternative energy sources which needs extensive capital borrowed from the stock market. This is a new area of business rarely articulated in popular media. The phenomenon is currently best known by a range of scientific and financial specialists. The sequel's storyline is set seven years after Gekko has served a prison term, following an excessive exposition around the dangers of rampant financial egotism. This storyline was culled from the initial *Wall Street* from the 1980s, which in turn was a homage/critique of capitalist greed that appears to ironically set up the systemic conflicts within corporate business culture, while at the same time upholding the economic bottom line. The sequel in turn afforded more up-to-date engagement with the current crisis that takes place 23 years after the original, essentially focusing on the 2008 Western financial meltdown.

The key visual motif, which encapsulates the opening credits, counterpoints the universal cityscape with the ups and downs of the Dow-Jones index. The urban skyline reflects the vagaries of the market and effectively demonstrates how everything is inter-connected – from the architecture and landscape, to the people playing the market, which runs the city. The iconic New York skyline essentially doubles as an organic signifier of the rise and fall of the money market and capitalism. Another related visual motif used in the film features the pulsating data-streams of financial information and the skill of reading the market 'ticker tape' of numbers, which can only be decoded by those master semiotic financial specialists who are in the know, while embracing a form of ethical agnosticism to anything outside of the crude logics of the market. All the time the master semioticians and financial wizards are gambling with other people's money. This exposition is crassly but effectively visualised later by a board game motif, where artificial blocks are all knocked down in sequence. Such crashes are set up as systemic and an inevitable feature of the capitalist system, which explicitly calls to mind cautionary ethical-environmental debates as a core building block and back-story in this parable around gambling with our future.

This sequel focuses in particular on the newly constituted 'clean tech' industry, which appears in the short term, at least, to create a solution to the energy crisis in industry, while requiring a major injection of capital and effective risk management. This in turn is contrasted with more conventional and unsustainable industries with their ever-decreasing reserves of carbon-based oil as the primary raw material for all forms of industrial activity, recalling other ecological readings of a primal oil narrative like *There Will be Blood* or the abuse of water sources in *Chinatown*.

The film creates the impression that extractive capitalism is less dependent on cohesive notions of rationality, much less the bonds of sustainability and are totally based on irrational/personal hunches and quick-thinking financial/gambling judgements – undercutting the pseudo-scientific illusion of technology, designed to rectify the unethical black art of financial dealing. Contextually Stone cites the well-known real-life American financial guru Warren Buffet who appears on tape speaking of an 'economic Pearl Harbor' and how we 'have to put the fires out'. Government power and control is essentially needed to protect the market, which for some raises the spectre of socialism by another name. But as Gekko prophetically suggests who the enemy is, this still remains less clear than in more easily defined global world wars. He goes on to talk about the definition of insanity, doing the same thing over and over again and getting the same result. Far from learning from nature, such business sharks simply feed off 'get rich quick' formulas and seldom if ever worry about broad-based precautionary principles, much less take into account any form of moral hazards, or alternatively striving to support more viable long-term sustainable and environmentally ethical projects or services. As a financial system of open governance, 'Wall Street' and the Western financial system generally would appear to have become totally irrational and uncontrollable.

In the filmic narrative of *Wall Street: Money Never Sleeps,* our young heir-apparent Jake – the apprentice influenced by his long working relationship with the founder of his firm Louis Zabel, as contrasted with his more pragmatic and ethically suspect future father-in-law Gekko – is apparently smitten by his intuitive belief in 'alternative energies' as the panacea for global problems. He regards this alternative 'clean energy' as the future for conventional (energy) business; the story thereby lures us into the now trendy business agenda of promoting green energy, all the while regarding the young apprentice as a pragmatic idealist.[11] His old mentor Zabel who took him into his KCI bank, finds its share prices going through the floor and tells his young protégé that there are 'no limits any more' and suggests with some bitterness that the world is all bullshit. 'Fear and the media drive everything', he prognosticates. Asked a straight question 'are we going under?', like a trainee Jedi master, Jake is told that he is posing the wrong questions; suggesting more radically that the whole system is going under. Consequently, as a visual correlative and to crudely slam home the didactic message, the *mise-en-scène* focuses on kids blowing artificial bubbles. How unsubtle can you get! But then Oliver Stone has always been blunt and direct, to say the least, in his often-preachy political/polemical and cautionary filmic tales.

At a packed meeting of the key stakeholders of all the big banks – reminiscent of a gangsters' meeting from *The Godfather* trilogy – we see evidence of the system trying to protect itself and requiring a scapegoat to be offered up. KCI bank is offered a very minimal lifeline of three dollars a share to stem the financial rot and takes the hit to stem the dangers of contaminating other companies in the consortium. While this trophy company was heretofore valued at over 80 dollars a share a few weeks previously, now it is apparently worth less than the actual bricks and mortar costs of the building that they currently occupied and paid for.[12]

Moral hazard: a particular business and ethical conundrum

The ethical notion of moral hazard is brought into the foreground of *Wall Street*'s narrative with inferences made that it might happen again. Essentially, executives who take risky resource and financial decisions, while not taking responsibility for the consequences of their actions, are by all accounts ethically suspect. Historically, an egocentric ethic permits individuals (or corporations) to extract and use natural resources to enhance their own lives and those of other members of society, limited only by the effects on their neighbours. Twentieth- and twenty-first-century capitalism and financial wheeling and dealing encapsulate the extremes of this form of egocentric ethics. Moral hazard remains more prevalent in such an environment and this is a primary ethical dilemma for business generally and capitalist practice in particular. Basically an entrepreneur makes a short-term decision about how much risk to take, leaving national governments and the general taxpayer to bear the ultimate cost if things go badly wrong. Consequently the businessperson or entrepreneur becomes *de facto* isolated from risk, or having to face any moral culpability and most certainly behaves differently to how they might if they were fully exposed to the total risk involved.[13]

Zabel effectively acts out such moral hazard scenarios and presumably he knew the rules of the financial game, including managing and dealing with such risks. But in the end he cannot take the incalculable chaos and shame any longer resulting from his actions and walks deliberately through the crowds towards the front of the platform and jumps in front of an oncoming train. News reports speak of an icon of Wall Street being lost.[14] Meanwhile, his nemesis Gekko remains a survivor, retaining much fewer moral scruples, while knowing how to protect himself, both psychologically and financially. In any case having served eight years in prison from previous unethical behaviour (portrayed in the original film), he apparently remains insulated from further fears around moral hazard.

This alternative father figure and business guru is re-introduced on his promotional book tour. Gekko's apparent recuperation and rehabilitation is set up as he speaks some 'home truths' to his mainly student admirers in the audience, presumably echoing the film director's thematic and ideological preoccupations also. He is introduced with some real biographical details, notably highlighting how since being released from prison in 2002, he has written and spoken publicly about the current state of the world economy. Also we are told how he is not allowed to trade on the US stock exchange, and the irony implied in naming his new book *Moral Hazard: Why Wall Street has Finally Come too Far*. Gekko's major speech is surprisingly full of very useful ethical assertions and testing moral evaluations of business practice that engage his audience. These include a provocative thesis describing the audience as 'the Ninja generation – no income, no assets, no job. You have a lot to look forward to! Greed is good – now it seems it's legal also'.

> You're all pretty much fucked ... Greed was good. America needed greed and risk-taking and leverage to get to become the super power we are, or were. And capitalism needs greed and risk and leverage to become the economic platform it has become ... But these same attributes that got us there are now the liabilities that threaten to destroy us. It's greed that caused the ratings agency to give the toxic loan a triple A rating, just because it was mixed up with good loans. ... But the beauty of the deal is that nobody is responsible; everyone is drinking from the same cool-aid. We're all part of it.

Moral hazard, as a litmus test around business probity, has not been used to offset business excess, which instead of being checked has reached a new level of precariousness, according to this wily and highly astute businessman, who has seen it all. Moving money around, leveraging, steroid banking, not worrying in the least about any form of moral hazard, remains particularly pertinent and a highly relevant allegory that speaks to the current Western (global) causes for depression/recession. Gekko can apparently prophetically see the unvarnished 'truth' and the reality of the current financial crisis, having been locked up behind bars for so long. The mother-of-all-evils, he affirms, is speculation, leveraging, borrowing to the hilt. 'It's systematic and malignant and it's global and like cancer, we have to fight back!'

Audiences might expect a 'road to Damascus' epiphany and a radical affirmation of the economic truth, or at least a strong testament around the need for transformation from selfish 'ego' to more altruistic values including ecological sustainability and an affirmation of a robust form of state regulation – particularly from such a left-field director. Instead, we get a glib throw-away punch-line that appears to relegitimise the status quo of consumer capitalism, or at best accept that there is no way out of the current system, with no real practical alternative to selfish egotism. 'I have three words', he teases, concluding his speech: 'buy my book.' Even appearing to promote an alternative agenda to the dominant modes of business practice, essentially results in a continuation of the same cycle of retrogressive modes of production and distribution. In the end it's all about sales and product, no matter what, and this perspective certainly foreshadows *The Wolf of Wall Street*'s deliberate evocation of a corrupt businessman getting away with it.

Furthermore, essentially questioning the environmental agency of the other main protagonist in the film and his active promotion of green technology, Nick Pinkerton (2010) in his review in *The Village Voice* is particularly critical of the casting of LaBeouf as Jake, who he believes does not have the acting ability, beyond projecting ambition through 'a pert frown and intent gum-chewing. He's flat and dull when he needs to gleam from both sides of a divided loyalty. There's no sense of moral suspense in Jake and James' (Bretton, Josh Brolin as devious boss of rival bank Churchill Schwartz) uneasy partnership.' Working in this 'good guy field of "saltwater fusion", he's no idealist. The only green is money, honey', he tells his fiancée. Nonetheless, while recognising such cogent and perceptive criticism, at least at a macro level, I would like to think Jake is embodied as a performative cypher, albeit not always a very convivial one, as he becomes hooked on drugs, all the while foregrounding the drive to promote alternative energy.

Later Gekko reaffirms to his new protégé and prospective son-in-law, 'money is a bitch' and speaks of how 'we are all slaves to the system'.[15] But as a de-facto 'commercial project' in itself, feeding into conventional Hollywood politics and hermeneutics, the film has to negotiate an acceptable 'happy ending', with foundational bonds of family finally affirmed and greed apparently put aside in favour of more altruistic agendas. All this feel-good mood creation simply reflects a necessary predisposition for a successful environmental agenda. Gekko consequently finally decides to pump his money (which he originally misappropriated of course) into the trendy new environmental financial bubble of clean tech, as popularised and supported by his son-in-law Jake. In some ways Jake can be read as metaphorically representing the fickleness of the environmental movement as it strives to withstand the dominant business model that very much leaves environmental and ethical concerns as an afterthought. One wonders has Gekko really seen the environmental light, or is he simply playing the market again and gauging the odds and prospects of increased clean technology as the safest bet to accumulate even more wealth.

At least from an environmental and creative imaginary perspective, the polarising and simplistic tension set up between unsustainable and indiscriminate (dirty) capitalism and what at least appears to be a pure clean-technology helps to underpin and dramatise the whole narrative's financial trajectory. While by any measure the environmental ethical debate in the film remains underdeveloped, nevertheless it is clearly positioned and foregrounded within the subtext of the whole film.

Two of the best and most insightful critical reviews of the film are by Roger Ebert from the *Chicago Sun-Times* (22 September 2010) and the aforementioned Nick Pinkerton. Ebert muses in conclusion, how he wished the film had been angrier. But 'maybe Stone's instincts are correct, and American audiences aren't ready for that. They haven't had enough greed'. Following on the back of the original *Wall Street* (1987) which was a wake-up call about the financial train-wreck the world's largest financial centre was heading for in that time period, one wonders of course has this sequel added anything new environmentally to the critical mix. Meanwhile Pinkerton remains even more critical in his review 'Wall Street Bails out the Bad Guys'. 'We're all mixed bags' is the conclusion of his piece. He cites Stone who told *Fortune* on *Wall Street's* twentieth anniversary that 'it's very hard to do a financial movie, to make stocks and bonds sexy and interesting'. Still he does his best with 'his beloved stop-motion scuttling clouds, eccentric cell-phone, split-screens and Bloomberg terminal readouts superimposed over images. The Dow Jones arches and plunges along downtown's skyline; a spiralling crane shot rises alongside Philip Johnson's Lipstick Building.'

Metaphorically and visually connecting a city skyline and the vagaries of the Stock Exchange remains a provocative juxtaposition for mass audiences who know little and care less about the complexity of the financial and money market, unless and until this directly impinges on their own lives. Such corporate capitalists and traders, who in one quick deal can radically reframe the physical environment, are conveniently ignored by political and media elites and simply perceived as functionaries performing acts of salesmanship. They perform like the 'barrow boys' of old within street markets, but who have been transported and elevated to deal instead with extremely expensive new tools of financial capitalism including derivatives, hedge funds, bonds and shares. These attributes of performativity and salesmanship, without necessarily worrying about what the consequences are for the 'real' economy and environment, have become the new heroic model for financial dealers to aspire to and at the same time not be worried about any environmental or ethical concerns.

Displaying and dramatising the growing disparity between the digitised online performance of financial capital and the apparently intangible real-life consequences of such awesome wheeling and dealing, affords this area of professional practice much fascination for the general public. Such scenarios exude a surfeit of cautionary ethical tales around moral hazard and suggest a full gamut of precautionary principles. Instead of dealing face-to-face with your customers in historical street markets, now forms of business are done at one remove, either on the phone or simply on the computer screen. Like the drone strikes and contemporary warfare strategy (as dramatised in the HBO television series *Homeland* for instance), the consequences of one's actions are never fully realised on a human scale.

This dissonance and disaggregation of causes and consequences is even more effectively dramatised in the commercially successful film *The Wolf of Wall Street*, where gross disparity of wealth and hyper-greed is further dramatised, assisted by the casting of Leonardo DiCaprio in the lead role, together with a smart script with lots of visual and sexual excess to ostensibly keep mass audiences amused.

By all accounts, *Wall Street: Money Never Sleeps*, in spite of some very strong thematic engagement with environmental ethics and recognising the need to support alternative energy sources, nevertheless remains an undercooked environmental back-story. Yet it still supports a tangible environmental back-story that is primarily addressed at a mass audience, who might not otherwise be receptive to sustainable environmental ethics, alongside its intrinsic cautionary messages. Such a complex issue as climate change, considered in the academic literature as a 'wicked' problem, has to be resolved across multiple dimensions and needs various trajectories including an appreciation of the effects of financial markets on global economics to get its message across. Consequently new forms of visual and aural signifiers can in turn help to feed into mass audiences' creative imaginary and assist in developing a potentially new aesthetic, if not necessarily a counter-cultural environmental ethic, to help explore the various options open to dealing with such global issues. The simple graphic analysis of the ticker tape as a signifier of the life-blood of the financial system, together with the Dow Jones iconic imagery reflected on the city skyline helps, if only unconsciously, to draw connections between excessive urban growth and capitalistic excess. But even more crudely and unsubtly, a provocative populist allegory of redemption is offered and dramatised by Martin Scorsese's recent commercially successful *The Wolf of Wall Street*.

The Wolf of Wall Street

Leonardo DiCaprio plays Belfort, a Long Island penny stockbroker who, like the earlier story of a Wall Street executive, served 36 months in prison for defrauding investors in a massive 1990s security scam. The film biography looks back to the early 1990s when he set up his brokerage firm with Donny Azoff. As their business status grew, the amount of substances they abused also extended, alongside their lies and abuse of systems of governance. They draw attention to themselves like no other business, throwing lavish parties for their staff when they hit the jackpot on high trades. This in turn led to a *Forbes* magazine cover feature, which gave him the nickname. It seems inevitable that such dubious ethical practices would get them caught in the end.

Key scenes that can be re-framed from an explicitly environmental ethical perspective include the cautionary tale of the Wolf's designer boat being capsized in high seas towards the end of the movie, echoing the hubris of such business executives and reminiscent of eco-filmic readings of the *Titanic* (see Brereton 2005). Having to drive his luxury boat in very rough seas to secure a financial deal, sets up an allegorical assertion around how the raw force of nature is pitted against the DiCaprio figure and his greed in trying to squeeze even more wealth from an inheritance. The power of the sea and the resultant high waves, as the business traders struggle to survive, would force most people to contemplate their life path and possible death. But the only thing the Wolf can contemplate is having some recreational drugs to 'cope with it all'. This is his initial response to all disasters, together with the successes and highs in his life. He simply needs to feel in control, unlike the more heroic and altruistic struggles of others, such as in *All is Lost* discussed in Chapter 2.

Like *Wall Street,* Scorsese's film also serves as a cautionary allegory around the irrationality of money markets, pushing to even greater excess Stone's cinematic critique discussed above. This comparison is invoked in a number of promotional videos turned documentaries that are used to set up the new brokerage company by our protagonist. These mini-documentaries recall 'business studies 101' while alluding to animals, in focusing on the differing responses to the 'artificiality' of the market. From a 'bull' market (buying shares as profits go up), to a 'bear' market (low activity, a wait and see approach), financial scenarios are effectively codified in an attempt to cope with all situations, while continuing to make an overall profit. Such signalling apparently of the logical and rational ethical choices within business philosophies, help to reify the naturalness of animals as short-hand explanations of this very artificial and endlessly experimental stock-trading environment. These are the broad possibilities or most appropriate ethical measures to follow in dealing with their otherwise artificial environment. The 'Wolf' also recalls allusions to the solitary animal examined in *Fantastic Mr Fox*, together with more negative cinematic allusions, such as the vicious wolves shown hunting down the survivors of a plane crash in *The Prey*. How the chief protagonist of this film 'survives' in his environment is reminiscent of the *mise-en-scène* of an exotic nature programme, emulating a carefully chosen wild animal who is usually in control of his habitat. Here, however, the chief protagonist at times appears totally out of control.

These very driven entrepreneurs in this financial environment do not necessarily respect any notion of property rights, certainly affording no hint of 'common ownership', much less worrying about doing the right thing for the common good. Some reviewers characterise the film as reminiscent of a form of Jeremiad, like in the classic *Citizen Kane* discussed earlier, portraying the rise and fall of a 'tragic' barrow boy and business leader, who wants to have it all. By all accounts this is a quintessential archetypical storyline in fiction, if not also in real life.

While there is no explicit selling of 'new energy companies' like in the *Wall Street* sequel discussed above, the chief protagonist and his entourage have even fewer moral scruples in this film than those in *The Godfather* mafia family discussed earlier. None of his partners, to put it mildly, have any responsive philosophy regarding protecting the future of the planet. This is so far from their single-minded preoccupation and fixation with making money, it might as well encapsulate a different species of life form. Essentially these blue-blooded amoral working-class wizards illustrate the dominant, but nonetheless pervasive logic – if you make enough money, you can secure a luxury house in a very prestigious area with 'lovely environments all around'. In other words such well-to-do non-citizens can apparently ignore the ethical demands and requirements for global citizenship, which include self-control to help protect the environment for the common good.

Meanwhile, reflecting their neoliberal logic, if you don't have much money and probably retain a surfeit of ethical values and maybe work in a 'public-service job', the Wolf and his followers assume such regulatory workers ought not to have any financial security. Like in the aforementioned gangster movie, the FBI agent – recalling the 'honest policeman – is set up as the foil for audiences who certainly can identify with the FBI officer as an all-round good citizen who is trying to catch him. Such a principled individual who apparently cannot be bribed and constantly emphasies the 'common good', legitimises the need for strict laws and enforced legislation, and is in turn reinforced by a character who is apparently destined to have a poor, albeit frugal lifestyle, as symbolised by the vagaries of using public transport. The Wolf caustically recounts his honest nemesis-imagined 'bony ass' riding the horrible dirty underground. Such an image paradoxically also calls to mind the public service communal benefits of public utilities, which are designed for the maintenance of a healthy environment, as regulations maximise utility and usage, as opposed to wasteful one-person car journeys. Yet the former mode of utilitarian transport is by all accounts painted by such busy and self-serving entrepreneurs as 'demeaning' and in turn a clear marker of deprivation and poverty. Meanwhile, the Wolf rides around in one of the most gas-guzzling and wasteful vehicles currently on the road.

The storyline is a critique of the values of spoilt rich teenagers who always demand a good time and never think of tomorrow, rather than taking on and endorsing the responsibilities of frugal citizen values that are in tune with their environment. Such caricatures of financial success have no concern or scruples whatsoever with regards to the need to control or protect the environment, recognising the prospect of hard choices that have to be made, which would curb resource consumption. Instead, the Wolf and many others believe that by having enough personal wealth and making money,[16] they can simply purchase a good environment and escape the pervasive logics of environmentalism.

At one level, this selfish logic appears totally philistine and at odds with the received thinking of all 'right-minded' environmentally aware citizens, alongside questioning what is promoted by environmental scientists and some pro-active environmental politicians. But, as various cultural historians affirm, the climate change juggernaut has not really turned the minds, much less the behaviour of most well-to-do Americans. Simply put, many believe, like the Wolf and his cohort, that the poor will always suffer as victims of climatic changes, with regard to water levels and other radical environmental conditions; while those who have money and power can always control their circumstances and move inland and/or up to high ground. Furthermore, as evident in a reading of *Chinatown* for instance, money and wealth can facilitate the literal rerouting of water sources and help control the environment to secure the needs and desires of those with the financial muscle to take this on. Consequently, ideological critiques would suggest that publics in the West have been indoctrinated by the power and potency of material acquisition and essentially accepting money and big finance as the solution to most problems – a key premise and preoccupation of a neoliberal philosophy.

This behaviour pattern and business logic is reaffirmed in the open-mouthed and rapt attention displayed by the final live audience who listen to the corrupt and now convicted Wolf, as he fulfils his 'speaking tour', echoing Gekko's earlier speech, delivered to college graduates. Here also the audience apparently want to embrace the myth of easy financial growth and rewards, and are not particularly worried, or concerned about the ethical means of getting there. Finding the magic formula to becoming rich remains enticing, in spite of the dangers for all concerned. As a somewhat one-sided cautionary tale, Scorsese projects 'our' easy seduction for the illusory capitalist message, while only hinting at the need to temper such selfish individuality or striving for material success, as a prerequisite for avoiding environmental catastrophe.

Such amoral (would-be) entrepreneurs do not by any measure embody a right-thinking philosophy or are the type of concerned citizens who appreciate the necessity of controlling scarce resources. 'They just want to party and have fun'. Frequently we see these 'fat cats' (recalling earlier gangsters made-good, like in the *Godfather* franchise) escaping to expensive all-in exotic locations to enjoy the idealised sunny climate and to dance, swim and make love. In other words adapting a totally epicurean morality, rather than accepting the responsibility of upright citizens, who respect the need for stoical restraint and living frugally and in tune with their environment. One can easily see however why this is such a difficult message and life style to sell.[17]

Incidentally having gone through the roller-coaster ride embracing all forms of immorality and wallowing in selfish hubris, the Wolf ends up becoming a 'motivation teacher' for others, like Gekko in the earlier film. In spite of his regressive and downward spiral, many citizens still aspire to be like him and hopefully also make loads of money. As he says: if I had to choose between 'poverty' and being 'rich', I know which way I would choose every time. It is clear this message is also the underlying motivation of everyone else that is listening so intently to his every word. One wonders alternatively, how one could possibly impart a more long-term corrective philosophy of stoicism and frugality, as a bulwark against such an appealing destructive mindset? The final image includes a cinematic pan around the lecture room observing all the faces listening to his amoral selling analogy.

Almost no explicit environmental scruples are featured in this comic pastiche and parody, which tries to have it every way. Yet, I would like to think the film draws attention to such ethical values through hyper-expression of a lack of and even absence of a counter-discourse, while at the same time recounting the truth of such a character's biographical trajectory. Only his first brunette wife has some ethical influence on the rampant economical entrepreneur, encouraging her husband to gravitate towards selling to 'rich schmucks', rather than the poor workers who most definitely need the money and cannot afford to gamble. Otherwise the environmental representation in the film presents a 'morality-free' zone of work and manipulation, with the instrument of 'cold calling' and psychological motivation tools such as the phone as an instrument of power, control, persuasion, passion and commitment, being effectively employed; recalling incidentally for another generation theatrical classics like *Death of a Salesman*, while appreciating the ever-present myth around what America is good at.

From the very start, the young apprentice Leonardo DiCaprio gets his first lesson from his boss Matthew McConnaghy, who perform a 'childish' but nonetheless macho beating of his chest routine with appropriate sounds and movement. This game is designed to anchor the salesman and consequently enable him to be able to perform at the top of his game. Feeding off the dreams of investors who strive to get rich quick, he is informed how they as 'brokers' are the key businessmen, who make the real killing, getting a percentage of *all* transactions. 'We feed off their greed, which is also their drug.'

The whole film can subsequently be read as presenting a provocative cautionary and allegorical business tale, speaking to the totalising allure of capitalism and instant wealth creation through financial wheeling and dealing; a job of work which does not involve, much less promote, any 'real' tangible output. Hence the environmental ethic and prospect of more wholesome financial business is conjured up simply by the pervasive absence of such core ethical values.

It has been argued that advertising's most important function is to keep industrial power constantly on display, to reiterate endlessly this power in our environment. It might be argued that this is a key function of the media in general (Riggs and Willoquet-Maricondi in Desser and Garths 2000: 332–3). Alternatively, however, in these readings I try to counter such dominant ideological arguments by suggesting such negative perceptions are so exaggerated that they can encourage audiences to recognise and even appreciate environmental alternatives and the need for altruistic values and considering the common good, using appropriate precautionary principles and taking into account appropriate moral hazards. Nonetheless, I would have to admit, such a counterintuitive and radical agenda is less evident when commodity production and consumption are 'represented as the means to resolve all conflicts and contradictions' and 'commodification must be seen as always an enhancement' (Riggs *et al.* in Desser and Garths 2000: 334).

Notes

1 Other more reflexive environmentally activist documentary parables including *Garbage Warrior* and *Growth Busters* will be textually analysed in a subsequent study, to foreground their evolving ethical agendas which are beginning to inform more mainstream cinema.

2 It is suggested by scholars like David Myers (*Exploring Social Psychology* fifth edition) that attempting to move societies in the direction of sustainability would be a modification of society comparable in scale to the agricultural and industrial revolutions. But while these two were gradual and largely unconscious, this one will have to be a fully conscious operation.

3 As Jackson illustrates, our current socio-economic thinking is locked into what he calls the 'iron cage' of consumerism, which is characterised by a severe lack of

macro-economic models that do not rely on growth, but rather are designed for functioning at a steady state (Jackson 2009: 100).

4   This almost religious orthodoxy of a narrow measure of economic success that dominates Western (business) values systems has to be turned on its head.

5   This aspect naturally causes severe problems in trying to create and maintain strict guidelines and terms of reference. As Tim Unwin postulates, 'it would be difficult to find a set of issues which symbolise more vividly the torment of a way of life gone astray, which captures more exactly the transformative urge propelling political and economic works', than those raised by modern ecology (cited in Norton 1991: 188).

6   The first *Wall Street* film directed by Oliver Stone and starring a very young Michael Douglas and Charlie Sheen, with his father also playing his screen father as a plane mechanic and running the union. We follow the ambitious young broker (Charlie Sheen) who is lured into an illegal, lucrative world of corporate espionage when he is seduced by the power, status and financial wizardry of Wall Street legend Gordon Gekko – played by Michael Douglas in his Oscar-winning performance: by all accounts a morality tale about the American dream gone wrong!

7   Christians speak of how materialist values make for less happy lives. While Czech poet-President Vaclav Havel (1990) affirmed 'if the world is to change for the better it must have a change in human consciousness'.

8   It is noted that the wider public is heavily swayed by their belief system that is the dominant social paradigm (DSP), in which business is complicit (see Kilbourne, McDonagh and Prothero 1997). The DSP is perceived or generally understood by the public to be the best mechanism to respond to problems of *what to do in society* especially around concerns many have about planet earth.

9   I would echo the comments of Harvey (2000: 214) in suggesting that for the business movie, anthropocentric values are *de rigeur*:

> The environment and ecological movements are full of competing and cacophonous claims as to the possible future of the human species on planet earth. Consider some of the major axes of difference. Ecocentric or biocentric views vie with naked anthropocentrism. Individualism clashes with collectivism (communitarianism). Culturally and historically-geographically embedded views (particularly those of indigenous peoples) sit uneasily alongside universal claims and principles (often advanced by scientists).

10 The *modus operandi* of this gangster narrative essentially incorporates murder as the final sanction, alongside the more all-pervasive code of silence, designed to protect those inside the family. As Chris Messenger argues, such family bonds appear to 'innoculate mob murders against any moral constraint' (Messenger 2002: 11).

11 While Gekko's daughter, who Jake is living with, works for a 'lefty website' with over 50,000 hits a day. She is by all accounts considered altruistic; the boyfriend on the other hand is simply playing the market, while committed to 'green technology' simply because of its intrinsic goodness but also because of its economic justification for making more money in the future.

12 How illogical and irrational are such forms of market fluctuation; effectively serving to concretise Marx's critique of the huge differential between *use* as against *exchange* values, which often has little to do with the reality, much less the truth of 'authentic' value(s).

13 For instance a very useful recent documentary *The Corporation* stops short of claiming capital as the corporate unconscious, but it never questions whether the nation-state, fundamentally grounded in private property-based sovereignty, is responsible for defining the material world specifically as private property and thus ready-made for exchange – for traffic. In this way, *The Corporation* resembles Michael Moore's *Capitalism: A Love Story* (2009).

14 Such a tragic incident, of course, is reminiscent of the equally destructive 1929 crash, when the popular myth suggests many financiers jumped to their deaths in response

to the then global crisis; a period which also resulted in fears of total disintegration of social norms.

15 Interestingly, while gender discourses are continuously implied throughout the narrative, these are not fully outlined, with men dominating the financial market – playing into essentialising notions of gender in some early eco-feminist writings. Yet some characters like Jake appear to reject such Darwinian and macho 'survival of the fittest' forms of capitalism and adapt more altruistic and holistic approaches to labour production.

16 Coincidentally envisaged of late in the West as a macro-economic tool of 'quantitative easing' involving printing more money, which has been adapted most recently by America and other Western states to cope with severe economic recession.

17 Incidentally, anecdotal evidence suggests that the film is very popular with Wall Street executives.

Bibliography

Belz, Frank-Martin and Peattie, Ken (2009) *Sustainability Marketing: A Global Perspective.* Hoboken, NJ: Wiley 2009.

Brereton, Pat (2005) *Hollywood Utopia: Ecology in Contemporary American Cinema.* Bristol: Intellect Press.

Desser, David and Garths, Jowett (eds) (2000) *Hollywood Goes Shopping.* Minneapolis, MN: University of Minnesota Press.

Dobson, A. (ed) (1995) *Green Political Thought.* London: Routledge.

Ebert, Robert (1987) 'Review of *Wall Street*', *Chicago Sun-Times* 11 December.

Ebert, Robert (1998) 'Review of *Citizen Kane*', *Chicago Sun-Times*, 24 May.

Ebert, Robert (2010) 'Review of *Wall Street: Money Never Sleeps*', *Chicago Sun-Times*, 22 September.

Gablik, S. (1991) *The Reenchantment of Art.* New York: Thames and Hudson.

Harvey, D. (2000) *Spaces of Hope.* Edinburgh: Edinburgh University Press.

Havel, V. (1990) 'Ten Ways to Shift Your Consciousness'. http://www.shift.is/2013/07/10-ways-to-shift-your-consciousness/

Jackson, Tim (2009) *Prosperity without Growth: Economics for a Finite Planet.* London: Earthscan.

Keller, David (ed) (2010) *Environmental Ethics.* Oxford: Wiley Blackwell.

Kilbourne, W., McDonagh, P. and Prothero, A. (1997) 'Sustainable Consumption and the Quality of Life: A Macromarketing Challenge to the Dominant Social Paradigm'. *Journal of MacroMarketing* 17(1): 4–24.

Kuttner, Robert (1997) 'Everything for Sale: The Virtues and Limits of Markets'. *The Freeman* 1 November. http://fee.org/freeman/detail/everything-for-sale-the-virtues-and-limits-of-markets-by-robert-kuttner

Levina, Marina and Bui, Diet-my T. (eds) (2013) *Monster Culture in 21st Century A Reader.* London: Bloomsbury.

McDonagh, Pierre and Brereton, Pat (2010) 'Screening not Greening: An Ecological Reading of the Greatest Business Moves'. *Journal of Macromarketing* 30(2): 133–146.

Messenger, Chris (2012) *The Godfather and American Culture: How the Corleones Became 'Our Gang'.* Albany, NY: State University of New York Press.

Myers, David (2012) *Exploring Social Psychology* 6th edition. Columbus, OH: McGraw Hill.

Nash, James A. (1997) 'On the Subversive Virtue: Frugality', in David Crocker and Toby Linden (eds) *An Ethics of Consumption: The Good Life, Justice and Global Stewardship.* Lanham, MD: Rowman and Littlefield Publishers

Norton, B.(1991) *Towards Unity Among Environmentalists*. Oxford: Oxford University Press.

Okun, Arthur (1975) *Equality and Efficiency: The Big Trade Off*. Washington DC: Brookings Institution Press.

Pinkerton, Nick (2010) '*Wall Street* Bails Out the Bad Guys', *The Village Voice*, 22 September.

Sagoff, Mark (1997) 'Carrying Capacity and Ecological Economics', in David Crocker and Toby Linden (eds) *An Ethics of Consumption: The Good Life, Justice and Global Stewardship*. Lanham, MD: Rowman and Littlefield Publishers.

Shultz, C. and Holbrook, M. (1999) 'Marketing and the Tragedy of the Commons: A Synthesis, Commentary, and Analysis for Action', *Journal of Public Policy & Marketing* 18(2): 218–222.

Speth, James Gustave (2008) *The Bridge on the Edge of the World: Capitalism, the Environment and Crossing from Crisis to Sustainability*. New Haven, CT: Yale University Press.

Warshow, Robert (1948) 'The Gangster as Tragic Hero', *Partisan Review*, February, 240–248.

8

END OF THE WORLD SCENARIOS AND THE PRECAUTIONARY PRINCIPLE

Overview

The iconic films discussed in this chapter appeared in cinemas during 2011. Both strive in varying ways to illustrate forms of environmental and ethical responses to 'end of the world' scenarios and how best to face up to such cosmic imbalance. As clearly coded cautionary tales, they can also be read, at least allegorically, as reflecting the urgent need to respond well in advance to upcoming catastrophic changes to our planet, which can in turn be ascribed to long-term concerns around climate change and global warming in particular.

Melancholia and *The Tree of Life* are cautionary tales around what might happen if we don't begin to seriously address major environmental and ethical issues. One could also argue that these provocative examples appeal to a pervasive nihilism and form of melancholia in the face of global environmental disaster. For the late Ulrich Beck in particular, environmental hazards can never be eliminated through the use of technological knowledge, although they can be anticipated. This theory claims that we now live in a highly troubled risk society that continues to find answers to these particular environmental problems using the logic of the nineteenth century heuristics.[1] Mark Smith summarises Beck's ideas:

> while the hazards of a technologically driven society in the late twentieth century penetrate every region and level of society, human beings remain wedded to the responses to environmental degradation which were more appropriate in the nineteenth century ... The scale and scope of human impacts upon the environment produce a range of complex and unanticipated consequences which cannot be contained effectively within the earlier guarantees and safety mechanisms.

(Smith 1998: 94)

Yet by all accounts, as Richard Maxwell and Toby Miller (2014) point out, Hollywood remains the biggest producer of conventional pollutants in the Los Angeles area.

> [W]hen you think of film and the environment, does your mind turn to how cinema has depicted nature and pollution? Do you revel in Adorno's conceit that cinema can provide an 'objective recreation' akin to dreaming about landscapes as if that would prettify urban existence?
>
> (Maxwell and Miller 2012: 271)

Such a bold assertion and reality check should always be kept in mind when eco-film scholars, as in this work, attempt to valorise the recuperative potential of cinema to promote a pro-environmental agenda. Maxwell and Miller remain especially cynical, for instance, when examining the work of directors like Danny Boyle and his claim that *The Beach* was essentially preoccupied with 'raising environmental consciousness' (Maxwell and Miller 2014: 4). They go on to conclude that a risk society 'organises what cannot be organised' by creating institutions to protect people from 'social, political, economic and individual risks'. Rather than 'being occasional, risk is now part of what it means to be modern' (Maxwell and Miller 2014: 7).

Risk society similarly rationalises and naturalises climate change, often seeking to promote a technological and geo-engineering solution to the problem.[2] Risk analysis assessment is often coupled with a range of precautionary principles, which were examined in Chapter 1.

Timothy O'Riordan and Andrew Jordan (1995) suggest in a paper 'The Precautionary Principle in Contemporary Environmental Politics' that like sustainability, the precautionary principle is 'nether a well-defined principle nor a stable concept'. While at least, such principles challenge the direction of authority of

> science, the hegemony of cost-benefit analysis, the powerlessness of victims of environmental abuse, and the unimplemented ethics of intrinsic natural rights and inter-generational equity.
>
> (O'Riordan and Jordan 1995: 191)

Nevertheless, as Norton (1991: 98) affirms, to fully take on board notions of risk society, much less analyse a range of precautionary principles and concerns over sustainability, remains an almost impossible balancing act. Calls for a coherent 'set of principles' are derived from core ideas around sustainability, but further calibrated in sufficiently specific terms to provide robust guidelines for day-to-day decisions and to help make policy choices affecting the environment. Precautionary principles most certainly could underpin these core principles, for they provide an intuitively simple guide to humans around how to intervene in environmental systems in a manner that is least damaging.[3]

Speaking to the dominance of climate change as the global environmental challenge, while witnessing extreme weather events across the globe, environmental risk ethics have become even more evident, pervasive and engaging across a wide range of contemporary films discussed in this volume. Such interconnecting tools, measures and perspective, can certainly help explain how contemporary narratives like *The Tree of Life* and *Melancholia* at least dramatise, if not signal, a new language of ethical environmental concern. This is especially evident within these examples of sublime and excessively visualised digital rendering of apocalyptic and extreme climatic weather conditions, which will be textually analysed throughout this chapter.

Interestingly, Seabrook (2002) proposes that our Western fascination with 'wild weather' is in part a matter of 'Christian guilt' with a growing public awareness of changes in the climate, making correlations to extreme weather anomalies. We appear to be moving to a position where 'extreme weather is taken as a sign of cosmic displeasure for our failure as stewards of the earth' (2002: 45), as most explicitly explored in the reading of *Noah*. This highly contested 'Old Testament' notion of 'cosmic displeasure' surprisingly resonates with many natural disaster films, most of which suggest in various superficial ways that *we* are mistreating 'nature' and are now on the verge of being mightily punished; they are 'guilt trips that we feel we deserve and are prepared to receive' (see for instance Sizemore 2014) – as long as they don't force us to actually scrutinise our lives and our institutions and to push for change. Such reductive moralisation of natural disaster in turn feeds into the concept of 'weatherporn', which is certainly ripe for scholarly analysis. As with pornography, the consumption of representations of extreme weather is about 'the illusion of control: one watches the forecast because one wants to know nature's secrets – to see through the eye of the hurricane' (Belmont 2007: 353; see also readings of films like *Twister* in Brereton 2005).

Hollywood cinema in general remains good at portraying effects, but finds it difficult to show causes, which might in turn address underpinning ecological and environmental problems. Causality is primarily a motivational agent of character and plot, propelling the narrative to a final resolution. However, following the growth in scientific knowledge and ecological awareness, science fiction texts of late have begun to appropriate a form of diegetic realism, through applying well-worn conventions of docudrama within the overall fictional style.

Sociologists such as Adam, Beck and Van Loon have identified how contemporary environmental problems are not always easily accessible to the senses, giving them an 'air of unreality' until 'they materialise as symptoms' (Allan *et al.* 2000: 3). Adam (1998) has argued further that the very nature of environmental problems – including issues around sustainability, which adds a further layer of complexity – means that they happen over a long period of time and are often invisible if not understood in this temporal manner.

To examine and articulate this difficult representative challenge, this chapter will focus on specific Hollywood/arthouse films which are ostensibly designed not to promote a predetermined agenda around environmentalism, nor are they designed to 'preach' to an audience – unlike more directly 'teacherly' environmental documentaries such as *An Inconvenient Truth* which strive to influence and affect audiences by promoting a radical proactive environmental agency.

Imagining ecological disaster: climate change beyond the disaster movie

Until recently, few eco-film scholars (David Ingram, Sean Cubitt, Adrian Ivakhiv, Alexa Weik von Mossner and Paula Willoquet-Maricondi are among those that come to mind) focused almost exclusively on a range of environmental representational debates. Yet the influence of other disciplines, most notably eco-criticism in literature and green cultural studies is now beginning to permeate film analysis. Working from the premise that climate change and global warming has become *the* most important contemporary political and social issue for this century, throughout this study I have explored how a wide constituency of (eco)-cinema has represented the pervasive threat posed by climate change in particular. These fears are particularly evident in this chapter, while creating new imaginaries and effectively speaking to the urgency of such debates.

Lisa Garforth, for instance, suggests that many recent films continue to address this growing ecological preoccupation of the modern world:

> [F]rom Danny Boyle's (2000) representation of the desert island as an Edenic paradise falling/transforming into paranoia and violence for jaded tourist consumers in *The Beach*, to the spectacular climate change epic *The Day After Tomorrow* (Emmerich 2004).
>
> (Garforth 2006: 26)

Furthermore, as suggested in earlier chapters, recent films including the polemical eco-film *The Age of Stupid*, alongside futuristic cautionary tales like *Wall-E* and *2012* all feature the long-term effects of climate change, collapsed into a very short screen-time and draw attention to growing ecological preoccupations within the world today. For many critics at present, it seems clear that anxieties and hopes about the future of nature reaching conditions approximating endemic crisis, are insistently finding their way into mainstream film, assisted, it must be said, by the dire, almost biblical and doom-laden, warnings of some environmental activists. But as David Ingram and others caution, Hollywood has made environmental apocalypse seem perversely attractive, as we frequently observe wild nature simply getting its own back on humans.

Nevertheless, the ideological or deconstructionist approach that has become dominant within critical film studies remains sceptical of Hollywood's broadly escapist classic narrative structure and its excessive use of spectacle and blockbuster special effects, alongside the idealisation and romantic evocation of nature in general. Many critics consistently affirm that in the end Hollywood serves simply to reify the dominant ideology and promote the status quo. But such analysis sometimes misses the multiple and even contradictory discourses at work in popular culture, including the exploration of new possibilities for an evolving form of ecological expression, together with a growing desire within contemporary culture and society for a more sustainable and less alienated existence.

I still, at least, want to believe that spectacular representations of landscape and cosmic catastrophe in mainstream Hollywood film call upon and often contain 'moments of transcendent possibility that illuminate profoundly other ways of being' and that this 'romantic utopian impulse', expressed through visions of the sublime remains 'what Hollywood has always been good at exploiting' (Brereton 2005: 39). In many ways, as Brian Butler affirms, this 'unapologetic quality of the Hollywood narrative can serve as a therapeutic tool because of the reluctance on the part of academics to promote any positive ideals' (Butler 2007: 62). Or, as suggested most pointedly:

> (W)hile academic theory has enormous difficulty articulating, much less legitimising, various foundational beliefs, Hollywood has no qualms whatsoever in promoting them.
>
> (Brereton 2005: 35)

In other words, mainstream movies, as affirmed throughout this volume, are also valuable as artefacts for 'seeing ecology' and imagining a broad strand encapsulated by the notion of sustainability.

Hollywood has certainly made environmental apocalypse perversely attractive. Environmentalists have as part of their arsenal adapted the old-Testament concept of doomsday with a perverse appeal, 'waking us from our humdrum existence'. People may even be emotionally attracted to apocalypse, according to Steven O'Leary, through a desire for consummation, narrative closure or absolute knowledge (O'Leary 1994: 66). So the ever-present set-piece of apocalyptic weather effectively exhibits the sublime power of wild nature, violent, chaotic, amoral and beyond human control. In these revenge-of-nature films, the problem with identifying with wild nature effectively functions across transgressing ethical norms, as we witness nature 'getting its own back' as it were, for its maltreatment at the hands of human beings. The spectator takes pleasure in the destructive forces of nature, from the safe distance of their cinema seat. Such films such as *The Day After Tomorrow* accordingly seek out particular forms of identification, not only with regards to wild nature, but also paradoxically with the forces of civilisation that try to control nature.

Incidentally, this meta-narrative also recalls James Lovelock's Gaia principle that the earth will heal itself as the storm passes. But the 'right-wing' version of this thesis implies that there is consequently no need to be especially protective towards the environment; simply 'leave it to Gaia' and it will solve the problem without human intervention. In his 2006 book *The Revenge of Gaia*, James Lovelock milks a literary metaphor, which echoes tropes long-established within the disaster movie:

> we suspect the existence of a threshold, set by the temperature or the level of carbon dioxide in the air, once this is passed, nothing the nations of the world do will alter the outcome and the Earth will move irreversibly to a new hot state. We are now approaching one of these tipping points, and our future is like that of the passengers of a small pleasure boat sailing quietly above the Niagara Falls, not knowing that the engines are about to fail.
>
> (Lovelock 2007: 7)

Hollywood scriptwriters are paid big money to develop such cautionary allegorical tales across blockbuster disaster movies; and even more reflexive and arthouse storylines, including *The Tree of Life* and *Melancholia*, can be read as also addressing such dangers.

Melancholia: extreme psychic and dystopic representations of climate change

In contrast to the late great Swedish director Ingmar Bergman, for example, whose European arthouse films focused on the angst of the unbeliever and the yearning to believe, von Trier's more secular films are about the angst of the believer and at the same time desiring not to believe. An apt observation by film critic Thomas Beltzer conveys some of von Trier's ambivalence towards Christian dogma and its corresponding ethical mindset.

> The Dogme 95 Manifesto of filmmaking encourages filmmakers to abuse their godlike dominance over their material, if not to behave like children. Such explicit yet at the same time elastic notions around work practice helps to create a radical film-making praxis and provides some interesting avenues for an environmental ethical agenda. This is certainly evident in the aesthetically rich narrative *Melancholia*, which apparently evolved out of von Trier's own mental health issues.[4]
>
> (Beitzer 2002)

There is a strong sense of life being lived post-sustainability in *Melancholia* – in the first shot Justine (Kirsten Dunst) blinks heavy, depressed eyelids as a rain of dead birds falls in agonising slow motion behind her. The prelude to the film continues by way of a montage of 16 colour-saturated, fantastic images of apocalypse set to the overture from Wagner's *Tristan und Isolde*: a bride wades through a jungle of oppressive tendrils. A charge of electricity emanates from Justine's fingertips. She stands Christ-like in the midst of a storm of moths.

Meanwhile her sister Claire (Charlotte Gainsbourg) sinks into the disintegrating green of a 'fantastic' golf course, which von Trier has said is symbolic of limbo (Sinnerbrink 2012: 4). A painting, Bruegel's 1566 'Hunters in the Snow' burns in the ashes. On the horizon, a magnificent planet, the errant Melancholia, rises to eclipse the sky. These images create, as Sinnerbrink has observed, a kind of 'uncanny tableaux vivant effect' as well as recalling a kind of popular fantasy art we might associate with genre fiction paperbacks and a 'mad new age movement' (Sinnerbrink 2012: 28).

Richard Wagner's music permeates the film, as the creator of the idealised *Gesamtkunstwerk* (total work of art) in the form of the nineteenth-century music drama. Wagner claimed that

> as a pure organ of the feeling, [music] speaks out the very thing which word speech in itself cannot speak out … that which, looked at from the standpoint of our human intellect, is the unspeakable.
> (Wagner, 1849/1964: 217 cited in Langer 1942)

According to Suzanne K. Langer: 'music has all the earmarks of a true symbolism, except one: the existence of an assigned connotation' and, though music is clearly a symbolic form, it remains an 'unconsummated symbol' (Langer 1942: 240). Therefore in order for a film to make the greatest possible impact, there must be an interaction between the verbal dialogue (consummated symbol), the cinematic image (also a consummated symbol) and the musical score (unconsummated symbol)' (see Lipscomb and Tolchinsky 2004).[5]

While the viewer (who only moments before was witness to the interplanetary collision of the prelude) already suspects that this star represents cosmic threat, the first half of the film ignores this and continues in its narrative, perhaps echoing the way we continue our own lives in the face of environmental catastrophe.

The blonde Justine is almost a psychic representation of the planet, having just got married, yet still apparently having the worries of the world on her shoulders. We are privy to a sublime image of a new planet rising in the skyline and getting bigger and bigger. In a revealing interview with the director on the DVD bonus feature, von Trier admits: 'I only write about myself', reflecting his own depression issues. von Trier sees himself in both of the sisters, almost as two sides of the same person and continues how it is refreshing to make a film about bad things, as you can gain something from it. While Claire represents the sane, normal human being, Justine is more prone to panic attacks and is very egocentric.

Theatre (tragedy) is one of the many devices the human race has developed to 'endure the unthinkable, that which is essentially beyond logos and representation' (Jeong and Dudley 2008: 8). This proposition is certainly evident in *Melancholia,* which records a form of 'anti-sublime in the ending' (Jeong and Andrew 2008: 8). The film uses visual styles such as montage, super slow-motion filming, a highly saturated palette and computer animation to bring to life an uncanny vision of the end of the world, which is inhabited viscerally by the audience. In both instances, the protagonist's psychology is indivisible from the *mise-en-scène,* and we are invited through the mechanism of cinema, to partake (and to delight, as many of these sequences possess unnerving beauty) in their mad, prophetic visions.[6]

Robert Sinnerbrink in a comparative analysis from 2014 argues von Trier presents an

> ironic critique of rational optimism: the conviction that, given our irrational faith in instrumental reason and fantasies of controlling nature through technology, the only foreseeable end is a scenario of world destruction. At the same time, it resonates with contemporary ecological anxieties concerning the threats to the biosphere and the environment, even the "unthinkable" thoughts of species extinction.
>
> (Sinnerbrink 2014: 122)

The contrast between the husband John's deluded rationalism, Claire's controlling anxiousness and Justine's nihilistic certainty can be read as a refusal on behalf of the film-maker to perpetuate the coupling of madness and unreason – von Trier's own battle with depression is certainly significant.

For other critics however, the acceptance of the finitude of the human race is not evidence of a nihilistic worldview, but rather speaks to the inherent optimism of the film. He takes this idea further and claims that if we are to resist the logics of totalitarianism, we all should reach this acceptance of finitude. Recalling the seminal study *A History of Madness* for instance, Foucault (2006) has observed the link between madness and a special kind of foreknowledge in the Dark Ages which has, in fact, persisted well into the classical period. It is precisely this bond between madness and nothingness that *Melancholia* seeks to restore. Here

> melancholia is evoked as a mood, an aesthetic sensibility, a way of experiencing time; a visionary condition and aesthetic experience that cinema has all but lost.
>
> (Sinnerbrink 2012)

Environmental re-reading

At a most basic textual level, there is an operatic/music video feel to the opening sequence with so many weird images that recall conventional markers of surrealism, as the stirring Wagnerian music rises to a crescendo. So many images of figures 'melting' into the landscape and images of a bride in a white gown pulling elements of earth/vegetation/decay in almost slow motion, as the female protagonist tries to move from screen left to right. In other vignettes she is helping a boy who is wading knee deep in soil/earth (as if it's porous) across a field. One of the most striking and memorable images from this visceral opening sequence remains however the iconic cosmic silhouette of the moon, framed alongside another alien planet called Melancholia approaching earth. Cosmic destiny and the recalibration of the long-established laws of nature being turned on their head, help to signal an inverted environmental ethical sensibility.

The beautiful landscape and manicured gardens and trees remind a cinephile of a modernist art classic, *Last Year in Marienbad* (as suggested in a 2011 reading by Manogha Dargis (2011)), subverting postwar perceptions/visualisations with shadows not falling naturally on all the trees in any uniform way. Here, also, natural and physical laws are subverted with nothing as it seems; especially witnessing the moon being symmetrically framed with another 'Melancholia' moon, and both in turn framed against the sun. This truly sublime and disturbing astronomical creative imaginary – which calls to mind the power and magic of early cinema like *Journey to the Moon* – is repeated several times throughout the spectacle of this 'end of the world' psychic exposition. For the purposes of this study however, this juxtaposition can clearly be decoded as a cautionary environmental and ethical planetary destruction tale.

Jungian analysis is probably a useful psychological tool for a broad-ranging ecological and ethical appreciation of such a film. Jung conceived the process of self-development (or individuation) as a primarily spiritual journey, and this perspective has been influential in a genre-implied dealing with the journey of self-knowledge. Furthermore, a preoccupation with the feminine experience of lycanthropy has characterised fantasy fiction since the 1930s, a phenomenon that lends some support to Spivack's speculation that fantasy is perhaps a 'feminine' form and is especially applied to readings of the moon.[7]

At a more prosaic and lexical level of engagement, the term melancholia is decoded and easily unpacked by Googling the word, which is parsed as meaning 'death melancholia', causing a deep form of depression.[8] But before Claire can assimilate this information by printing off the definition for future examination, the electricity goes off. Rather than the 'normal' representation of electricity, much less explaining physical phenomena via the easily accessed Google definitions, we are privy to a perverse form of scientific 'cinema of attractions'. The lightning sparks from Claire's outstretched fingers, having some cosmological connections with the 'death star', all of which is reminiscent of iconic early film classics including *Metropolis*. The ubiquitous power of computers and, in particular, Google as an über-database and repository of human knowledge is certainly of little use here, when the world is facing total annihilation from a strange planet, hidden behind the sun, as it hurtles majestically towards the earth.

But the unseen expert 'scientists' reassure the general public that by their calculations Melancholia will miss the planet, resulting in a 'fly-by' event. The alpha male of the house John is played by *24*-star Keifer Sutherland, who in that cult television series always finds a way to solve conspiratorial problems. In this story, however, John remains somewhat one-dimensional with no psychic inner life and therefore is unable to cope. His problems are of course compounded when life and nature are radically pushed out of kilter. Worries regarding a risk society has by all accounts been dramatised through its ultimate manifestation of facing total annihilation.

Claire's story: she appears, like her sister, to be 'easily depressed' and worried, but not in the explicit psychotic way as her sister, Justine. Claire announces several times in frustration how she 'really hates her sister'. The iconic image – as she lies naked, almost offering her body to some deity, real or imagined, by the lakeshore and lit by the bright Melancholia moon – embodies a recreation of her sister's potent imagination. Again recreating the iconic tragic and romantic image from British art with the subject as victim immersed in water, affirming her transcendent soul in the iconic painting of Ophelia. This evocative image appears to particularly upset Claire, who spies her from a distance, being in turn transfixed by such purity and raw presentation of self; and consequently she does not interfere in this scene of perfection. Apparently Justine has deep power and 'sees the light' both literally and metaphorically, almost fulfilling a deep psychic fantasy.[9]

While being extremely nurturing in the conventional sense, as explored in the earlier eco-feminist chapter, Claire remains unsure how to relate to such cosmic circumstances and easily believes her husband John when he 'comforts' her with the proposition that all will be well in the end. She wants to believe in the rationality of science – albeit foregoing worries about any impending natural disaster. But in the end the apparent split personality of Justine is more knowing and more in tune with life's macro 'forces', including what might at a stretch be considered also as global environmental concerns. Justine announces with a strong sense of certainty, and against what by any measure would be regarded as common sense, her essentially intuitive feelings around how almost nobody will actually miss this planet! – at the same time acknowledging that there is no life-force possible on any other planet. I know this, she affirms, with apparent total confidence.

By all accounts this remains a depressingly negative mindset. Is it worth thinking, much less being ethical, at all in such a scenario, especially if there is nothing out there in the cosmos? Such a profound questioning, yet surprisingly affirmative spectre of anti-belief and (empty) spectacle, neatly dovetails with the much more life-affirmative evocation of a spiritual form of rapture and closure in *The Tree of Life,* to be discussed below.

And yet there is Claire's son, the object of any mother's affections, over which she is called upon to display her deep, nurturing instinct. This instinct permeates much mainstream cinema and is for instance also echoed and mirrored in possibly the most nihilistic example of environmental ethics, namely *The Road,* which was discussed elsewhere in this volume. By facing absolute rock bottom, we as a human species can travel no further. For some audiences this might signal the beginnings of fresh hope. If only for the children, one has to keep up some pretence. But how can these protagonists create or play with the notion of a 'safe space' in such a dystopian environment? As an audience we also find it hard to connect with the tone and mood of such a dystopian situation where there is no hope. Surveying such nihilism and anti-utopian and anti-ecological sentiment, what is the point of it all? Nonetheless, like the counterintuitive trajectory of horror movies, the spectacle in itself serves in ways as being both therapeutic and engaging with regard to how it speaks to and for its empathetic audiences.

Justine and her sister must uncover ways of coping with global disintegration, which is beyond any normal sense-making schema or human comprehension. Consequently, such a traumatic narrative serves by default to encourage audiences to try to comprehend the stark (Old Testament) elemental realities of life, while struggling with the prospect of their terminal fate. This prospect is dramatised by some unnatural extra-terrestrial logic, or some extreme form of cosmological transformation or malfunction, resulting in catastrophic destruction. Paradoxically, I suppose, the least prescient of the victim's worries centre around the slow working out of climate change scenarios, while actually facing immediate cosmic catastrophe.

Nevertheless, I would suggest, this storyline can also function as a cautionary tale about the end of the world and by extension the radical effects of climate change. It thereby sets up in a dramatic manner how to psychically and ethically 'cope' with such cosmic eventualities. Justine remains the knowing melancholic one, who apparently 'identifies' with eminent catastrophe, yet cannot cope with her 'real life', including marriage, family and work life. But in the end she becomes the most resigned, as they construct a ritualised solution for coping with the situation by building a 'primitive' spiritual pre-Christian tepee of joined sticks which all three family members step into and hold hands as they face their destiny.

One wonders, incidentally, why the director still found it necessary to actually include the final nihilistic vision of total destruction. It was always clearly signalled in the text that global catastrophe was imminent. Maybe von Trier sought to labour this personal tragedy, coupled with global annihilation as both come together. Human agents are left with no ethical choice in such psychologically charged 'end of world' narratives, and become literally and aesthetically swamped by the inevitability of total destruction.

Bruno Latour most usefully speaks of how we began with feeling so powerless, because of the total disconnect between the range, nature and scale of the phenomena and the set of emotions, habits of thoughts and feelings that would be necessary to handle crises such as these. How are we to behave sensibly when there is no ground control station anywhere to which we could send a message for help? 'Houston, we have a problem'? (Latour 2011). Recalling a mayday message that is often not heard in time, or is sometimes misinterpreted – as in a reading of *Gravity* discussed in Chapter 4 – it seems that in *Melancholia*:

we might rather all be quietly enjoying the solitary spectacle of the planet crashing into our Earth from the derisory protection of a children's hut made out of a few branches by Aunt Steelbreaker. If as in the West, just when the cultural activity of giving a shape to the Earth is finally taking a 'literal' and not a symbolic meaning, resorted to a totally outmoded idea of magic as a way to forget the world entirely.

(Latour 2011: 5)

In this amazing final scene, Latour suggests that hyper-rational people fall back onto what old primitive rituals are supposed to do – protect childish minds against the impact of reality. A counter-reading, I suggest however, might also speak of the elusive power and unity of community (or *agape* meaning a deep form of unconditional love) and even recalling the fractured notion of family in the face of forces greater than all of us. von Trier might even have grasped just what happens after the empty/romantic sublime has disappeared, again echoing an 'Old Testament' mindset, which has apparently come back into fashion with blockbusters like *Noah* and even *The Tree of Life* discussed later.

All in all, as reaffirmed by Latour, when the trumpets of judgement resonate in your ear, you fall into melancholia!

No new ritual will save you. Let's just sit in a magic hut, and keep denying, denying, denying, until the bitter end. What if we had shifted from a symbolic and metaphoric definition of human action to a literal one? After all, this is just what is meant by the anthropocene concept: everything that was symbolic is now to be taken literally.

(Latour 2011: 5)

Cultures used to 'shape the earth' symbolically, now they do it for good. Furthermore, the very notion of culture went away along with that of nature. 'Post natural, yes, but also post cultural' (Latour 2011: 11). This need to reimagine and reconstitute human's role in climate change is a big ask for the creative imaginary of film and other art formats.

The film's ending is also particularly insightful with Justine appearing calm, and Claire asserting – 'I want [us] to be together when it happens'. I want to do the right thing – while in response Justine is dismissive, recalling cheap sentimental and nostalgic responses to such a catastrophe: 'How about a song – Beethoven's ninth – we could light some candles – have a glass of wine – that would make me happy.' Justine concludes, recalling any rationale analysis, that her sister's plan 'is a piece of shit'. Both sisters' responses are of course valid and totally identifiable in their own ways.

While Claire's son, the embodiment of innocence, like the boy in *The Road* who also sees the deeper truth, recognises: 'I'm afraid that the planet will hit us anyway' and 'there is no place to hide'. But like the father's evocation of a 'fire within us' in *The Road*, Claire here recalls the notion of a 'magic game' and conspires to recreate a utopian possibility for her son and, one could insinuate, society in general. Consequently, the boy cuts up sticks and coincidentally the audience is privy to the ground on which they stand alive with insects scurrying around, also waiting, preparing 'and knowing' the end is nigh. All of nature appears connected and co-present in fearful harmony.

Essentially they create a symbolic 'tree house of sticks' to metaphorically protect them and do the ethically right thing as they re-create a human community while about to meet their final end, or their maker, depending on which value system one believes in. They hold hands and the boy closes his eyes, like in a theatrical performance. As the music swells to a fever pitch, they wait for the end. As in several films explored in this volume, the power of human hands to create bonds of unity and demonstrate pure love remains evocative and compelling, in spite of Latour and other critical reservations. As a mother cries, Justine looks on stoically with eyes wide open. The boy's eyes remain tightly shut. The audience is entreated to witness a close-up of the huge (alien and digitised) planet Melancholia coming into extreme close-up, before final destruction and the screen goes blank.

Interestingly, Clive Hamilton (2010) offers the strange and terrifying assertion that it's hope that we should abandon if we wish to enter into any transaction with Gaia. Hope, unremitting hope, is for him the source of our melancholia and the cause of our cognitive dissonance. In this environmental reading, however, I would counter that hope and witnessing forms of endurance become strangely therapeutic and in turn speak to a deep ecological form of stoical discourse. The final evocative sequence is reminiscent of the power of 'innocence' to appreciate and frame such ecocidal events, displayed also in other dystopian narratives like *The Road*.

Psychological imbalance and seeing the truth in nature

In his already cited *History of Madness*, Michel Foucault tracks centuries of madness: 'it is still true today that our scientific and medical knowledge of madness rests implicitly on the prior constitution of an ethical experience of unreason' (Foucault 2006).

In film, pathologies become character tropes, such as the psychotic serial killer, the hyperactive teen-delinquent, the depressed housewife, the happy fool, or the knowing psychic in *Melancholia* and *The Tree of Life*. Such films use the trope of mental illness or madness as an allegory or metaphor, a vehicle for the critique of our dominant social system. *Melancholia* and *The Tree of Life* both emphasise links between madness, prophecy and apocalypse which is restated in order to form a greater critique about a specific, post-global financial crisis together with environmental concerns as a key moment in late capitalism (Kermode 2012: 8).

For instance, Deleuze and Guattari insist that forms of schizophrenia are not only a product of capitalism, but also its external limit, and that accessing schizophrenia as a process will allow us to decode the despotic 'flows of signification' which are part of the repressive power of capitalism. Here madness disturbs rather than locates meaning. Schizophrenia then, 'is a tool of resistance, and as it is held as both a limit of and a potential antidote of capitalism, schizophrenia also becomes an apocalyptic concept, which can be used to measure the rise of (cosmic) environmental concerns and subsequent ethical concerns and issues' (Doyle 2007: 23). In these two films, Doyle astutely asserts, they form a metaphoric schema indicating the impossibility of clarity of mind or indeed any form of normality in late capitalism, as well as remaining intact as an experience for the sufferer and those around them.

The Tree of Life: sublime environmental endings

On first viewing the film, I was taken by its explicit reference to Rachael Carson's *Silent Spring* and the DDT wars in the 1950s, as an unmarked lorry is witnessed pumping out DDT insecticide, with kids jumping all around behind inhaling the fumes. I've never seen such an explicit play on conflictual ecology. Philosophically, nature is presented as 'selfish' and will do what it takes to survive – like the patriarchal male – unlike the iconic nurturing mother with its instinct for selfless love and devotion as its primary ethic. At the outset, *The Tree of Life* connects at a very deep level with loss (both personal and global), framed through environmental ethics and cosmology, which can incidentally be contrasted with the more commercial and semiotically less sophisticated *Avatar* and its evocation of the 'home tree', explored in an earlier chapter.

Throughout the film, again like in *Avatar*, trees serve as a barometer of nature and speak to iconic/allegorical visions of environmental/ethical purity. Ever since antiquity, trees have been used as symbols and literal embodiments of religious beliefs for mankind. One special symbolic tree shared by many cultures is the tree of life, which of course has deep religious significance. Compared to flowers and mountains, it is often suggested, trees are closer to man's own nature (McReynolds 2013: ix).

Some critics however dismiss the final *mise-en-scène*, which is even more unsettling for some viewers than *Melancholia*, as a crude evocation of a fundamentalist type of rapture – further denoted environmentally by flocks of birds trying to escape the cosmological 'end of world' scenario, together with the sea conventionally ebbing from the shoreline. All the family, together with presumably their greater community are lined up – as in a theatrical set piece – waiting to act out their final moments. Time passes as night comes around and almost instantaneously we are back into sunrise. A facemask appears floating in the water, suggesting the Platonic ending of appearances and the truth of self-revelation. A prayer to endings and new beginnings is affirmed by further images of a door opening, hands and movement and the affirmation of movement into another world; 'I can hear my son'. We are finally treated to the beautiful luxurious colours of a mature sunflower field literally following the sun to capture its rays and life-giving energy – very much echoing the glorification of natural and primal power of the sun's rays to afford life to the planet.[10]

Then we are back to reality and the older reflective brother, who is the architect, travelling down a very large glass-fronted skyscraper and further echoing the 'technological sublime' (Nye 1994), by being treated to a long static shot of a literal and metaphorical [Brooklyn] bridge to another time/space before the film closes enigmatically and fades to black.

McAteer (2013) reads the film from a largely theological and Christian standpoint; one which I think is necessary to fully appreciate its positive values, unlike the more pessimistic evocation of *Melancholia* discussed above. I believe, following McAteer, that the film provides a useful model for considering how a narrative, non-documentary film might present an all-embracing argument around environmental ethics and speak to a cosmological end of the world scenario and its implications for all of nature including mankind.[11]

Mrs O'Brien (Jessica Chastain) accompanied by idyllic images of nature, alongside a farm setting announces:

> The nuns taught us there are two ways through life: the way of nature and the way of grace. You have to choose which one you'll follow. Grace doesn't try to please itself. It accepts being slighted, forgotten, and disliked. It accepts insults and injuries. Nature only wants to please itself. And others to please it too. [It] likes to lord it over them. To have its own way....

But nature itself, particularly in the colloquial sense of the totality of living things is depicted in the narrative as more in tune with the 'ways of grace', if not also symbolic of the divine dimension of creation. The main protagonist Jack has become an architect, who consequentially seeks to mould and control space, living in modern-day Houston.

Visually and metaphorically, a large tree's prominent inclusion in the suburban *mise-en-scène* seems to parallel the lives of the human characters and provides an environmental and temporal timeline for the story's development. The image of the tree – or more dramatically evoked through Home Tree in *Avatar* – seems to anchor the human lives at key moments in their development and even recall the process of 'evolution'. In other words, one could posit a clear manifestation of nature, as embodied by the iconic tree as tightly wrapped up into a human narrative.

Mrs O'Brien's character and personality is that of a free spirit and diviner of nature. In many instances her presence on the screen provides a symbolic representation of human absorption in nature, while also serving to articulate humanity's connection with the supernatural makeup of creation. In one outdoor scene she draws her son's attention to the sky, saying 'That's where God lives'. In another, she reminds the boy 'you'll be grown before the tree is tall'.

In a voiceover, the father, Mr O'Brien, after he loses his job, speaks of how he wanted to be loved because:

> I was great, a big man. Now I'm nothing. Look at the glory around us. Trees, birds. I lived in shame. I dishonoured it all and didn't notice the glory.

In an endearing scene of family connectivity shortly after however, he embraces Jack heartily, saying: 'You're all I have … You're all I want to have'. Both father and mother symbolically evoke very deep ecological aspects concerning appropriate modalities around engaging with nature.

The final episode, already alluded to, transitions forward to the present life of adult Jack, where he experiences something like a spiritual reconciliation, if not a religious epiphany. Jack appears in a metaphorical or dream sequence of the afterlife, reunited with his parents and brothers. This sequence is bookended by crosscuts showing Jack ascending (suggestively, up to heaven) then descending (back to earth) in an elevator in a skyscraper. Jack's awakening seems to crystallise in an outdoor scene that follows. He appears at the ground level, looking upward at the very building he both works in and designed. He seems to revel in the play of light, clouds and sky reflected on the face of the glass tower (Loht 2014).

Most especially the film's historical framing of the birth of the universe and the dawn of biological life through its mini-history of the planet and a somewhat jarring life-on-earth nature mini-documentary, serves as a backdrop for human life and humanity's earthly sojourn and is considered most indulgent and out of synch with the rest of the film by many critics. By virtue of juxtaposing these macro-micro elements, *The Tree of Life* defines human life cinematically as a moment within a larger cycle of cosmic and biological genesis and destruction. Certainly this large spatial and temporal canvas can be considered the ultimate template for framing long-scale time and setting up spatial environmental ethical representations around the interconnectivity of all life forms. In ways it serves as the polar opposite to the nihilism of *Melancholia*.

Offering a vision that is both intimate and enormous, *The Tree of Life* details the middle-class upbringing of Jack as a boy in Waco, Texas. Malick chooses to disclose intimate moments of family life in fragmented and non-chronological sequences, while interspersing them with explosive images of cosmic drama, hurtling the viewer through space, into the depths of the ocean and onto primordial shores, as the birth of the universe is laid open. Such images could be read as a teacherly parable on the origins of life. Snapshots of childhood are framed within a broader moral canvas, using earthly symbols of Christianity (church gatherings, the father's talent as a pipe organist, prayers at mealtimes), interspersed with allusions to Jack's mother and father as metonymic archetypes of, respectively, grace and nature.

As already suggested, it is in watching the last fifteen minutes of the film that most reviewers lose their admiration for the work. The adult Jack walks on a beach of the spirit and passes through an empty doorframe to attain spiritual growth. He ambles beside all the people of his life, alive and dead – including his younger self – and embraces his loved ones. As McCarthy writes, 'a sense of reconciliation and closure is sought by the sight of flowers and disparate souls gathering on a beach in a way that uncomfortably resembles hippie-dippy reveries of the late 1960s' (2011). Critics tend to read such forms of closure as cheap and synthetic, simply pandering to populist kitsch visions of such intangible experiences. Read this way, the ending to *The Tree of Life* is merely an aesthetic gimmick, akin to representing the God figure using magical lightscapes, as most recently evident in the unsophisticated Old Testament parable *Noah*.

Furthermore, certain tropes such as the glowing crystal that apparently symbolises God also come perilously close to a semiotic shorthand of a vague form of 'spirituality' and hazy mysticism recalled by so-called new age gurus. As Sterritt suggests,

> From the prayers at the beginning to the sermon in the middle and the vision of heaven at the end, Malick's film is wrapped in a religiosity that secular humanists will find nostalgic and naïve.
>
> (Sterritt 2011: 52)

It is of course relatively easy to critique such apparently second-hand religious metaphors, if they are not examined, much less embraced, within the context of what the director is attempting to get across.

According to some commentators, such a project – which at its core emphasises faith in the unknown, above the ontology of direct experience – positions religion as pivotal to understanding ethics. 'Levinas claims that God is glimpsed in the ethical experience,' writes Urbano; and continues, 'For him ethics provides an opening and a clearing where the trace of God can be discerned' (Urbano 2012: 50). Urbano is referring to Levinas' assertion that ethics is an optic of the Divine; and that at the same time ethics is a spiritual optics.

The closing scene of rapture can most fruitfully be read in deeply religious ways as most specifically a representation of all stages of man including a state that is seldom visualised or appreciated, namely a metaphysical and deep-seated environmental ethical sensibility. In marked contrast to the impending 'nothingness' of *Melancholia*, *The Tree of Life* 'provides reassurance and hope of everlasting eternity (the Christian promise of the afterlife), dramatically quelling the film's evocation of pain that is established in the first part of the film' (French and Shacklock 2014: 344). The older Jack meets and embraces those people who meant so much to him throughout his life – including his boyhood self – as he walks around the seashore. Everyone here appears to accept their destiny and is at one with nature. This is a state that the main protagonists in *Melancholia* seek to aspire to. But despite one's religious or alternative secular reading of this sequence, one wonders if the reader needs to have some quotient of faith, to fully connect with this form of ultra-utopian closure. In any case taking into account its articulation of a deeply religious and transcendent sensibility, the film promotes a less selfish sense of agency and by extension signals a deep quotient of environmental ethics. Such a reading appears to be more pronounced and tantalising, as it allows audiences to connect with the film on a multi-sensory and aesthetic level, which goes beyond any reasoned analysis.

Concluding remarks

Holmes Rolston (1988) explores the rational grounds upon which human beings might be said to have ethical commitments to nonhuman creatures, objects and a radical sense of selflessness. He asserts that the decisive question here is whether and how we can determine these to have long-term residual value. For instance the love of nature and horse riding which the main protagonists enjoy, seem to disappear at the end of *Melancholia*. Present life is literally and metaphorically representative of millennia upon millennia of creative transformation, as evident in *The Tree of Life*. Hence, for Rolston, an ethical outlook on human duties towards natural objects and creatures requires first appreciating them as individual containers of creation: we live in an 'inventive universe'.

We confront a *projective nature*, one restlessly full of projects, including stars, comets, planets, moons, radically changing skyscapes and also rocks, crystals, rivers, canyons, seas. The life in which these astronomical and geological processes culminate is still more impressive if only from a vicarious 'cinema of attractions' perspective. But it is also of a 'piece with the whole projective system' as visualised through a huge array of cinematic experiences that most particularly seeks to represent various forms of cosmic imbalance, which can be traced at one level to various forms of psychological imbalance and by extension a call to mine deep fissures around environmental ethics. Something is clearly out of kilter between humans and nature. Facing up to global apocalypse remains the most pervasive creative imaginary such films seek to engage with.

> Everything is made out of dirt and water, stellar stuff, and funded with stellar energy. One cannot be impressed with life in isolation from its originating matrix. Nature is a fountain of life, and the whole fountain – not just the life that issues from it – is of value.
>
> (Rolston 1988: 197)

In short, if natural things are to be seen as possessing intrinsic value, whether they are animate or inanimate, this value stems from the natural history each expresses within its evolutionary makeup. *The Tree of Life* with its mini nature documentary on the history of the cosmos can be read as foregrounding this evolutionary and historical context for all living things, especially trees, as part of a cosmic environmental and consequentially ethical plane of experience. A standpoint Rolston encourages is phenomenological and somewhat Heideggerian in spirit, because it emphasises that any insight into ethical duties and responsibilities towards nature first requires an openness and yielding of oneself to nature's projective disclosure. This openness does not generate a systematic set of norms or commands with regard to environmental science so much as it lays the foundation for well-informed action. The main protagonists in these narratives have to face up to the dramatic effects of cosmological imbalance, which in turn speaks in varying ways to its different audiences and the representation of environmental questions.

If 'Doomsday is no longer … a day of spiritual reckoning but a possibility imminent in our society and economy' (Giddens 2009: 228), we must ask what representations of doomsday means today. It is our contention that the effectiveness of these 'end of the world' films is based on a range of communicative processes, which elicit ostensibly timeless emotional engagements that are grounded in the cultural prevalence of risk anxiety and melancholic orientation to social and political loss.

Such dramatic 'end of the world' films, which have become a feature of recent Hollywood cinema, express historical and social anxieties and fears especially through the interpersonal focus of their narratives. They are indicative of a historically specific Janus period in the political life of postmodern Western and Westernised societies. While acknowledging the climate scientist Mike Hulme's worries that 'the discourse of catastrophe is in danger of tipping society into a negative, depressive and reactionary trajectory' (cited in Skrimshire 2008), I would counter, however, that such creative imaginaries at the very least call attention to such climatic catastrophe and at the same time afford fruitful reflection, if not necessarily serving as clear models for future action.

While such broad-based textual analysis of cinema is fine in itself, in examining a range of environmental/ethical aesthetics and concerns, as environmental scholars we must continually ask what impact do such texts have in creating an explicit awareness of climate change. Scholars like Allison Anderson point out that certain issues gain public legitimacy 'through their capacity to become icons or symbols for a wide range of concerns that people can easily identify with' (Anderson 1997: 5–6). While others like Julie Doyle go on to maintain that in the case of climate change predictions, the lack of explicit visible evidence of this problem makes it difficult for the issue to be linked to an established set of symbolic imagery (Doyle 2007: 133). Probably there is enough cogent visual evidence of late to effectively narrate this cautionary environmental global problem. In any case commercial eco-cinema I believe helps to make such issues easily identifiable and make visible complex environmental problems. But there is always a danger of environmental issues becoming simply topical and populist, while finding it difficult to sustain their energy, as the broad ecological church pulls in various directions.

Notes

1 This is somewhat reminiscent of *Star Trek's* fixation with traditional modernist and renaissance mindsets (see Brereton 2005).
2 The United States, by any measure of analysis, presents a clearly coded risk society, 'with 50 per cent of the population participating in stock-market investments'. The insurance cost alone of September 11 2001 have been calculated at 21 billion dollars according to Maxwell and Millar (2014) and they go on to cite that in 2005 alone, US residents spent over 1.1 trillion dollars on insurance – more than they paid for food, and more than a third of the world's total insurance expenditure (Maxwell and Miller 2014: 10).
3 Most recently, the West Germans in the 1970s applied the term as a way to justify policies to tackle acid rain, global warming and pollution of the North Sea. They regard such precepts as a positive facilitation of economic growth rather than a break on it. Certainly there is need for a search for more meaningful relationships between precaution, sustainable development and global citizenship (O'Riordan and Jordan 1995: 312).
4 Steven Shaviro (2012) affirms also from an 'insider's' perspective that the film really captures depression in a very accurate manner.
5 Music remains of course in almost all cinematic forms a *leitmotif*, which is defined by Whittall (2003) as 'a theme, or other coherent musical idea, clearly defined so as to retain its identity if modified on subsequent appearances, whose purpose is to represent or symbolise a person, object, place, idea, state of mind, supernatural force or any other ingredient in a dramatic work'.
6 In some ways, Justine epitomises the hypocrisy of success in late capitalism. She is unreasonably wealthy in a world of economic collapse. She even works in advertising (often heralded as the corporate coloniser of art) convincing people of their desire for unnecessary things. But she is also a melancholic who cannot bear to enter into the pretence that everything will be okay..
7 As asserted in a recent study, 'generally the moon is feminine and its trek across the night sky has been likened to the travels and travails of the feminine psyche' and goes on to observe that the cycles of the moon and of menstruation are closely linked in most cultures. As Barbara Creed has pointed out, the werewolf's monthly full-moon transformation is an obvious parallel with the female menstrual cycle. Creed argues that the werewolf is consequently a feminised figure (in Du Coudray, 64).
8 At another, more human-centred level, melancholia is defined and remains of course a psychological condition, first characterised by Hippocrates as an excess of black bile.
9 In spite of her worries and concerns, Claire tries to keep it all together, as she sorts out the wedding and deals with her sister's deep depression. This process is visualised through a bathing scene for instance which is reminiscent of the Bergman chamber classics *Cries and Whispers* or *Persona* when she attempts to give Justine a wash, alongside feeding her like a baby, with her favourite nut-roast meal to help prise her out of her deep melancholia.
10 This is evidenced also in Malick's languorous recreation of the colonisation of America in *The New World*, which ends with a very conventional evocation of environmental sustainability, featuring a low-angle camera shot looking up at trees reaching up to the sparkling light of the sun.
11 *The Tree of Life* can be read – as suggested in an essay by Brereton and Furze (2014) focusing on its transcendent qualities – as an example of how film is able to transcend reason, introducing the enticing prospect that the images projected on a cinema screen are equivalent to the human, cultural elements upon which Levinas, in particular, often focuses on, so that Malick's consistent return to images of nature project the same power over the observer as, say, the encounter with the human *visage* in Levinas.

Bibliography

Adam, B. (1998) *Timescapes of Modernity: The Environment and Invisible Hazards*. London: Routledge.

Allan, S., Adam, B. and Carter, C. (2000) *Environmental Risks and the Media*. London: Routledge.

Anderson, Joseph D. (1997) *Reality of Illusion An Ecological Approach to Cognitive Film Theory*. Carbondale, IL: Southern Illinois University Press.

Beitzer, Thomas (2002) 'Lars von Trier' *Senses of Cinema*. http://sensesofcinema. com/2002/great-directors/vontrier/

Belmont, Cynthia (2007) 'Ecofeminism and the Natural Heroine', *Women's Studies: An Interdisciplinary Journal* 36(5): 349–372.

Brereton, Pat (2005) *Hollywood Utopia: Ecology in Contemporary American Cinema*. Bristol: Intellect Press.

Brereton, Pat and Furze, Robert (2014) Transcendence and *The Tree of Life*: Beyond the Face of the Screen with Terrence Malick, Emmanuel Levinas and Roland Barthes, *Journal for the Study of Religion, Nature and Culture* 8(3): 329–351.

Butler, Brian (2007) 'Seeing Ecology and Seeing as Ecology: On Brereton's *Hollywood Utopia* and the Anderson's *Moving Image Theory*, *Film Philosophy* 11(1) 61–69.

Dargis, Manogha (2011) 'This is How the End Begins'. *The New York Times,* 30 December. http://www.nytimes.com/2012/01/01/movies/awardsseason/manohla-dargis-looks-at-the-overture-to-melancholia.html?_r=0

Doyle, J. (2007) 'Picturing the Clima(c)tic: Greenpeace and the Representational Politics of Climate Change Communication'. *Science as Culture* 16(2): 129–150.

Du Coudray, Chantal Bourgault (2003) 'The Cycle of the Werewolf: Romantic Ecologies of Selfhood in Popular Fantasy'. *Australian Feminist Studies* 18(40): 57–72.

Foucault, Michel (2006) *History of Madness*. London: Routledge.

French, Sarah and Shacklock, Zoe (2014) 'The Affective Sublime in Lars von Trier's *Melancholia* and Terrence Malick's *The Tree of Life*', *New Review of Film and Television Studies* 12(4): 339–356.

Garforth, L. (2006) 'Review of Pat Brereton's 2005 *Hollywood Utopia: Ecology*', *Contemporary American Cinema: Organisation and Environment* 3: 5–26.

Giddens, A. (2009) *The Politics of Climate Change*, second edn. Cambridge: Polity Press.

Hamilton, Clive (2010) *Requiem for a Species: Why We Resist the Truth about Climate Change*. London: Earthscan.

Jeong, Seung-Hoon and Andrew, Dudley (2008) 'Grizzly Ghost, Bazin and the Cinematic Animal'. *Screen* 49(1); 1–12.

Kermode, Mark (2012) 'DVD Round Up', *The Guardian,* 15 January. http://www.theguardian.com/film/2012/jan/15/mark-kermode-dvd-round-up

Langer, S. (1942) *Philosophy in a New Key: A Study of the Symbolism of the Reason, Rite and Art*, third edition. Cambridge, MA: Harvard University Press.

Latour, Bruno (2011) 'Waiting for Gaia: Composing the Common World through Arts and Politics'. A lecture to the French Institute, London. http://www.bruno-latour.fr/sites/default/files/124-GAIA-LONDON-SPEAP_0.pdf

Lipscomb, Scott and Tolchinsky, David (2004) The Role of Music Communication in Cinema, in Dorothy Miell, Raymond MacDonald, and David J. Hargreaves (eds) *Music Communication*. Oxford: Oxford University Press.

Loht, Shawn (2014) 'Film as Ethical Philosophy, and the Question of Philosophical Arguments in Film – A Reading of *The Tree of Life*', *Film Philosophy* 18: 164–183.

Lovelock, James (2007) *The Revenge of Gaia: Why the Earth is Fighting Back and How We Can Still Save Humanity*. Santa Barbara, CA: Allen Lane.

Maxwell, Richard and Miller, Toby (2012) 'Film and the Environment: Risk Off-screen', in Mette Hjort, *Film and Risk*. Detroit, MI: Wayne State University.

McAteer, John (2013) 'The Problem of the Father's Love in *The Tree of Life* and the Book of Job'. *Film and Philosophy* 17: 137–150.

McCarthy, Todd (2011) 'The Tree of Life: Cannes Review'. *Hollywood Reporter.* 16 May. http://www.hollywoodreporter.com/movie/tree-life/review/188564

McReynolds, Lindsay (2013) 'The Biological Tree of Life in Modern Literature and Art'. Thesis, Baylor University, Waco TX.

Norton, B (1991). *Towards Unity Among Environmentalists*. Oxford: Oxford University Press.

Nye, D. (1994) *American Technological Sublime*. Cambridge, MA: MIT Press.

O'Leary, S. (1994) *Arguing the Apocalypse: A Theory of Millennial Rhetoric.* Oxford: Oxford University Press.

O'Riordan, Timothy and Jordan, Andrew (1995) 'The Precautionary Principle, Science, Politics and Ethics'. CSERGE Working Papers. Norwich: CSERGE, University of East Anglia.

Rolston, Holmes (1988) *Environmental Ethics: Duties to and Values in the Natural World.* Philadelphia, PA: Temple University Press.

Seabrook, John (2000) 'Selling the Weather'. *The New Yorker.* 3 April, 44–53.

Shaviro, Steven (2012) 'Melancholia, or, The Romantic Anti-Sublime', *Sequence*, 1.1. http://reframe.sussex.ac.uk/sequence1/1-1-melancholia-or-the-romantic-antisublime/

Sinnerbrink, Robert (2012) 'Cinematic Belief: Bazinian Cinephilia and Malick's *The Tree of Life*'. *Angelaki: Journal of the Theoretical Humanities* 17(4): 95–117.

Sinnerbrink, Robert (2014) 'Anatomy of Melancholia'. *Angelaki: Journal of the Theoretical Humanities* 19(4): 111–126.

Sizemore, Vic (2014) 'God, Guilt and Aronofsky's Noah Part 1'. Patheos blog 23 July. http://www.patheos.com/blogs/goodletters/2014/07/god-guilt-and-aronofskys-noah-part-1/

Skrimshire, Stafan (2008) 'Curb your Catastrophism', *Red Pepper.* http://www.redpepper.org.uk/curb-your-catastrophism/

Smith, M. (1998) *Ecologism; Towards Ecological Citizenship*. Milton Keynes: Open University Press.

Sterritt, David (2011) 'Days of Heaven and Wako: Terrence Malick's *The Tree of Life*'. *Film Quarterly* 65(1): 52–57.

Urbano, C. (2012) 'Levinas Interfaith Dialogue', *The Heythrop Journal* 53(1): 148–161.

Whittall, A. (2003) Leitmotif. *The New Grove Dictionary of Music Online*. Oxford: Oxford Music. http://www.oxfordmusiconline.com/public/book/omo_gmo

9

ENVIRONMENTAL ETHICS

Concluding remarks

Overview: environmental ethics and mass audiences

Biologists often tell us that humans are full of selfish genes, consequently they are constituted by human nature to act primarily in terms of self-interest (Rolston 1994: 223). Many of the narrative, thematic and textual studies in this volume seek to question such a general assertion. Back in another time, at the foundation of the environmental movement during the late 1950s and 1960s, Rachel Carson (1962) argued that social issues needed a moral language articulated in the public media before minds could be changed and society move forward. Her extraordinary career demonstrates that when common problems are understood, not just technically but most essentially ethically, then constructive social action becomes possible.

Environmental ethics even if crudely mediated through fictional narratives has a significant future as long as there are moral agents on the planet with values at stake in their environment and these can be represented on film. Environmental alarms started some time ago with prophets such as Aldo Leopold, Rachel Carson, John Muir, and David Brower and have over recent decades become daily news (Rolston in Keller 2010: 561). We now need new prophets to promote this agenda and a film medium that in turn produces provocative environmental ethical narratives that can at least complement this process of active engagement with audiences across the world and from all spheres of life.

By any measure, the current crisis in the financial and natural world has created a new and much more divisive tipping point, with global implications for the future of our energy consumption system in particular. Unfortunately, there do not appear to be enough prophets or perceptive cross-disciplinary scholars like Carson who also catch the imagination of mass audiences and communicate what is happening to our fragile environment. In any case, we need more hopeful solutions for our future existence and fictional creative imaginaries to help examine these, if only at an allegorical and metaphorical level. Many of the films discussed in this volume – chosen primarily for being mainstream and contemporary – provide a useful touchstone in signalling how the entertainment film industry can develop a more proactive engagement with this very complex area of environmental ethics and its consequences for the planet. But at the outset I would state that much more dynamic, hard-hitting and aesthetically innovative imaginaries are needed to help provide more political, as well as ethical responses while encouraging behaviour change. Referring to digital futures and new modes of developing environmental literacies such as indicated in *The Age of Stupid*, while at the same time understanding audiences' engagement with such narratives, will be signalled towards the latter end of the chapter.

Recalling Wendell Berry's *Think Little* as a classic statement on environmental activism (1975), instead of using emotional appeals to simply blame others and motivating audiences by guilt and fear, Berry encourages the people's voice to be acknowledged and rooted in personal change.[1] Trying to move beyond 'cheap' forms of emotional empathy, to more sustained, provocative and even hopeful scenarios, remains a challenge for media communications, from online and mainstream journalism, to more small-scale eco-documentaries, together with big-budget fictional meta-narratives that have been the focus of this volume. All these approaches in various combinations are badly needed to speak to niche and mass audiences across the world.

For the moment, at least, contemporary Western societies remain predominantly influenced and anchored within broadly anthropocentric principles. Consequently ecological scholars fear that ethical and environmental problems cannot be systemically resolved, until there is a radical change in this overall philosophical and ethical predisposition. While this study would not totally agree with this general assertion, nonetheless as a matter of urgency, long-term global planning and management has to make a radical paradigm shift and privilege a more ecocentric, or earth-centred approach that puts nature and the environment first, before GDP and economic growth maximisation, for the long-term survival of the planet. While at the same time recognising the danger of being too prescriptive, even polemical, ecocentric ethics encapsulates and radically calls attention to the often hidden social processes underlying our comfortable Western lifestyles.[2]

Susan McFarland argues for instance for the need to construct happy ending narratives and the development of productive forms of environmental agency or activism in the audience. A high number of the readings in this volume focus on narrative closure and possible ethical implications for audience interpretation. McFarland writes however that the

> movie industry's desire for happy endings preclude the kind of ending
> that a genuinely environmental film would have – one that makes us rise

up and leave the theatre with a sense of urgency, a clearly defined action plan, and a desire to make a difference.[3]

(McFarland 2009: 103)

By all accounts, this is probably too much to expect from an entertainment and commercially driven mainstream cinema.[4]

The environmental ethical lens explored in this volume, stresses the particular affective nature and broad scope of film spectatorship. The spectator's perceptual and sensory engagement with film is, by all accounts, regarded as foregrounding ethical considerations from an environmental perspective and not simply as a general moral groundwork and barometer of good living.

Examining a broad range of contemporary films, this book has attempted to demonstrate how well-established methodological and theoretical ethical propositions might be called upon and reframed to strengthen an environmental ethical approach to reading film. Films as far apart as *The Constant Gardener* and *The Hunger Games* can at a stretch be read as suggesting a form of egalitarianism – promoting less selfishly prescribed anthropocentric worldviews – and alternatively examining a range of provocative environmental ethical positions and values, encapsulated, somewhat simplistically, around 'doing the right thing' *with* and *for* nature.

Nature remains constructed as a complex web of adapted fits across a broad-based series of ecosystems. Such a trajectory, feeding off notions around the close relationship between humans and nature, clearly promotes a robust environmental ethical starting point.

Being ethical sometimes means having to place the interests of others above our own and that means that certain of our interests will not be satisfied, at least not in the same degree that they might have been had we no ethical concern.

(Rolston 1994: 227)

The struggle to encourage audiences to see beyond their selfish interests remains paradoxically what hero-worshipping, spectacular-driven mainstream Hollywood cinema has been good at. For example, from *Casablanca* in the 1940s to *Terminator 2* in the early 1990s and up to *Elysium*, a contemporary science fiction fantasy discussed in this volume, many types of cinema have over the decades become proficient at speaking to such concerns. This capacity and potentiality of the creative imaginary to speak to mass audiences ought to be fully recognised and mined to help discover new communicative ways to instil more effective interventions, both for the environmental and ethical benefits of society in general.

Probably the most explicit and 'successful' nature film of late remains *Avatar*, which has been discussed in several chapters in this volume. Cameron's film actively cues its story to set up and create an environmental and clearly coded ethical message for his intended audience. Of course this does not necessarily guarantee that such intentions are always clear to the audience, much less successful in affecting behaviour, as suggested by various other scholars who have extensively analysed the film, including studies by Ivakhiv (2013), Elsaesser (2011) and a full volume edited by Bron Taylor (2013).

Film/media studies: a turn to green environmental ethics

Eco-cinema strives to have a social, political and material impact and is slowly being considered as an agent for knowledge dissemination, consciousness-raising, public and ethical debate, and even political action, in response to the ever-growing environmental challenges facing the planet. At the same time, what is currently needed to help progress an environmentally sustainable future are, of course, visually and ecocritically literate viewers. These viewers need to be able to discern, challenge and adapt to the ways in which our erstwhile more normative and regressive representations of nature and of human/nature relations tend to reinforce and re-produce 'business as usual' values and worldviews that further contribute to the degradation of our ecosystems. Recent scholarly eco-cinema volumes (including Rust *et al.* 2013 and Weik von Mossner 2014) have gone some way towards developing this subdiscipline's *modus operandi* and outline effective textual analysis strategies towards signalling varying ways that mainstream cinema can be most cogently read and appreciated from an environmental perspective.

Furthermore, in addition to espousing, codifying and legitimating a 'progressive' ecological cinema – a project I have been closely involved with since writing *Hollywood Utopia* (2005) – if we are to help create an environmentally sustainable future, we must have *active* and *environmentally literate* audiences. We must also be capable of discerning and ethically incorporating our new-found engagement with eco-citizenship, where representations of nature and environmental science are framed and acted upon; all the while recognising, of course, the naïve illusion that simply providing more finely tuned creative imaginaries, coupled with a more critically engaged and literate citizenship, will automatically ensure a prescribed quotient of transformation in the environmental condition. Imbalances of power and injustice remain ever present and are not overcome simply by utopian models of expression. Nevertheless, cataloguing and outlining a growing corpus of what can be described loosely as environmentally inflected cinema is a necessary first step in this process. Meanwhile, of course, moving from a critical and literate engagement with environmental ethics to actual behavioural change demands a radical transformation, which, by all accounts, is much more difficult.

A 'tipping point' for environmental ethics and radical transformation

One must recognise the dangers of academic analysis being perceived as emanating from a tunnel-visioned activist or from a polemical point of view, rather than appreciating a range of deeply held positions by various stakeholders and constituencies around the need to balance and marshal scarce resources. Eco-centric ethics most certainly remind us of the hidden social and environmental processes underlying our comfortable Western lifestyles, as opposed, most notably, to the primal poverty and lack of basic resources of the Third World. It should be considered alongside the overall price paid for damage to the natural environment, if such core ethical precepts are not adapted and taken on wholeheartedly across the globe.[5]

As explored in Chapter 7, the 'iron cage' of consumer capitalism essentially transmutes a once-healthy pattern of desires into greed and avarice. With escalating opportunities for consumerism, driven by markets in search of profits, the human race in response needs more self-discipline, an alternative set of values, alongside robust forms of environmental regulation. This tension and the exponential growth of a virulent form of neoliberal capitalism, which has radically increased divisions of wealth and power between the 1 per cent financial elite, who own and control a majority of the wealth and the rest of us, is sharply manifested through textual analysis of the *Wall Street* franchise and *The Wolf of Wall Street*.

Incidentally, the fundamental flaw with regard to various conceptions of 'sustainable development' is evident when the earth is simply conceptualised as a resource, which is set out only to be exploited in various ways. The underlying conviction embedded in the sustainable biosphere model is simply that the current trajectory of the industrial, technological, commercial world is generally wrong, because it will inevitably overshoot and destroy the planet (Rolston in Keller 2010: 567). These multi-faceted debates have in turn fed directly into an environmental and ethical critical analysis of Hollywood itself across this volume.[6]

The challenge therefore involves reimagining various forms of more benevolent and sustainable development and showing how these can be actualised on film. The ethic of consuming less, for instance, as explored through a discussion of the notion of frugality as a progressive environmental value, suggests a radical reshifting and regearing of established economic, political and cultural norms. The inherent dangers of an otherwise 'business as usual' philosophy, legitimating the status quo and perpetuating a range of severe inequalities between the elite rich and various marginal groups, needs to be kept in mind at all times. Certainly embracing less carbon-based industrial development and consequently less overall financial growth remains unfortunately for many in powerful positions a counterintuitive and impossible starting point for transformation. But to help build a future model for sustainable development and living, 'excessive' and, by all accounts, unsustainable lifestyles across the Western world in particular will have to radically change, and the mass media including film can play a significant role in (re)imagining such long-term transformation.

Yet strategies that encourage feelings of guilt can also become counterproductive in effectively stagnating real change, according to communication research. Other more process-driven, staged evolution and less emotionally fixated strategies need to be called upon to encourage Western consumers to change, or at least modify their behaviour, on the back of more profound systemic change across the 'real' power brokers of multinational corporations and national governments. It is certainly important for film to rise to the challenge and communicate such truly awesome environmental issues with corrective actions, using effective images, words and language through powerful and engaging storylines. Most significantly, new and provocative narratives and creative imaginaries need to be developed to help speak to such an evolving radical and ethical mind-set across contemporary mass cultures. Motivating through education and across the range of eco-literacy and ethical teaching, using the stimulus of fictional creative narratives, help provide models to interrogate and discover what environmental alternatives might look like in the future.

Creating iconic environmental imagery in representing the earth

The iconic Apollo photographs are just one concrete example by which people all over the world have become able to apprehend planet earth's sublime beauty and organic symmetry. A powerful visualisation of the earth and its inherent environmental values continues to draw audiences, as evidenced by the recent success of *Gravity* and other mainstream science fictional narratives.[7] In the 'end of the world' narratives discussed in Chapter 8, through films like *Melancholia* and *The Tree of Life* there is evidence of a strong appeal to the sublime act of cosmic creation and destruction and how it sets up tangible environmental and ethical impacts on the viewing audience. This primal macro-environmental appeal, even shock, at witnessing 'end of the world' scenarios certainly has even more resonance and potency, as *we* hopefully face up to the awesome prospect of the long-term effects of climate change.[8]

Environmental fictional narratives are constantly trying to find appropriate metaphors and provocative modes of address to get across growing concerns about major global issues like climate change. Hence images of our planet as sublime, yet clouded by waste junk out in space, serves as a useful and tangible objective correlative that speaks to the complexity of environmental issues for mainstream audiences. *Gravity,* and most recently *Interstellar,* have created powerful sublime spatial images for audiences to connect with.

Promoting environmental ethics across the chapters

Environmental criticism provides the literary-minded critic with a storehouse of individual and collective metaphors through which the socially transformative workings of the 'environmental imagination' can be fruitfully analysed. American eco-critic Lawrence Buell – from whose scholarship the term came into existence – convincingly suggests that the environmental imagination engages a set of aesthetic preferences for eco-criticism which is not necessarily restricted to environmental realism or for that matter romantic (first wave environmental) nature writing. It is especially attentive to those forms of fictional and non-fictional writing that highlight nature and natural elements (such as landscape, flora and fauna etc.) as self-standing agents, rather than simply support structures for human action in the world (Buell 1995). This recognition of the broad scope of generic and narrative formats, alongside calling to mind those audio-visual texts that most overtly and explicitly address environmental issues on film, are most useful for this study.

Yet, as Morton provocatively asserts, when you mention the environment, you risk sounding boring or judgemental or hysterical or a mixture of all of these attributes.

> Nobody likes it because when you mention the environment, you bring it to the foreground. In other words, it stops being the environment. It stops being that thing over there that surrounds and sustains us. … When you think about where your waste goes for example, your world starts to shrink. … This is the basic message of criticism that speaks up for environmental justice.
>
> (Morton 2007: 1)

And this remains a difficulty also for this study. Driven by the commercial imperative and need to maximise audiences and their pleasure, film frequently tries to be all things to everyone and hence sometimes loses the specificity of its address in its attribution of causes and effects.

The Enlightenment revolutionary idea that one can radically change the world is of course deeply rooted in the Romantic ideal, as is the notion of a worldview itself (*Weltanschauung*). Contemporary scholars certainly need to hold on to such a belief, rather than dallying with the 'luxury' of a postmodernist, relativistic worldview if they want their scholarship within eco-film research to have measurable and long-lasting effects. At the same time, putting something called 'Nature' on a pedestal and admiring it from afar, again according to Morton in a flurry of excessive hyperbole, ends up doing for the environment what he claims patriarchy does for the figure of woman, and is certainly not the way to proceed. Morton probably oversteps the logic of his argument, however, with such a provocative proposition and critique. If fully accurate, one would expect and presume that Western culture was continuously swamped by explicit nature imagery, alongside various forms of eco-cinema. By any measure, this is clearly not the case. In fact it would appear that hyper-romantic evocation of nature across the full gamut of contemporary cinema is probably less dominant now than in previous times.

Nevertheless, the selection of film analysis across the chapters has emphasised the on-going environmental potential of mainstream and often non-explicitly romantically framed nature cinema, as they and other examples help to keep environmental ethical concerns in the public consciousness. The opening literature chapter for instance sought to explain and privilege key environmental ethical concepts, such as the tragedy of the commons, the precautionary principle, the land ethic and lifeboat ethics among others, while illustrating how these in turn might connect with and speak to contemporary film study. Furthermore, the dominance of an anthropomorphic sensibility across all aspects of filmic representation certainly serves as a critique of some of the films alluded to throughout the subsequent chapters.

Chapter 2 examined some of the most tantalising recent eco-narratives across mainstream contemporary cinema, while posing the question, in what ways do highly evolved and self-aware beings relate to nature? Exploring, for instance, how characters like Robert Redford in *All is Lost* and Tom Hanks in *Captain Phillips* find new ways of relating to and dealing with nature in extremis. Is it possible one wonders to return to more ecologically attuned ways of inhabiting nature, and what would be the cultural prerequisites for such a change? These and other questions are also featured in studies of eco-criticism and further explored through a small sample of texts in subsequent chapters. Eco-criticism, with its triple allegiance to the scientific study of nature, the scholarly analysis of cultural representations and the political struggle for more sustainable ways of inhabiting the natural world, was born in the shadow of such debates. However, it must be finally asserted that such open-ended questions do not lead to clearly defined narratives, much less environmental and ethical resolutions in these films. Nonetheless, such questions are effectively examined and call attention to the dilemma of coping with nature in extremis and consequently signal new ways of promoting various forms of environmental and ethical agency. The contentious closure of *Captain Phillips,* in particular, which appears to forget the ethical agency and injustice towards the Third World pirates, brings such issues into sharp focus.

Deep ecology is often associated with a valuation of wild and rural spaces, promoting self-sufficiency and a sense of place, while promoting local knowledge. Most pointedly this tapestry of connections is visualised and allegorised through contemporary lifeboat tales, like *All is Lost* and *Captain Phillips*. New generations can learn to tap into these primal survival tales, which ostensibly call attention to humans' need to be at one with and learn from nature. Such narratives and spectator engagement certainly helps to foreground some of the most important ontological debates around environmental ethics.

The rehistoricisation of the wilderness concept suggested by the environmental historian William Cronon, is undoubtedly one of the most important critiques used in this volume. Unlike ecological movements in other parts of the world, Cronon argues that environmentalism in the United States, for example, tend to hold up an ideal of landscapes untouched by human beings as the standard against which actual landscapes are measured. But of course this standard is problematic both in its relation to the past and also for the future. It conceals the fact that the apparently transhistorical ideal of wilderness only acquired connotations of the sublime and sacred in the nineteenth century and that the cultural valuation of pristine and uninhabited areas led to the displacement of native inhabitants and in some cases to the creation of official 'wild-life' parks. Far from seeing nature in its original state, such wilderness was the product of very predetermined colonial and cultural processes (Heise 2008: 507). This (post)colonial aspect of the manifestations of nature and environmental ethics was most specifically addressed in Chapter 3.

Chapter 3 focused on representations of food, indigenous people and farming, examining how contemporary representation of so-called 'primitive' cultures and in some cases their food consumption helps break down cross-cultural barriers, while most noticeably obfuscating racial and other environmental debates that focus on all forms of injustices. As argued elsewhere, earlier mainstream Hollywood texts like *The Emerald Forest* and *Dances with Wolves*, serve to privilege what can loosely be characterised as a form of Western ecological guilt, while at the same time highlighting growing ethical concerns for *our* unsustainable planet. Nonetheless, the rhetoric of these constitutionally inscribed (in America in particular) humanist and ethical values has yet to create radical change in the 'real politics' of the world, measured against the growing manifestation of social injustices and global poverty, as examined across other chapters and here in this chapter through detailed readings of historical and allegorical tales like *Apocalypto* and *The Road*.

Unlike the growing literature around nature and environmental studies, food surprisingly remains under-theorised from a cultural, much less from an ecological and ethical perspective. Threats to the food supply chain amidst a world of scarcity and plenty, together with the search for bodily sustenance at the global and local level, set up a major thematic preoccupation of films discussed in this chapter. This struggle for basic sustenance has also become a dominant motif across post-apocalyptic science fiction in particular and most explicitly calls attention to the related ethical and environmental values of food.[9]

'We have tended to view nature as a Kodachrome still life, much like a tourist-guide illustration. But nature is a moving picture show' (Botkin 1992: 6). This well-worn idea is taken up in earlier critiques of eco-criticism, like Dana Phillips's *The Truth of Ecology* (2003), which lambasts environmental scholars for 'adhering to an obsolete notion of ecological science and for transferring ecological terms to literary study by means of mere metaphor' (Phillips 2003: 42).[10] Phillips is certainly right in cautioning eco-critics against undue metaphorisation, moralisation, or spiritualisation of scientific concepts and in calling for more up-to-date scientific and environmental literacy. But film study by its very nature remains preoccupied with allegories and metaphors but ought to be cognisant of such dangers while reading these texts. Nevertheless, I would have to suggest that the benefits of powerful evocations of the 'creative imaginary' evident through thematic and textual analysis of a range of narratives, speaking to a range of environmental and ethical debates, while using various allegorical, mythic and metaphorical tropes, far outweigh such inherent dangers in communicating to mass audiences.

Chapter 4 focused on various aspects of eco-feminism and how this permeable lens can be applied to recent science fiction films. Val Plumwood most cogently talks of 'ecological denial' and of 'the reality of our embeddedness in nature' (Plumwood 2002: 97). Yet feminism's conceptual starting point, the significance of gender distinctions, generally puts it at odds with deep ecology's somewhat dangerous propensity to think in terms of holisms like 'nature' or 'man' or even 'humankind', alongside its emphasis around identification of self as echoing and fulfilled through identification with nature. Such conceptualisations of nature can serve simply to re-affirm inequalities and sometimes even at one extreme lead to valorising a fascistic worldview (see Brereton 2001). On the contrary Plumwood retorts,

> [T]he basic concept required for an appropriate ethic of environmental activism is not that of identity or unity (or its reversal in difference) but that of *solidarity* [which] requires not just the affirmation of difference, but also sensitivity to the difference between positioning oneself *with* the other, and positioning oneself *as* the other.
>
> (cited in Buell 2005: 108, emphasis in original)

The films discussed in this chapter including *The Hunger Games* and *Elysium*, all in their own way address this notion of gendered otherness.

'The womanising of nature and the naturalising of women' remains a core preoccupation with eco-feminist criticism (Bullis 1996: 125). Ironically, however, this feminist critique of androcentric modes of environmental imagination has also had the effect of putting *eco*-feminsts on the defensive within feminism, as Stacy Alaimo points out in a candid discussion of 'Feminist Theory's Flight from Nature' (Alaimo 2000). All in all it would be most efficient and critically effective to many feminist, anti-racist and post-colonialist scholars focused around environmental justice to pull together and construct the most effective model for addressing such trans-national 'wicked' environmental problems like climate change.[11] Eco-feminist theorising pervades the study of environmental ethics, most particularly from a 'duty of care' perspective. Much more eco-feminist theorising can certainly help deepen the study of environmental film, as we move discussion to the more contentious analysis of animals in film.

Chapter 5 focused very broadly on the ethical valuation of animals on film and gauges them against an anthropomorphic measure of engagement.[12] Consequently such techniques are frequently critiqued by deep environmentalists as positing a very safe and uncontentious approach to animals and nature, which do little towards promoting critical environmental and ethical engagement.[13]

Focusing on representations of non-cuddly animals, this chapter tends to agree with Jacques Derrida that the Western idea of 'the animal' itself has contributed greatly to the plight of living animals. There is a growing body of work on the 'ethical question of the animal' and on representations of animals and animality in human cultures. Scholars like Cary Wolfe have begun to think in terms of the 'posthumanities' and the animal is most certainly returning to the humanities (Welling and Kapel in Garrard 2012b: 105). This chapter's close reading of contemporary reflexive animal classics like *Grizzly Man* and *Fantastic Mr Fox*, dramatises and analyses some of these contentious issues and debates. Audiences most certainly have to confront the animal in humans and visa versa, while at the same time beginning to appreciate the central importance of the representation of animals in examining the duty of care *we* have for animals, which remains a core constituency of environmental ethics in film and in real life.

From the extremes of Disney's anodyne, hyper-anthropomorphic animals in successful tales like *March of the Penguins*, through more reflexive ecological agents and on to more explicit critiques in reflexive (real-life animal) texts, like Herzog's *Grizzly Man* and the more ironic and playful *Fantastic Mr Fox*, such films are read as having re-imagined a wider spectrum and continuum of animal-human representations on film, which in turn have greater resonance for exploring a less monolithic and even, one could hypothesise, non-anthropomorphic visions of environmental ethics.[14]

The so-called creative imaginary of film, with its capability to speak philosophically, culturally and politically to mass audiences, can help to both mirror and illuminate such ecological issues and realities, while at the same time providing at least a metaphorical platform for portraying more ethical and sustainable long-term solutions to animal husbandry and food production.

Chapter 6 focused on representations of Third World peoples, albeit from a Western and Hollywood perspective, through a case study of Africa. It is suggested the African peoples, like so-called indigenous cultures discussed earlier, have a particular sacred respect for natural phenomena, like mountains, rivers, the sea and, of course, trees, alongside the sun, moon and stars. Everything remains personal and alive for such a vivid nature-based culture. This philosophy around everything being connected, as a first principle environmental ethic, resonates across many of the films discussed in this and other chapters. Most pointedly, the so-called primitivism of the legends attached to the peoples of (southern) Africa in films like *The Constant Gardener* are connected with a particular type of animism that speaks to a very deep environmental ethical worldview, which has been apparently lost in the West. This is emphasised through a close and detailed reading of the closure of this film.

It must be constantly acknowledged that far too much eco-filmic discourse comes from a very narrow Western-centric philosophical framework. Calling on African, Asian and other Eastern philosophies and other alternative ecologies of nature, will in the future become a major source of scholarship across the broadening parameters of eco-cinema studies. If such an all-inclusive mindset and religious worldview were to take hold for instance, it might initiate and legitimate a radically new and ecologically benign form of nature worship within mainstream cinema, as signalled in a relatively Western conceptualisation of such possibilities in *Life of Pi*. Unfortunately at present, we have a long way to go before we can harvest the fruits of such a trans-global vision, including 'Eastern' and 'Southern' as well as 'Western' modes of altruistic and eco-sensitive and spiritual/philosophical discursive modes of signifying and engaging with nature. A good start has been made however in studies like *Transnational Ecocinema* (Gustafsson and Kääpä 2013) and another focused on Indian and other non-Hollywood cinema, edited by Rayson K. Alex *et al.* (2014).

No more are crudely constructed binaries that polarise post-colonial/ Western, ideology/ecology as simple uni-directional frames or debates helpful in articulating, much less constructing progressive forms of engagement. Instead such binaries need to be re-appraised and re-coded, as world cinemas fluctuate across the three-dimensional nexus of local/global, indigenous and transnational polarities and feed into more complex debates around the periphery/centre and erstwhile reductive divisions between Third, First and other world cinematic outputs. The crudely constituted shorthand of the West as an imperialist coloniser and the even more restrictively constituted bulwark of the continent of Africa as a passive postcolonial space, have to be reappraised and reconstituted, so that scholars can approach complex notions like environmental ethics and universal sustainability, through more considered and balanced evaluation. In turn we can learn how such frames might be usefully reconstituted, rearticulated and repoliticised through a firm commitment to universal justice and global ethical responsibility. Furthermore, by developing a more productive and reflexive sense of place through civic identity and environmental connectivity, film as a fictional medium can in particular help re-imagine and even promote a more benevolent cooperative series of protocols across our polarised planet earth.

Chapter 7 focused on probably the most contentious area of environmental and ethical concern, alongside Third World injustices, namely neoliberal economic and 'business-as-usual' structures that promote what is described as an anti-ecological worldview. Moving away from a preoccupation with the continuous economic growth paradigm remains the biggest environmental and ethical challenge for contemporary society. Fictional film certainly has a role to play in helping to document and frame how to activate this major transformation. It is precisely the prospect of expecting never-ending growth that exacerbates climate change as a global problem for the long-term security and safety of the planet. Tim Jackson's influential book *Prosperity without Growth: Economics for a Finite Planet* (2009) for example clearly calls attention to how this economic model of seeking unstoppable growth will lead to environmental catastrophe.

The *Wall Street* franchise and most recently *The Wolf of Wall Street* discussed extensively within this chapter, certainly appear at the outset very far away from any sense of embracing deep-ecological values, or even promoting more benevolent protocols of business practice. Nonetheless, these somewhat one-sided cautionary tales effectively dramatise, if only through omission, the large gap between what might be characterised as pro-environmental business models, as against a more avaricious form of neoliberal capitalism that remains dominant at present.

When academics refer to the 'anthropocene', they specify a period in which human activity has ruled the earth. 'It would probably do little good to reinstate a notion that for instance Gaia will wreck "her" mythical violence upon us as punishment' because of our inability to protect the planet. Such an Old Testament fearful approach is evident in recent reimagined mythic blockbusters like *Noah* that address contemporary audiences who usually don't like being preached at. Alternatively in *The Age of Stupid:*

> Armstrong's opening sequence of the making of the universe and our own fragile globe struggle [suggests] that there is a mystery which cannot be reduced to myth. Perhaps this realisation would guarantee the first steps of global intelligence over global stupidity.
>
> (Lord 2012: 12)

Geoff Mead (2014) in a review piece in *The Guardian* titled 'Sustainability needs new narratives between catastrophe and Utopia' is certainly apt in mentioning deep ecology scholar Thomas Berry who affirms:

> [I]t's all a question of story. We are in trouble just now because we do not have a good story. We are in between stories. The old story, the account of how we fit into the world, is no longer effective. Yet we have not learned the new story.
>
> (Berry 2015)

This new story must involve connection with our fragile environment and looking beyond our own selfish desires.[15] In *Wall Street* the evocative use of the Dow Jones index and the fluctuation of stocks and shares on the financial market place through direct visual connections with the growth and development of American cities, help to clearly draw parallels and connect these albeit very different phenomena for a mass audience and signal clear ethical and environmental consequences of such excessive and risky business behaviour. This volume, while recognising and hopefully adding to the growing corpus of studies that help to unpack a range of environmental narratives that can be gleaned from mainstream cinema, at the same time calls for more and radically progressive and innovative stories that speak to the worsening environmental and ethical dilemma we all face. Some of the most explicit and cogent Hollywood narratives that address these concerns over the last decade have been so-called 'end of the world' narratives.

Chapter 8 explores 'end of the world' narratives *Melancholia* and *The Tree of Life* that most clearly address the real and present dangers we face, by dramatically (re)presenting various forms of environmental ecocide. By all accounts, one of the aims of critical environmental literature analysis of such filmic texts is to get at the 'nature' of the text in the double sense: its possible meaning (remaining conscious of course that eco-critical interpretation is always provisional), and its specific way of referring to the natural (scientific) world. The heightened romantic imagery presented in these environmental morality tales feed off a long history of poetic and literary pastoralism coupled with dystopic foreboding. These apocalyptic environmental cautionary tales speak to contemporary fears and worries that marry personal psychological and global planetary imbalances, using the shorthand of catastrophic environmental destruction.

Note, a key concept within the preliminary analysis of such landscapes, both before and after a catastrophe, remains that of vulnerability.[16] Protagonists as constructed in these narratives are particularly vulnerable through their own psychological imbalance and also end up trying to cope with a radically unstable world – both cosmically and in other more personal ways. As suggested by several contemporary cross-disciplinary scholars, an economic and social disaster, translated into profound and visible injustices, is usually the antecedent of natural disasters and humanitarian crises (Hewitt 1983).

Adrian Ivakhiv is most succinct in capturing the pleasures and tensions of such narratives when he announces:

> [I]f I claim that I have been moved by *Melancholia* – I have been moved along with that image and have in some sense lived and experienced it.... [providing] exercise of real imagination, which means the development of a kind of muscle that poises me for an engaged responsiveness to a certain present or future possibility.[17]
>
> (Ivakhiv 2013: 337)

Melancholia certainly remains one of the most finely tuned examples of this form of creative engagement, which serves also to promote debate around environmental ethics. *The Tree of Life* also raises major epistemological and ontological questions around humans' deeply felt spiritual relationship with and worries concerning their environment and nature in general. Concurrently, many of the films examined in this volume have sought in varying ways to call attention to and promote this potency, but sometimes it must be said with less successful results. Nevertheless, all extend the corpus of narratives that can be fruitfully examined through a range of environmental and ethical questions.

Implications for future analysis of eco-cinema

At a theoretical level and echoing the conclusion of many of these readings, I am taken by Kääpä who affirms that overall, 'cinema is distinctly anthropocentric and [an] anthropogenic machine' but at the same time 'it is also one that fosters a concrete connection with the public and the politics of the society in which the films are produced' (Kääpä 2014: 236). In spite of trying to fight against this predisposition, environmental mainstream cinema at least is most frequently pulled back towards embracing this 'normative' position. But as Lawrence Buell suggests in addressing the anthropocentric/biocentric conundrum, it is:

> entirely possible without hypocrisy to maintain biocentric values in principle, while recognising that in practice these must be constrained by anthropocentric considerations, whether as a matter of strategy or as a matter of intractable human self-interestedness.
>
> (Buell 2005: 134)

Mainstream narrative film is seldom, if ever, dogmatic in its positioning and certainly from these readings I probably concur with Buell's concluding assertions.

Kääpä's final judgement on the matter is also apposite, when he says:

> to capture the ways ecological film culture operates as a complex sphere of contesting perspectives, as well as critiquing the underlying hegemonic ideological framework, we need to be able to confront our own idealism and our embeddedness in the constitutive ideological structures we criticise. While explicit environmental rhetoric and rethinking of existing anthropocentric paradigms is absolutely vital to the ongoing development of the field, ecocinema needs to be understood as both an anthropocentric *and* ecocentric form of communication, both reflecting the often unconscious constitutive ideologies of the society, as well as challenging the limitations these ideological formations pose for contemporary policy and awareness level of the general public.
>
> (Kääpä 2014: 239, emphasis added)

The focus of many of the readings in this volume involved unpacking how various narrative tropes and especially closures of contemporary mainstream cinema, consciously or more often unconsciously, end up questioning the dominant hegemonic norms of anthropomorphism. Hopefully this process in itself promotes and helps to create a more productive alternative environmental vision. At the same time we have to accept the impure and often irrational nature of human activity, as it pulls against the strictures of more clearly defined ethical norms and values.

Evolving environmental film research and foregrounding digital futures

Bill McKibben's *The Age of Missing Information* (1992) provocatively warns that 'far from enjoying an Information Age', we live in a period of 'Unenlightenment', cut off from lessons taught by nature such as the:

> [S]ubversive ideas about how much we need, or what comfort is, or beauty, or time, that you can learn from one of the great logoless channels and not the hundred noisy ones or even the pay per view.
>
> (McKibben 1992: 23)

It can be suggested that scholarly activity in communications worries about the loss of 'analogue' reality and a perceived closer connection to truth-making within our real lived environment, as more and more time is spent online across digital spaces and traversing the audiovisual delights of prolific websites such as YouTube and the like.

Katherine Hayles for instance examining new digital media aesthetics in 'Simulated Nature and Natural Simulations' suggests that the functionality of virtual reality (VR) programmes and other simulations depends on an intimate fit between technology and nature, which in turn implies a critique of the poetics of authenticity.

> If nature can be separated from simulation in a clear-cut way, then we risk believing that nature is natural because it is unmediated, whereas simulation is artificial because it is constructed.[18]
>
> (Hayles in Cronon 1996: 418)

Science fiction most obviously articulates and plays off such debates and constructions. *The Hunger Games,* for instance, which has been extensively examined in this volume is both a reality television game and very much a reconstruction of nature. Nonetheless its very constructedness, at the same time calls to mind a range of environmental and ethical concerns, which are far from simply simulations of an otherwise artificial reality that recreate the 'environmental realness' of habitats like forests, being simply reconstructed for audience amusement as in a theme park.

Yet it must also be noted, as Jean Baudrillard claims in his influential *Simulacra and Simulations* (1981), that communication technologies are capable of infinite replication and wide dissemination of information and have initiated a world of simulation that now functions to supplant the real world (see Garrard 2012a: 190). This growth of all forms of simulation from Second Life to video games which inform some of the films discussed in this volume, such as *Elysium*, exacerbated by a market-driven digital media, has important aesthetic implications regarding the continued efficacy of representing the 'truth' around extremes of nature and climate change in particular. Most pointedly a greater arsenal of digital special effects can now be employed across the full gamut of film production. The excessive ability to (re)construct, replicate and simulate the reality of nature in extremis can, in turn, allow audiences to remain cynical, or at least very cautious when environmental science tells us to be worried about the effects of climate change. The 'creative imaginary' of digital cinema remains, by all accounts, a multi-edged tool and aesthetic modality, as it sets up a range of cross-connecting cautionary tales.

At the same time, as the late Ulrich Beck points out, inflecting the planet simply through global risk generates new political strategies as well as actors, including encouraging audiences to see environmental problems from a different perspective than they normally would. This also calls to mind the 'judo politics' of Greenpeace who are 'designed to mobilise the superior strength of environmental sinners against themselves' (Garrard 2012a: 193). All of the possibilities and potentialities across so-called 'smart' new media protocols and filmic aesthetics feed off the ubiquitous rise of so-called 'database logics' (Manovich 2001), and the ability to easily make connections using the power of computers and 'big data', as evident in contemporary film and media (Brereton 2012). While at the other end of the spectrum of scientific agency, Mike Hulme's equally influential *Why we Disagree about Climate Change* (2009) foregrounds differences over the level of prestige and actual reliability of science, the attribution of value to climate stability, the role of government in society and even calling upon various divergent religious beliefs espoused by mass audiences. Perceptions of environmental risk are, by all accounts, not simply predetermined by increased digital capability and the drive towards even greater verisimilitude and reality making. They also vary both individually and across divisions of gender, race and social class, according to Hulme, with privileged white males the most likely to perceive 'nature as tolerant, rather than fragile', and striving at the same time to minimise the danger from climate change (Hulme 2009: 188–9).

Smart digital environmental allegories: *The Age of Stupid*

Examples like the hyper digital (smart) *The Age of Stupid* that portrays a futuristic 'climate chaos' development as the consequence of ignorance and greed, remains somewhat counterproductive, according to Hulme, who argues that such narratives are primarily designed to frame climate change as a 'mega-problem awaiting, demanding, a mega-solution' (Hulme 2009: 333). Alternatively one must appreciate human activities, feeling and beliefs are thoroughly entangled with the cultural idea of climate. Environmental problems and ethical concerns are not simply a 'knowledge deficit' problem. Hence polemical creative imaginaries may be less effective in speaking to mass audiences, as such complexities are not taken into account through such polemical narratives. Consequently, in this study, conventional mainstream films are explored instead for their quotient of often unconscious engagement with such issues, emanating from a belief that such narratives tend to be more influential in the longer term by building up a range of environmental ethical protocols and cues. These speak to majority audiences within their comfort zones, using tools of identification and empathy, and especially through narrative closures across a range of storylines. Such narratives also speak across broad thematic concerns of (post)modern, smart and other cinemas, including engagement with nature and the environment, both at a simulated digital and analogue level.[19]

Essentially, Hulme concludes that we should consider climate change as one of a range of global 'wicked problems', which 'afflict open, complex, and imperfectly understood systems, and are beyond the range of mere technical knowledge and traditional forms of governance' (Hulme 2009: 334). Hulme's striking reconceptualisation of climate change as an imaginative opportunity, rather than simply a problem to be 'solved', also suggests new directions for proactive eco-criticism. For instance, examining historical and cross-cultural perceptions of risk, analysing representations of climate change in literature and film (without looking simply for the best and most effective model) and most particularly exploring the relationships concerning our climate predicament, have also to be eco-film's major preoccupation (see Hulme 2009: 340–64).

Again I would concur with Sean Cubitt who suggests '[T]hat attention to the past is especially necessary when the environment appears in crisis, a crisis that in various ways denies the possibility of a future'. Neither 'apocalypse nor utopia will arrive the day after tomorrow. The process is longer, slower, more banal'. Welling up from popular media however 'are visions and stories that unveil a common awareness of complexity. Sloganeering is no response. The yearning and the love are real enough, as are the fears, and most of all the sense that the world has grown into a fabulously interconnected web' (Cubitt in Rust *et al.* 2013: 139). Eco-film scholars and a broad swathe of films explored in this volume seek out and promote this more productive strategy and strive to promote the deep ecological mantra that 'everything is connected', which in turn hopefully promotes a proactive environmental ethical perspective. However, illustrating, much less proving that such creative imaginaries have a measurable and direct affect on audiences is open to question.[20]

Changing audience practices and environmental ethical values: hitting the sweet spot

Pietari Kääpä in a special issue of *Interactions: Studies in Communication and Culture* (2013) outlines how scholars like Benjamin Thevenin perceive the commercial roots of much eco-rhetoric as a potential fallacy, as dictated by an 'Adornian' appreciation of the culture industry. This study compares the audience addressed across modes of Hollywood animation as against a case study of Hayao Mayazaki's evocative *Princess Mononoke* (1997) and uncovers how such provocative narratives help to construct a 'new' ecological nature narrative capable of producing complex viewings in a way that confronts their taken-for-granted beliefs in environmental narratives and in turn provokes audiences to see humanity's nature embeddedness anew (Kääpä 2013: 110).

Furthermore, Chris Tong helpfully proposes four modes of viewing eco-cinema: activist, allegorical, evocative and realist (Tong 2013: 113).[21] Tong suggests that we aught to reframe the term 'audience' as a 'gathering', which is inclusive of all points of view. Yet for some long-established eco-scholars like Scott MacDonald and others, according to Tong, recognising such evocations as promising ubiquity is not the point, and mobilisation is not finally the goal for eco-cinema. Instead he recognises such evocations as promoting some form of relief from the demands of modern society and in cultivating a sense of appreciation for places and landscape. 'This attitude towards ecocinema is not unlike certain aesthetic practices with gardens and ink paintings in traditional Chinese culture' (Tong 2013: 116). While probably a bit unfair in his assessment, at least eco-scholars have to be shaken out of their (literary) textual fixation and develop robust new models of analysing film from a wide range of environmental perspectives, as scholars like Alexa Weik von Mossner and others are proactively interrogating at present.

For Tong, viewing cinema ecologically is very far removed from the uni-directional nature of first wave eco-criticism and involves coexisting with it. 'It feels like being seduced' without 'succumbing to persuasion or being provoked to reject it'. Viewers of ecocinema find themselves hanging out in the 'sweet spot' between 'the suspension of disbelief and the distancing effect, between the cinematic world and the extra-cinematic world' (Tong 2013: 116). One wonders of course if for instance Katniss's evocation as an eco-warrior in the earlier extensive reading of *The Hunger Games*, corresponds with how new generational audiences play into the intertextual reality televisual games.

This volume has probably unconsciously attempted to uncover such a 'sweet spot' in the broad range of exposition around narration and identification discussed above, while often reading 'against the grain' of conventional narrative analysis to help uncover a (deep) ecological thematic preoccupation and subtext; a non-common-sense project that could be simply dismissed as not part of the film's intentionality. Lacanian film theorists most notably 'call this process the oscillation between the unregulated desires of the Imaginary and the culturally sanctioned meaning-making of the Symbolic' (McGowan and Kundle 2004: xi–xxix). Viewing what can be characterised as environmental film from this so-called 'sweet spot' can in turn be considered as deeply political and provocative, not just conforming to a predetermined psychological model of spectator activity, while hopefully at the same time promoting a very explicit form of active environmental agency and engagement.

As film and media scholars concerned with the environment, we can help re-construct new modes of audience understanding which can engender an inclusive dialogue around eco-cinema; a dialogue that keeps us attuned to the sense of coexistence that is the hallmark of ecological thinking (Tong 2013: 123). Calling to mind the much-discussed *An Inconvenient Truth* and its chief protagonist – a politically powerful, rich, white man Al Gore – it has been suggested by some critics that the documentary film in the end fails to model the diversity necessary to create and maintain a sustainable and ultimately successful campaign against global climate change (Selheim 2011: 135).[22]

Environmental and ethical scholar Holmes Rolston wonders out loud, can and should humans win or lose when they 'do the right thing' by for instance caring for nature and for animals etc. Life is defined by many in the modern world as simply a utilitarian model of economics, foregrounding value gain and value loss. 'There must be winners and losers among the humans who are helped or hurt by the conditions of their environment'. Nevertheless, it can more fruitfully be suggested that caring

> properly for the natural world can combine with a strategy for sustainability, a win–win solution. A bumper sticker reads: 'recycling, everyone wins'. That is almost an aphoristic model for the whole human-nature relationship. If we are in harmony with nature, everyone wins.
>
> (Rolston 1994: 218)

Of course other scholars contest this somewhat simplistic and relatively easy and utilitarian correlation around use/benefit. Nonetheless where possible such 'easy gains' ought to be highlighted, as like most things, once you go deeper, the problems and difficulties appear to proliferate and often serve to deaden any resolve to uncover clear systemic and effective solutions.

If eco-cinema studies were to extensively employ an active audience research approach, it would also have to confront challenging academic and ethical questions such as: What constitutes collaborating with the culture industry's 'research agenda'? What ethical issues are present in the use of human subjects for research? What would it mean to make viewers the 'primary' concern, allowing their mentalities to evolve on their own? Or how would studies of grassroots, non-commercial or independent efforts with regards to eco-cinema contribute to a resistance against the culture industry? (Tong 2013: 121).

Scientists and other specialist stakeholders continue to find it hard to understand the heuristics and dynamics of the public *agora*, beyond ascribing an often untheorised notion that the media is needed to fulfil a 'knowledge deficit'. This is an attempt to proselytise various publics around the inherent benefits of protective environmentalism and at the same time highlight caution around simply replicating fears and concerns around climate change. But, of course, like Pandora's Box, the media, including the creative imaginary of film, remain an unpredictable and very imperfect 'public sphere' – even if not further bounded by an ever-present commercial imperative – and can certainly proselytise both for and against a green agenda, while also sparking audiences to respond in sometimes contradictory ways, often bearing little relationship to the original intent.

Nonetheless, as environmental communications scholars, we need to constantly explore and explain how such filmic texts might encode various shades of environmental and ethical expression and over time must also take on this much more difficult project of unpacking and empirically measuring audience responses to film and media generally. Gauging the mass psychological and cognitive responses to such global challenges is necessary, in framing and understanding the power and impact of fictional (as well as documentary) texts, as they extend their reach and appreciation around broad-based ethical and environmental issues.

The creative imaginary of film can and does help to bring into focus many of these complex issues and concerns and one hopes this conjunction will be continued, as the corpus of what is described as eco-cinema grows into the future. More abstract, and at the same time, concrete metaphors and objective correlatives of the primary green issues around environmental ethics will be constructed over time and help humans as global citizens to continue to rescue and appreciate that 'everything is connected'. This alone will serve to create a more actively engaged and environmentally sensitive global citizenship. But of course all these strategies need finally to be coupled with effective political praxis.

Notes

1 Alasdair MacIntyre's *After Virtue* (1981) offers a similar critique in historical terms. One great mistake of the Enlightenment Project, he says, was 'the tendency to think atomistically about the human action and to analyse complex actions and transactions in terms of simple components' (MacIntyre 1981: 204). MacIntyre advocated a new perspective on moral philosophy rooted in the way humans actually experience life and how they interpret it, that is, in community.

2 Such polarising ethical philosophies are especially evident on the ground in the Third World, which explicitly marks the overall price paid for damage to the natural environment, if such radical re-evaluations of environmental values are not addressed. It has been suggested in previous research that the creative imaginaries of films like *Waterworld, The Day After Tomorrow* and *Artificial Intelligence* (see Brereton 2012) all depict male heroes working to restore life or love against a backdrop of the global consequences of climate change. These environmental preoccupations include rising seas covering the earth, the next ice age, our out-of-control scientific advances, coupled with human alienation, among other cautionary tales. Currently we need more varied and less formulaic filmic creative imaginaries to address the growing complexity of environmental ethical problems, some of which have been addressed by this study.

3 That film should explicitly agitate for an environmental political cause remains a big ask for a mainstream risk-averse Hollywood industry. One recalls the polemical aesthetic of Russian filmmaker Sergei Eisenstein promoting a newly forged communist state at the beginning of the twentieth century.

4 While O'Brien worries that my earlier use of the aesthetic of Ernest Bloch to help foreground happy endings as a utopian prefiguration of a more benign relationship between human beings and the rest of the natural world (2013: 11), can engender a naïve form of utopian wish fulfilment. Nonetheless this approach continues to inform my environmental analysis and echoes a long line of narrative specialists

who believe that the narrative structure and particularly the ending of films play a key role in creating meaning for the viewer.

5 For instance it is suggested the 27 Bali Principles of Climate Justice (2002) redefine climate change from an environmental justice standpoint, using as a template the original 17 Principles of Environmental Justice (1991) created at the First National People of Colour Environmental Summit.

6 Films from the six 'majors' dominate the American movie landscape, accounting for 76 per cent of films released in 2012. Ingram (2004) for instance observed that one way studios can address environmental problems *and* cater to corporate ownership is to approach the subject from a *mainstream* environmental perspective, which places 'environmental concerns within the needs of a capitalist economy to sustain commodity consumption, profit maximisation and economic growth' (Ingram 2004: 13).

7 According to Yearley, such powerful image making reinforces this globalisation of the imagination across all aspects of finance, communications, culture, business and politics. As eco-critics interpret the meaning and intrinsic nature of the earth, they will increasingly have to engage at the same time with globalised political conflicts (Garrard 2012b: 185).

8 Kate Soper's seminal *What is Nature* for instance propagates the view that 'it is not language that has a hole in its ozone layer' (Soper 1998: 151). Her neat and memorable phrase has been cited by a number of critics to exemplify and emphasise literal truth, rather than through social construction, which in turn marks eco-criticism out from other literary critical schools (Barry 2002: 252). But, according to Garrard, Soper may have picked the wrong example to make her point. The 'hole in the ozone layer' is actually a good example of the scientific and cultural construction of global environmental problems, since the term 'hole' and 'layer' is strictly metaphorical in this context. The latter of course is an area of increased concentration of ozone, which is actually present throughout the atmosphere. As Hanningan observes, 'images of the ozone hole are really simulated graphic maps' (in Garrard 2012a: 188).

9 When hunger takes a literal rather than a metaphorical form, it propels actions that serve to define what it is to be human – or to be inhuman. Food and water scarcity leads both to brutality and kindness in science fiction films such as *The Omega Man* (1971) or *Mad Max 2* (1982) for instance.

10 For example Rachel Carson's influential indictment of pesticide overuse in *Silent Spring* (1962) skilfully uses tropes of the pastoral, biblical apocalypse, nuclear fear (in her comparisons of chemical contamination with radioactive fallout), and 1950s anti-Communism ('a grim spectre has crept upon us almost unnoticed' (cited in Heise 2006: 512)).

11 See, for instance, the Principles of Environmental Justice set forth in 1991 First National People of Colour Environmental Leadership Summit held in Washington DC: 'Environmental justice requires that we, as individuals, make personal and consumer choices to consume as little of Mother Earth's resources and to produce as little waste as possible; and at the same time make the conscious decision to challenge and reprioritise our life-styles to insure the health of the natural world for present and future generations' (http://www.ejnet.org/ej/principles.html).

12 Luc Jaquet's *March of the Penguins,* for example, features as its lead actors a colony of Emperor penguins in Adélie Land, Antarctica. Filmed over a course of a year, the film portrays the annual drama of the penguins' journey, while facing ice-filled oceans and harsh winds. Such Disneyesque animated animals are clearly anthropomorphised and made as cuddly and appealing to children as possible.

13 John Berger's famous claim recorded in 'Why look at Animals' (1980) that 'the look between animal and man, which may have played a crucial role in the development of human society a century ago, has been extinguished' (Berger 1980: 26). Many contemporary scholars have argued that Berger's 'look', while lost or co-opted

in many contexts, lives on elsewhere and can be recovered by city-dwellers and suburbanites willing to 'meet the gaze of living, diverse animals and in response undo and redo themselves and their knowledges' (Haraway 2008: 21).

14 Incidentally Mahatma Gandhi's early publications about the necessities of local sovereignty, limited consumption, equality for all sentient life, compassion, ecological sustainability and *satyagraha* were an inspiration to many, including the 1970s Chipko movement against logging in the Himalayas (see Shiva 2000: 69–70). Gandhi's work was of course very influential on Arne Naess – who wrote his PhD dissertation on Gandhism – and inspired many other theorists of environmental ethics (Guha 2000: 19–24).

15 Berry for instance envisioned a new 'ecozoic era' wherein people would 'treat nature as a subject rather than an object to be manipulated and controlled' (Watling 2014: 365). Many other scholars however dismiss the so-called 'entertainment adventures' as having little to teach us. It's time to slacken our grip on the hero's journey (almost a male archetype) and look to other types of story to guide us. Probably the Hollywoodised West needs to look to the proverbial East, alongside taking on board other aesthetic formats to speak to and to connect with more mainstream jaded audience sensibilities.

16 See Vygotsky's *Psychology of Art* (1971: 6) which talks of a contradiction, on the one hand a desire to differentiate ourselves from the landscape and, on the other, our desire to be a part of that landscape.

17 Cinema will hopefully continue to help us think and feel these radical environmental changes, and in its best forms will do this in ways that help us shape their direction as well. Cinema, as I have argued throughout this study, and as Nadia Bozak outlines in her recent book *The Cinematic Footprint: Lights, Camera, Natural Resources,* is in many ways a thoroughly ecological process (see also Ivakhiv 2013: 338).

18 For instance Ursula Heise's influential *Sense of Place and Sense of Planet* (2008) suggests that 'Google earth's database imagery may well be the latest and postmodernist avatar of modernist collage, which has now turned global, digital, dynamic, and interactive' (Heise 2008: 67).

19 Humanity has been described as a 'mythoepic' species (see Watling 2009), who need stories and narratives to explain the world. 'Stories of nature – how it is perceived, imagined, and socially constructed – thus carry great importance in how humanity treats it' (Watling 2014: 364).

20 What Marx said of history can be said equally of the environment: 'people make nature, but not under conditions of their own choosing'. The Gaia hypothesis is now a familiar example of this green logic: 'constrained to consume what humanity produces, nature as subject creates a history and a future in which humanity may have no part. Nature in this instance takes responsibility for itself, but not for us. Its intelligence and agency are inhuman' (Cubitt 2005: 142).

21 Tong's four distinctive modes of viewing eco-cinema can be used as a template for future analysis and is explained as follows:
- *Activist* – Examining what is the purpose and function of the film? What is the relationship between the film and the film-maker's agenda? What responses does the filmmaker anticipate from the viewers? A large proportion of eco-scholars have sought to establish a growing corpus of eco-cinema and have striven to develop and adapt a range of useful critical tools to help decode eco-textual analysis, which also feeds into Tong's other modes of viewing.
- *Allegorical* – Film performs a metafilmic critique, in addition to functioning as a medium in which entities are presented as cognitive content. By what (and whose) standards should the film be judged? For example, *The China Syndrome* is viewed not only as a Hollywood thriller about the threat of nuclear meltdown, but also as a sensational critique of the nuclear power industry. Attempts to specifically codify an environmental ethical reading certainly feed into this trajectory, as evidenced in this volume, alongside displaying other modes of reading.

- *Evocative* – Redefines the relationship between the viewer and other entities by means of evoking an alternative world, as explored in films like *Avatar* or *Wall-E* discussed in this volume.
- *Realist* – The camera stands in for the viewing subject, giving the film an illusory quality of immediacy. What are the 'real world' sources for the film and how is the film an interpretation of these sources? For instance mainstream films like *Erin Brokovich* which is based on a real-life activist, dramatising her work on behalf of residents affected by water contamination caused by the Pacific Gas and Electric Company, together with others like *Promised Land* based on fracking, *The Cove, An Inconvenient Truth, March of the Penguins* and many others explored in this volume that construct an arguably 'realist' narrative and aesthetic.
22 Yet surprisingly environmentalists in America and elsewhere have not been, for the most part, very open to or inclusive of women or people of colour alongside working classes who are often not taken into account (cited in Selheim 2011: 136). Instead mainstream film often serves to reinforce the current status quo of environmentalism. Nonetheless, I would hope that there are more fruitful examples as explored in this volume.

Bibliography

Alaimo, Stacy (2000) *Undomesticated Ground: Recasting Nature as Feminist Space*. Ithaca, NY: Cornell University Press.

Alex, Rayson K., Deborah, S. Susan and Sachindev, P.S. (eds) (2014) *Culture and Media: Ecocritical Exploration*. Cambridge: Cambridge Scholars Press.

Barry, Peter (2002) *Beginning Theory: An Introduction to Literary and Cultural Theory*. Manchester: Manchester University Press.

Baudrillard, Jean (1981) 'Simulacra and Simulations', in *Selected Writings* ed. Mark Poster. Redwood, CA: Stamford University Press.

Berger, John (1977) *About Looking*. London: Vintage Press.

Berry, Thomas (2015) 'A Question of Story'. Awakin.org http://www.awakin.org/read/view.php?tid=1002

Berry, Wendell (1975) 'A Continuous Harmony: Essays, Cultural and Agricultural'. *The Whole Earth Catalogue*. http://www.barrylou.com/thinkLittle.pdf

Botkin, D (1992) *Discordant Harmonies: A New Ecology for the Twentieth Century*. Oxford: Oxford University Press.

Bozak, Nadia (2011) *The Cinematic Footprint. Lights, Camera, Natural Resources*. New Brunswick, NJ: Rutgers Press.

Brereton, Pat (2001) 'Utopian and Fascist Aesthetics: An Appreciation of "Nature" in Documentary/Fiction Film'. *Capitalism, Nature Socialism* 12(4): 33–55.

Brereton, Pat (2005) *Hollywood Utopia: Ecology in Contemporary American Cinema*. Bristol: Intellect Press.

Brereton, Pat (2012) *Smart Cinema: DVD Add-ons and New Audience Pleasures*. Basingstoke: Palgrave.

Buell, Lawrence (1995) *The Environmental Imagination: Thoreau, Nature Writing and the Formation of American Culture*. Cambridge, MA: Harvard University Press.

Buell, Lawrence (2005) *The Future of Environmental Criticism: Environmental Crisis and Literary Imagination*. Malden, MA: Blackwell Publishers.

Bullis, C. (1996). 'Retalking Environmental Discourses from a Feminist Perspective: The Radical Potential of Ecofeminism', in J.G. Cantrill and C.L. Oravec (eds), *The Symbolic Earth: Discourse and Our Creation of the Environment*. Lexington, KY: University of Kentucky Press.

Carson, Rachel (1962) *Silent Spring*. London: Penguin.

Cronon, William (1996) *Uncommon Ground: Rethinking the Human Place in Nature*. New York: Norton.

Cubitt, Sean (2005) *EcoMedia*. New York: Rhodopi.

Garrard, Greg (2012a) *Ecocriticsm,* second edn. London: Routledge.

Garrard, Greg (ed) (2012b) *Teaching Ecocriticism and Greening Cultural Studies*. Basingstoke: Palgrave.

Gibson-Wood, Hilary and Wakefield, Sarah (2013) 'Participation: White Privilege and Environmental Justice: Understanding Environmentalism among Hispanics in Toronto'. *Antipode* 45(3): 641–662.

Guha, Ramaghandra (2000) *Environmentalism: A Global History*. New York: Longman.

Haraway, Donna (2008) *When Species Meet: Post Humanities vol. 3*. Minneapolis, MN: University of Minnesota Press.

Heise, Ursula K. (2008) *Sense of Place and Sense of Planet: The Environmental Imagination of the Global*. Oxford: Oxford University Press.

Hewitt, Kenneth (1983) *Interpretations of Calamity*. Winchester, MA: Allen and Unwin.

Hulme, M. (2009) *Why We Disagree about Climate Change: Understanding Controversy, Inaction and Opportunity*. Cambridge: Cambridge University Press.

Ivakhiv, Adrian (2013) *Ecologies of the Moving Image: Cinema, Affect, Nature*. Waterloo, Canada: Wilfred Laurier University Press.

Jackson, Tim (2009) *Prosperity without Growth: Economics for a Finite Planet*. London: Earthscan.

Kääpä, Pietari (ed) (2013) *Interactions: Studies in Communication and Culture* 4(2) Special issue.

Kääpä, Pietari (2014) *Ecology and Contemporary Nordic Cinemas: From Nation-building to Ecocosmopolitanism*. London: Bloomsbury Academic.

Keller, David (ed) (2010) *Environmental Ethics*. Hoboken, NJ: Wiley Blackwell.

Lord, Catherine Mary (2012) 'Precarious Planet: Ecological Violence in the Age of Stupid'. *Excursions Journal* 3(1). http://www.excursions-journal.org.uk/index.php/excursions/article/view/62

MacIntyre, Alastair (1981) *After Virtue*. Notre Dame, IN: University of Notre Dame Press.

Manovich, Lev (2001) *The Language of New Media*. Cambridge, MA: MIT Press.

McFarland, Sarh (2009) 'Dancing Penguins and a Pretentious Racoon: Animated Animals and 21st Century Environmentalism', in Sarah McFarland and Ryan Hediger (eds), *Animals and Agency: An Interdisciplinary Exploration*. Boston, MA: Brill.

McGowan, Todd and Kundle, Sheila (eds) (2004) *Lacan and Contemporary Film*. New York: Other Press.

McKibben, Bill (1992) *The Age of Missing Information*. New York: Random House.

Mead, Geoff (2014) 'Sustainability Needs New Narratives Between Catastrophe and Utopia', *The Guardian*, 30 April.

Morton, Timothy (2007) *Ecology: Without Nature: Rethinking Environmental*. Cambridge, MA: Harvard University Press.

O'Brien, Adam (2013) 'Book Review of *Beyond Green: Ecocinema Theory and Practice*', *Senses of Cinema* June. http://sensesofcinema.com/2013/book-reviews/beyond-green-ecocinema-theory-and-practice-edited-by-stephen-rust-salma-monani-and-sean-cubitt/

Phillips, Dana (2003) *The Truth of Ecology*. Oxford: Oxford University Press.

Plumwood, Val (2002) *Environmental Culture*. London: Routledge.

Rolston, Holmes (1994 [1988]) *Environmental Ethics: Duties to and Values in the Natural World*. Philadelphia, PA: Temple University Press.

Rust, S., Monani, S. and Cubitt, S. (eds) (2013) *Ecocinema, Theory and Practice*. AFI Film Readers. London: Routledge.

Selheim, Megan Elizabeth (2011) 'Towards a Political Economy of Activist Documentary'. Masters Thesis of Fine Arts in Science and Natural History Filmmaking. Montana State University.

Shiva, Vandana (2000) *Staying Alive: Women, Ecology and Development*. London: Zed Books.

Soper, Kate (1998 [1995]) *What is Nature? Culture, Politics and the Non-Human*. Oxford: Blackwell.

Taylor, Bron (2013) *Avatar and Nature Spirituality*. Waterloo, Canada: Wilfrid Laurier University Press.

Tong, Chris (2013) 'Ecocinema For All: Reassembling the Audience'. *Interactions: Studies in Communications and Culture* 4(2): 113–128.

Vygotsky, Lev (1971) *Psychology of Art*. Cambridge MA: MIT Press.

Watling, T. (2009) *Ecological Imaginations in the World Religions: An Ethnographic Analysis*. New York: Continuum.

Watling, T. (2014) 'Religion, Ecology, Science and Wisdom: Constructive Dialogue on the Environment'. *Journal for the Study of Religion, Nature and Culture* 8(3): 1–11.

Weik von Mossner, Alexa (ed) (2014) *Moving Environments: Affect, Emotion, Ecology and Film*. Waterloo, Canada: Wilfrid Laurier University Press.

Wolfe, Cary (2003) 'In the Shadow of Wittgenstein's Lion: Language, Education, Ethics and the Question of the Animal', in Cary Wolfe (ed) *Zoontologies: The Question of the Animal*. Minneapolis, MN: University of Minnesota Press.

GLOSSARY

biophilia an innate affinity human beings have for other forms of life. Romantic art constantly calls on our extreme 'love of nature' to get audiences to connect with a deep appreciation of nature.

communitarianism is based on the belief that a person's social identity and personality is moulded by community relationships, which in turn underpins much environmental philosophy.

deep ecology ethics based on non-anthropocentric belief systems. Cultural practices are placed in the context of a greater living cosmos and decisions are assessed in light of the effects on the broader living organism of which the self is a part.

deontology is a moral theory that emphasises one's duty to do a particular action, because the action itself is inherently right and not through any sort of calculation, such as the consequence of the action. Because of this non-consequentialist bent, deontology is often contrasted with utilitarianism, which defines the right action in terms of its ability to bring about the greatest aggregate utility.

eco-feminism encourages an ethical perspective that challenges patriarchal structures that have often equated women with nature. It generally challenges social and environmental relations to become more inclusive of the 'other', which includes women, nature, the poor and non-whites.

postmodern environmentalism an area that resists absolutes as a way out of what is considered the environmental crisis. Encourages a dialogue with cultural, gender and class 'differences' and offers an analysis of language, text and discourse in the construction of the environmental crisis.

social ecology   ethics based on a non-hierarchical relationship among people and nature. Cultural practices are challenged to become egalitarian and promote equity and move away from oppressive relationships of domination.

utilitarianism   is a theory that suggests that an action is morally right when the action produces more total utility for the group as a consequence that any other alternative. Sometimes this has been shortened to the slogan: 'the greatest good to the greatest number'.

virtue ethics   derived from the writings of Aristotle, virtue ethics consider the entirety of human life and the practices, habits, and knowledge that go into it as a whole, and into the connections with others, that supposedly autonomous individuals already rely upon.

FILMOGRAPHY

Title	Director	Year
11th Hour	Leila Conners	2007
12 Monkeys	Terry Gilliam	1995
2012	Roland Emmerich	2009
28 Days Later	Danny Boyle	2002
A Bug's Life	John Lasseter	1998
After Earth	M. Night Shyamlan	2013
AI: Artificial Intelligence	Steven Spielberg	2001
All is Lost	J.C. Chandor	2013
An Inconvenient Truth	Davis Guggenheim	2006
Another Earth	Mike Cahill	2011
Antz	Eric Darnell	1988
Apocalypse Now	Francis Ford Coppola	1979
Armageddon	Michael Bay	1998
Avatar	James Cameron	2009
Babel	Alejandro G. Inarritu	2006
Bambi	David Hand	1942
Behind Enemy Lines	John Moore	2001
Being There	Hal Ashby	1979
Blade Runner	Ridley Scott	1982
Braveheart	Mel Gibson	1995
Butch Cassidy and the Sundance Kid	George Roy Hill	1969
Capitalism: A Love Story	Michael Moore	2009
Captain Phillips	Paul Greengrass	2013
Castaway	Robert Zemeckis	2000

Title	Director	Year
Children of Men	Alfonso Cuaron	2006
Chinatown	Roman Polanski	1974
Citizen Kane	Orson Welles	1941
City of God	Fernando Meirselles	2002
Clockwork Orange	Stanley Kubrick	1971
Contagion	Steven Soderberg	2011
Dante's Peak	Roger Donaldson	1997
Dawn of the Planet of the Apes	Matt Reeves	2014
Doctor Doolittle	Betty Thomas	1998
Do the Right Thing	Spike Lee	1989
Dumbo	Ben Sharpsteen	1941
Earth	Alastair Fothergill	2007
Elysium	Neill Blomkamp	2013
FernGully: The Last Rainforest	Bill Kroyer	1992
Fight Club	David Fincher	1999
Finding Nemo	Andrew Stanton	2003
Food Inc	Robert Kenner	2008
Funny Games	Michael Haneke	1997
Garbage Warrior	Oliver Hodge	2007
Gattaca	Andrew Nicol	1998
Godzilla	Gareth Edwards	2014
Gorillas in the Mist	Michael Apted	1988
Grand Canyon	Lawrence Kasden	1991
Gravity	Alfonso Cuaron	2013
Green Card	Peter Weir	1990
Grizzly Man	Werner Herzog	2005
Growth Busters	Dave Gardner	2011
Happy Feet	George Miller	2006
Interstellar	Christopher Nolan	2014
In Time	Andrew Niccol	2011
Into the Wild	Sean Penn	2007
Jurassic Park	Steven Spielberg	1993
Jurassic Park: The Lost World	Steven Spielberg	1997
Koyaanisqatsi	Godfrey Reggio	1982
Last Year in Marienbad	Alain Resnais	1961
Life of Pi	Ang Lee	2012
Logan's Run	Michael Anderson	1976
Lord of the Rings	Peter Jackson	2001
Mad Max 2	George Miller	1982

Title	Director	Year
Man of Aran	Robert Flaherty	1934
March of the Penguins	Luc Jacquet	2009
Master and Commander	Peter Weir	2003
Melancholia	Lars von Trier	2011
Men in Black	Barry Sunnenfeld	1997
Mosquito Coast	Peter Weir	1986
Mud	Jeff Nichols	2012
Nanook of the North	Robert Flaherty	1922
Noah	Darren Aronofsky	2014
Oblivion	Joseph Kosinsky	2013
Omega Man	Boris Sagal	1971
Out of Africa	Sydney Pollock	1985
Pi	Darren Aronofsky	1998
Pilgrim Hill	Gerard Barrett	2014
Pirates of the Caribbean	Gore Verbuski	2003
Planet Earth	David Attenborough	2006
Pocohantas	Mike Gabriel	1995
Powaqqatsi	Godfrey Reggio	1988
Promised Land	Gus Van Sant	2012
Quantum of Solace	Mark Forster	2008
Requiem for a Dream	Darren Aronofsky	2000
Rise of the Planet of the Apes	Rupert Wyatt	2011
Silent Running	Douglas Trumbull	1971
Strike	Sergei Eisenstein	1925
Take Shelter	Jeff Nichols	2011
The Beach	Danny Boyle	2000
The Color Purple	Steven Spielberg	1985
The Constant Gardener	Fernando Meirelles	2005
The Corporation	Mark Achbar	2003
The Cove	Louie Psihoyos	2009
The Descendants	Alexander Payne	2011
The Emerald Forest	John Boorman	1985
The Godfather	Francis Ford Coppola	1971
The Graves of Wrath	John Ford	1941
The Hobbit: An Unexpected Journey	Peter Jackson	2012
The Hunger Games	Gary Ross	2012
The Impossible	B.A. Bayona	2012
The Last King of Scotland	Kevin McDonald	2006
The Life Aquatic	Wes Andeson	2004

Title	Director	Year
The New World	Terrence Malick	2005
The Passion of the Christ	Mel Gibson	2004
The Powerdown Show	Cultivate.ie	2013
The Prey	Eric Hensman	2015
The Road	John Hillcoat	2009
The Searchers	John Ford	1956
The Tree of Life	Terrence Malick	2011
The Wolf of Wall Street	Martin Scorsese	2013
The Yearling	Clarence Brown	1946
There Will be Blood	Paul Thomas Anderson	2007
Titanic	James Cameron	1997
Transcendence	Wally Pfister	2014
Twister	Jan de Bont	1996
UP	Pete Docter	2009
Up in the Air	Jason Reitman	2009
Walkabout	Nick Roeg	1970
Wall Street	Oliver Stone	1987
Wall Street: Money Never Sleeps	Oliver Stone	2010
Warhorse	Steven Spielberg	2011
We Bought a Zoo	Cameron Crowe	2011
Whale Rider	Niki Caro	2002
World War Z	Marc Foster	2013

INDEX

Taylor & Francis eBooks

from Taylor & Francis

Helping you to choose the right eBooks for your Library

Add to your library's digital collection today with Taylor & Francis eBooks. We have over 50,000 eBooks in the Humanities, Social Sciences, Behavioural Sciences, Built Environment and Law, from leading imprints, including Routledge, Focal Press and Psychology Press.

Free Trials Available

We offer free trials to qualifying academic, corporate and government customers.

Choose from a range of subject packages or create your own!

Benefits for you

- Free MARC records
- COUNTER-compliant usage statistics
- Flexible purchase and pricing options
- All titles DRM-free.

Benefits for your user

- Off-site, anytime access via Athens or referring URL
- Print or copy pages or chapters
- Full content search
- Bookmark, highlight and annotate text
- Access to thousands of pages of quality research at the click of a button.

eCollections

Choose from over 30 subject eCollections, including:

Archaeology	Language Learning
Architecture	Law
Asian Studies	Literature
Business & Management	Media & Communication
Classical Studies	Middle East Studies
Construction	Music
Creative & Media Arts	Philosophy
Criminology & Criminal Justice	Planning
Economics	Politics
Education	Psychology & Mental Health
Energy	Religion
Engineering	Security
English Language & Linguistics	Social Work
Environment & Sustainability	Sociology
Geography	Sport
Health Studies	Theatre & Performance
History	Tourism, Hospitality & Events

For more information, pricing enquiries or to order a free trial, please contact your local sales team:
www.tandfebooks.com/page/sales

www.tandfebooks.com